Cannibalism

Contents

Chapter 1

Cannibalism

For non-human cannibalism, see Cannibalism (zoology). For other uses, see Cannibal (disambiguation).

Cannibalism, Brazil. Engraving by Theodor de Bry to illustrate Hans Staden's account of his captivity in 1557.

Cannibalism is the act or practice of humans eating the flesh or internal organs of other human beings. A person who practices cannibalism is called a cannibal. The expression "cannibalism" has been extended into zoology to mean one individual of a species consuming all or part of another individual of the same species as food, including sexual cannibalism.

The Island Carib people of the Lesser Antilles, from whom the word cannibalism derives, acquired a long-standing reputation as cannibals following the recording of their legends in the 17th century.[1] Some controversy exists over the accuracy of these legends and the prevalence of actual cannibalism in the culture. Cannibalism was widespread in the past among humans in many parts of the world, continuing into the 19th century in some isolated South Pacific cultures, and to the present day in parts of tropical Africa. Cannibalism was practiced in New Guinea and in parts of the Solomon Islands, and flesh markets existed in some parts of Melanesia.[2] Fiji was once known as the 'Cannibal Isles'.[3] Cannibalism has been well documented around the world, from Fiji to the Amazon Basin to the Congo to Māori New Zealand.[4] Neanderthals are believed to have practiced cannibalism,[5][6] and Neanderthals may have been eaten by anatomically modern humans.[7]

Cannibalism has recently been both practiced and fiercely condemned in several wars, especially in Liberia[8] and Congo.[9] As of 2006, the Korowai were one of very few tribes still believed to eat human flesh as a cultural practice.[10] It is also still known to be practiced as a ritual and in war in various Melanesian tribes. Historically, allegations of cannibalism were used by the colonial powers as a tool of empire to justify the subjugation of what were seen as primitive peoples.[11] Cannibalism has been said to test the bounds of cultural relativism as it challenges anthropologists "to define what is or is not beyond the pale of acceptable human behavior" .[1]

Cannibalism has been occasionally practiced as a last resort by people suffering from famine, including in modern times. A famous example is the ill-fated Westward expedition of the Donner Party, and more recently the crash of Uruguayan Air Force Flight 571, after which some survivors ate the bodies of dead passengers. Also, some mentally ill people obsess about eating others and actually do so, such as Jeffrey Dahmer and Albert Fish. There is resistance to formally labeling cannibalism as a mental disorder.[12]

1.1 Etymology

Cannibalism derives from *Caníbales*, the Spanish name for the Caribs,[13] a West Indies tribe that formerly practiced cannibalism,[14] from Spanish canibal or caribal "a savage". It is also called *anthropophagy*.

1.2 Reasons

In some societies, especially tribal societies, cannibalism is a cultural norm. Consumption of a person from within the same community is called endocannibalism; ritual cannibalism of the recently deceased can be part of the grieving process,[15] or a way of guiding the souls of the dead into the bodies of living descendants.[16] Exocannibalism is the consumption of a person from outside the community, usually as a celebration of victory against a rival tribe.[16] Both types of cannibalism can also be fueled by the belief that eating a person's flesh or internal organs will endow the cannibal with some of the characteristics of the deceased.[17]

In most parts of the world, cannibalism is not a societal norm, but is sometimes resorted to in situations of extreme necessity. The survivors of the shipwrecks of the *Essex* and *Méduse* in the 19th century are said to have engaged in cannibalism, as are the members of Franklin's lost expedition and the Donner Party. Such cases generally involve necrocannibalism (eating the corpse of someone who is already dead) as opposed to homicidal cannibalism (killing someone for food). In English law, the latter is always considered a crime, even in the most trying circumstances. The case of *R v Dudley and Stephens*, in which two men were found guilty of murder for killing and eating a cabin boy while adrift at sea in a lifeboat, set the precedent that necessity is no defence to a charge of murder.

There are numerous examples of murderers consuming their victims, often deriving some degree of sexual satisfaction from the act of cannibalism. Notable examples include Albert Fish, Issei Sagawa and Jeffrey Dahmer. These individuals are usually considered to be mentally ill, although the compulsion to eat human flesh is not formally listed as a mental disorder in the *Diagnostic and Statistical Manual of Mental Disorders* (DSM).[12] Cases of autophagia, or self-cannibalism, have also been reported.

A cannibal feast on Tanna, Vanuatu, c. 1885-9

In pre-modern medicine, the explanation given by the now-discredited theory of humorism for cannibalism was that it came about within a black acrimonious humour, which, being lodged in the linings of the ventricle, produced the voracity for human flesh.[18]

1.3 Medical aspects

A well known case of mortuary cannibalism is that of the Fore tribe in New Guinea which resulted in the spread of the prion disease kuru.[19] Although the Fore's mortuary cannibalism was well documented, the practice had ceased before the cause of the disease was recognized. However, some scholars argue that although post-mortem dismemberment was the practice during funeral rites, cannibalism was not. Marvin Harris theorizes that it happened during a famine period coincident with the arrival of Europeans and was rationalized as a religious rite.

In 2003 a publication in *Science* received a large amount of press attention when it suggested that early humans may have practiced extensive cannibalism.[20][21] According to this research, genetic markers commonly found in modern humans worldwide suggest that today many people carry a gene that evolved as protection against the brain diseases that can be spread by consuming human brain tissue.[22] A 2006 reanalysis of the data questioned this hypothesis,[23] as it claimed to have found a data collection bias, which led to an erroneous conclusion.[24] This claimed bias came from incidents of cannibalism used in the analysis not being due to local cultures, but having been carried out by explorers, stranded seafarers or escaped convicts.[25] The original authors published a subsequent paper in 2008 defending their conclusions.[26]

1.4 Myths, legends and folklore

Cannibalism features in the folklore and legends of many cultures and is most often attributed to evil characters or as extreme retribution for some wrong. Examples include the witch in "Hansel and Gretel", Lamia of Greek mythology and Baba Yaga of Slavic folklore.

A number of stories in Greek mythology involve cannibalism, in particular cannibalism of close family members, for example the stories of Thyestes, Tereus and especially Cronus, who was Saturn in the Roman pantheon. The story of Tantalus also parallels this.

The wendigo is a creature appearing in the legends of the Algonquian people. It is thought of variously as a malevolent cannibalistic spirit that could possess humans or a monster that humans could physically transform into. Those who indulged in cannibalism were at particular risk,[27] and the legend appears to have reinforced this practice as taboo.

1.5 As used to demonize colonized or other groups

See also: Blood libel

Unsubstantiated reports of cannibalism disproportionately relate cases of cannibalism among cultures that are already otherwise despised, feared, or are little known. In antiquity, Greek reports of cannibalism, (often called *anthropophagy* in this context) were related to distant non-Hellenic barbarians, or else relegated in Greek mythology to the 'primitive' chthonic world that preceded the coming of the Olympian gods: see the explicit rejection of human sacrifice in the cannibal feast prepared for the Olympians by Tantalus of his son Pelops. All South Sea Islanders were cannibals so far as their enemies were concerned. When the whaleship Essex was rammed and sunk by a whale in 1820, the captain opted to sail 3000 miles upwind to Chile rather than 1400 miles downwind to the Marquesas because he had heard the Marquesans were cannibals. Ironically many of the survivors of the shipwreck resorted to cannibalism to survive.

However, Herman Melville happily lived with the Marquesan Typees for a time after the other two tribes on the island told him they were cannibals. In his semi-autobiographical novel *Typee*, he reports seeing shrunken heads and having strong evidence that the tribal leaders ceremonially consumed the bodies of killed warriors of the neighboring tribe after a skirmish.

William Arens, author of *The Man-Eating Myth: Anthropology and Anthropophagy*,[28] questions the credibility of reports of cannibalism and argues that the description by one group of people of another people as cannibals is a consistent and demonstrable ideological and rhetorical device to establish perceived cultural superiority. Arens bases his thesis on a detailed analysis of numerous "classic" cases of cultural cannibalism cited by explorers, missionaries, and anthropologists. He asserted that many were steeped in racism, unsubstantiated, or based on second-hand or hearsay evidence.[29] Arens' findings are controversial, and have been cited as an example of postcolonial revisionism.[30]

Conversely, Michel de Montaigne's essay "Of cannibals" introduced a new multicultural note in European civilization. Montaigne wrote that "one calls 'barbarism' whatever he is not accustomed to" .[31]

1.6 History

See also: List of incidents of cannibalism

Among modern humans, cannibalism has been practiced by various groups.[22] It was practiced by humans in Prehistoric Europe,[32][33] South America,[34] among Iroquoian peoples in North America,[35] Maori in New Zealand,[36] the Solomon Islands,[37] parts of West Africa[14] and Central Africa,[14] some of the islands of Polynesia,[14] New Guinea,[38] Sumatra,[14] and Fiji.[39] Evidence of cannibalism has been found in ruins associated with the Anasazi culture of the Southwestern United States as well (at Cowboy Wash in Colorado).[40][41]

1.6.1 Pre-history

There is evidence, both archeological and genetic, that cannibalism has been practiced for tens of thousands of years.[42] Human bones that have been "de-fleshed" by other humans go back 600,000 years. The oldest *Homo sapiens* bones (from Ethiopia) show signs of this as well.[42] Some anthropologists, such as Tim White, suggest that ritual cannibalism was common in human societies prior to the beginning of the Upper Paleolithic period. This theory is based on the large amount of "butchered human" bones found in Neanderthal and other Lower/Middle Paleolithic sites.[43] Cannibalism in the Lower and Middle Paleolithic may have occurred because of food shortages.[44] It has been also suggested that removing dead bodies through ritual cannibalism might been a means of predator control, aiming to eliminate predators' and scavengers' access to hominid (and early human) bodies.[*][45] Jim Corbett proposed that after major epidemics, when human corpses are easily accessible to predators, there are more cases of man-eating leopards,[*][46] so removing dead bodies through ritual cannibalism (before the cultural traditions of burying and burning bodies appeared in human history) might have had practical reasons for hominids and early humans to control predation.

In Gough's Cave, England, remains of human bones and skulls, around 15,000 years old, suggest that cannibalism took place amongst the people living in or visiting the cave,[*][47] and that they may have used human skulls as drinking vessels.[*][48][*][49]

Researchers have found physical evidence of cannibalism in ancient times. In 2001, archaeologists at the University of Bristol found evidence of Iron Age cannibalism in Gloucestershire.[*][50] Cannibalism was practiced as recently as 2000 years ago in Great Britain.[*][51] In Germany, Emil Carthaus and Dr. Bruno Bernhard have observed 1,891 signs of cannibalism in the caves at the Hönne (1000 – 700 BC)[*][52]

1.6.2 Early history

Cannibalism is mentioned many times in early history and literature. Cannibalism was reported by Flavius Josephus during the siege of Jerusalem by Rome in 70 AD,[*][53] and according to Appian, the population of Numantia during the Roman Siege of Numantia in the 2nd century BC was reduced to cannibalism and suicide.[*][54]

St. Jerome, in his letter *Against Jovinianus*, discusses how people come to their present condition as a result of their heritage, and then lists several examples of peoples and their customs. In the list, he mentions that he has heard that Atticoti eat human flesh and that Massagetae and *Derbices* (a people on the borders of India) kill and eat old people. [*][55]

Herodotus in "*The Histories*" (450s to the 420s BC[*][56]) claimed, that after eleven days' voyage up the Borysthenes (Dnieper River in Europe) a desolated land extended for a long way, and later the country of the Man-eaters (other than Scythians) was located, and beyond it again a desolated area extended where no men lived.[*][57]

1.6.3 Middle Ages

Reports of cannibalism were recorded during the First Crusade, as Crusaders were alleged to have fed on the bodies of their dead opponents following the Siege of Ma'arrat al-Numan. Amin Maalouf also alleges further cannibalism incidents on the march to Jerusalem, and to the efforts made to delete mention of these from western history.[*][58] During Europe's Great Famine of 1315–1317 there were many reports of cannibalism among the starving populations. In North Africa, as in Europe, there are references to cannibalism as a last resort in times of famine.[*][59]

The Moroccan Muslim explorer Ibn Batutta reported that one African king advised him that nearby people were cannibals (although this may have been a prank played on Ibn Batutta by the king to fluster his guest). However Batutta reported that Arabs and Christians were safe, as their flesh was "unripe" and would cause the eater to fall ill.

For a brief time in Europe, an unusual form of cannibalism occurred when thousands of Egyptian mummies preserved in bitumen were ground up and sold as medicine.[*][60] The practice developed into a wide-scale business which flourished until the late 16th century. This "fad" ended because the mummies were revealed actually to be recently killed slaves. Two centuries ago, mummies were still believed to have medicinal properties against bleeding, and were sold as pharmaceuticals in powdered form (see human mummy confection and mummia).[*][61]

In China during the Tang dynasty, cannibalism was supposedly resorted to by rebel forces early in the period (who were said to raid neighboring areas for victims to eat), as well as both soldiers and civilians besieged during the rebellion of An Lushan. Eating an enemy's heart and liver was also claimed to be a feature of both official punishments and private vengeance.[*][62] References to cannibalizing the enemy has also been seen in poetry written in the Song dynasty, (for example, in *Man Jiang Hong*) although the cannibalizing is perhaps poetic symbolism, expressing hatred towards the enemy.

While there is universal agreement that some Mesoamerican people practiced human sacrifice, there is a lack of scholarly consensus as to whether cannibalism in pre-Columbian America was widespread. At one extreme, anthropologist Marvin Harris, author of *Cannibals and Kings*, has suggested that the flesh of the victims was a part of an aristocratic diet as a reward, since the Aztec diet was lacking in proteins. While most pre-Columbian historians believe that there was ritual cannibalism related to human sacrifices, they do not support Harris's thesis that human flesh was ever a significant portion of the Aztec diet.[*][63][*][64][*][65] Others have hypothesized that cannibalism was part of a blood revenge in war.[*][66]

1.6.4   Early modern era

Physical evidence was found recently for cannibalism in the Jamestown Colony in 1609, which is also documented in written records of the colony.[*][67]

European explorers and colonizers brought home many stories of cannibalism practiced by the native peoples they encountered. The friar Diego de Landa reported about Yucatán instances,[*][68] and there have been similar reports by Purchas from Popayán, Colombia, and from the Marquesas Islands of Polynesia, where human flesh was called "long pig".[*][69] According to Hans Egede, when the Inuit killed a woman accused of witchcraft, they ate a portion of her heart.[*][70] It is recorded about the natives of the captaincy of Sergipe in Brazil: "They eat human flesh when they can get it, and if a woman miscarries devour the abortive immediately. If she goes her time out, she herself cuts the navel-string with a shell, which she boils along with the secondine, and eats them both." [*][71]

The 1913 *Handbook of Indians of Canada* (reprinting 1907 material from the Bureau of American Ethnology), claims that North American natives practicing cannibalism included "... the Montagnais, and some of the tribes of Maine; the Algonkin, Armouchiquois, Iroquois, and Micmac; farther west the Assiniboine, Cree, Foxes, Chippewa, Miami, Ottawa, Kickapoo, Illinois, Sioux, and Winnebago; in the South the people who built the mounds in Florida, and the Tonkawa, Attacapa, Karankawa, Caddo, and Comanche (?); in the Northwest and West, portions of the continent, the Thlingchadinneh and other Athapascan tribes, the Tlingit, Heiltsuk, Kwakiutl, Tsimshian, Nootka, Siksika, some of the Californian tribes, and the Ute. There is also a tradition of the practice among the Hopi, and mentions of the custom among other tribes of New Mexico and Arizona. The Mohawk, and the Attacapa, Tonkawa, and other Texas tribes were known to their neighbours as 'man-eaters.'"[*][72] The forms of cannibalism described included both resorting to human flesh during famines and ritual cannibalism, the latter usually consisting of eating a small portion of an enemy warrior.

As with most lurid tales of native cannibalism, these stories are treated with a great deal of scrutiny, as accusations of cannibalism were often used as justifications for the subjugation or destruction of "savages". However, there were several well-documented cultures that engaged in regular eating of the dead, such as New Zealand's Māori. In an 1809 incident known as the Boyd massacre, about 66 passengers and crew of the *Boyd* were killed and eaten by Māori on the Whangaroa peninsula, Northland. Cannibalism was already a regular practice in Māori wars.[*][73] In another instance, on July 11, 1821 warriors from the Ngapuhi tribe killed 2,000 enemies and remained on the battlefield "eating the vanquished until they were driven off by the smell of decaying bodies".[*][74] Māori warriors fighting the New Zealand government in Titokowaru's War in New Zealand's North Island in 1868–69 revived ancient rites of cannibalism as part of the radical Hauhau movement of the Pai Marire religion.[*][75]

Other islands in the Pacific were home to cultures that allowed cannibalism to some degree. In parts of Melanesia, cannibalism was still practiced in the early 20th century, for a variety of reasons —including retaliation, to insult an enemy people, or to absorb the dead person's qualities.[*][76] One tribal chief, Ratu Udre Udre in Rakiraki, Fiji, is said to have consumed 872 people and to have made a pile of stones to record his achievement.[*][77][*][78] Fiji was nicknamed the "Cannibal Isles" by European sailors, who avoided disembarking there. The dense population of Marquesas Islands, Polynesia, was concentrated in the narrow valleys, and consisted of warring tribes, who sometimes practiced cannibalism on their enemies. W. D. Rubinstein wrote:

> It was considered a great triumph among the Marquesans to eat the body of a dead man. They treated their captives with great cruelty. They broke their legs to prevent them from attempting to escape before being eaten, but kept them alive so that they could brood over their impending fate. ... With this tribe, as with many others, the bodies of women were in great demand.[*][4]

This period of time was also rife with instances of explorers and seafarers resorting to cannibalism for survival. The survivors of the sinking of the French ship *Méduse* in 1816 resorted to cannibalism after four days adrift on a raft and their plight was made famous by Théodore Géricault's painting Raft of the Medusa. After the sinking of the *Essex* of Nantucket by a whale, on November 20, 1820, (an important source event for Herman Melville's *Moby-Dick*) the survivors, in three small boats, resorted, by common consent, to cannibalism in order for some to survive.[*][79] Sir John Franklin's lost polar expedition is another example of cannibalism out of desperation.[*][80] On land, the Donner Party found itself stranded by snow in a high mountain pass in California without adequate supplies during the Mexican-American War, leading to several instances of cannibalism.[*][81] Another notorious cannibal was mountain man Boone Helm, who was known as "The Kentucky Cannibal" for eating several of his fellow travelers, from 1850 until his eventual hanging in 1864.

The case of *R v. Dudley and Stephens* (1884) 14 QBD 273 (QB) is an English case which dealt with four crew members of an English yacht, the *Mignonette*, who were cast away in a storm some 1,600 miles (2,600 km) from the Cape of Good Hope. After several days, one of the crew, a seventeen-year-old cabin boy, fell unconscious due to a combination of the famine and drinking seawater. The others (one possibly objecting) decided then to kill him and eat him. They were picked up four days later. Two of the three survivors were found guilty of murder. A significant outcome of this case was that necessity was determined to be no defence against a charge of murder.[*][82]

American consul James W. Davidson described in his 1903 book, *The Island of Formosa*, how the Chinese in Taiwan ate and traded in the flesh of Taiwanese aboriginals.[*][83]

Roger Casement, writing to a consular colleague in Lisbon on August 3, 1903 from Lake Mantumba in the Congo Free State, said: "The people round here are all cannibals. You never saw such a weird looking lot in your life. There are also dwarfs (called Batwas) in the forest who are even worse cannibals than the taller human environment. They eat man flesh raw! It's a fact." Casement then added how assailants would "bring down a dwarf on the way home, for the marital cooking pot ... The Dwarfs, as I say, dispense with cooking pots and eat and drink their human prey fresh cut on the battlefield while the blood is still warm and running. These are not fairy tales my dear Cowper but actual gruesome reality in the heart of this poor, benighted savage land." [*][84]

1.6.5 World War II

Many instances of cannibalism by necessity were recorded during World War II. For example, during the 872-day Siege of Leningrad, reports of cannibalism began to appear in the winter of 1941–1942, after all birds, rats and pets were eaten by survivors. Leningrad police even formed a special division to combat cannibalism.[*][85][*][86]

Some 2.8 million Soviet POWs died in Nazi custody in less than eight months of 1941–42.[*][87] According to the USHMM, by the winter of 1941, "starvation and disease resulted in mass death of unimaginable proportions".[*][88] This deliberate starvation led to many incidents of cannibalism.[*][89]

Following the Soviet victory at Stalingrad it was found that some German soldiers in the besieged city, cut off from supplies, resorted to cannibalism.[*][90] Later, following the German surrender in January 1943, roughly 100,000 German soldiers were taken prisoner of war (POW). Almost all of them were sent to POW camps in Siberia or Central Asia where, due to being chronically underfed by their Soviet captors, many resorted to cannibalism. Fewer than 5,000 of the prisoners taken at Stalingrad survived captivity.[*][91]

The Australian War Crimes Section of the Tokyo tribunal, led by prosecutor William Webb (the future Judge-in-Chief), collected numerous written reports and testimonies that documented Japanese soldiers' acts of cannibalism among their own troops, on enemy dead, and on Allied prisoners of war in many parts of the Greater East Asia Co-Prosperity Sphere. In September 1942, Japanese daily rations on New Guinea consisted of 800 grams of rice and tinned meat. However, by December, this had fallen to 50 grams.[*][92]:78–80 According to historian Yuki Tanaka, "cannibalism was often a systematic activity conducted by whole squads and under the command of officers".[*][93]

In some cases, flesh was cut from living people. An Indian POW, Lance Naik Hatam Ali (later a citizen of Pakistan), testified that in New Guinea: "the Japanese started selecting prisoners and every day one prisoner was taken out and killed and eaten by the soldiers. I personally saw this happen and about 100 prisoners were eaten at this place by the Japanese. The remainder of us were taken to another spot 50 miles (80 kilometres) away where 10 prisoners died of sickness. At this place, the Japanese again started selecting prisoners to eat. Those selected were taken to a hut where their flesh was cut from their bodies while they were alive and they were thrown into a ditch where they later died." [*][94]

Another well-documented case occurred in Chichi-jima in February 1945, when Japanese soldiers killed and consumed five American airmen. This case was investigated in 1947 in a war crimes trial, and of 30 Japanese soldiers prosecuted, five (Maj. Matoba, Gen. Tachibana, Adm. Mori, Capt. Yoshii, and Dr. Teraki) were found guilty and hanged.[*][95] In his book *Flyboys: A True Story of Courage*, James Bradley details several instances of cannibalism of World War II Allied prisoners by their Japanese captors.[96] The author claims that this included not only ritual cannibalization of the livers of freshly killed prisoners, but also the cannibalization-for-sustenance of living prisoners over the course of several days, amputating limbs only as needed to keep the meat fresh.[97]

1.6.6 New Guinea

The Korowai tribe of south-eastern Papua could be one of the last surviving tribes in the world engaging in cannibalism.[38] However, recent reports suggest that certain clans have been coaxed into encouraging tourism by perpetuating the myth that it is still an active practice.[98]

1.6.7 Africa

During the 1892–1894 war between the Congo Free State and the Swahili-Arab city-states of Nyangwe and Kasongo in Eastern Congo, there were reports of widespread cannibalization of the bodies of defeated Arab combatants by the Batetela allies of Belgian commander Francis Dhanis.[99] The Batetela, "like most of their neighbors were inveterate cannibals." [100] According to Dhanis' medical officer, Captain Hinde, their town of Ngandu had "at least 2,000 polished human skulls" as a "solid white pavement in front" of its gates, with human skulls crowning every post of the stockade.[100]

In April 1892, 10,000 of the Batetela, under the command of Gongo Lutete, joined forces with Dhanis in a campaign against the Swahili-Arab leaders Sefu and Mohara.[100] After one early skirmish in the campaign, Hinde "noticed that the bodies of both the killed and wounded had vanished." When fighting broke out again, Hinde saw his Batetela allies drop human arms, legs and heads on the road.[101] One young Belgian officer wrote home: "Happily Gongo's men ate them up [in a few hours]. It's horrible but exceedingly useful and hygenic ... I should have been horrified at the idea in Europe! But it seems quite natural to me here. Don't show this letter to anyone indiscreet." [102] After the massacre at Nyangwe, Lutete "hid himself in his quarters, appalled by the sight of thousands of men smoking human hands and human chops on their camp fires, enough to feed his army for many days." [100]

In the 1980s, Médecins Sans Frontières, the international medical charity, supplied photographic and other documentary evidence of ritualized cannibal feasts among the participants in Liberia's internecine strife to representatives of Amnesty International who were on a fact-finding mission to the neighboring state of Guinea. However, Amnesty International declined to publicize this material; the Secretary-General of the organization, Pierre Sane, said at the time in an internal communication that "what they do with the bodies after human rights violations are committed is not part of our mandate or concern". The existence of cannibalism on a wide scale in Liberia was subsequently verified.[103]

The self-declared Emperor of the Central African Empire, Jean-Bédel Bokassa (Emperor Bokassa I), was tried on October 24, 1986 for several cases of cannibalism although he was never convicted.[104][105] Between April 17, and April 19, 1979 a number of elementary school students were arrested after they had protested against wearing the expensive, government-required school uniforms. Around 100 were killed.[106] Bokassa is said to have participated in the massacre, beating some of the children to death with his cane and allegedly ate some of his victims.[107]

Further reports of cannibalism were reported against the Seleka Muslim minority during the ongoing Central African Republic conflict.[108][109]

Cannibalism has been reported in several recent African conflicts, including the Second Congo War, and the civil wars in Liberia and Sierra Leone. A UN human rights expert reported in July 2007 that sexual atrocities against Congolese women go "far beyond rape" and include sexual slavery, forced incest, and cannibalism.[110] This may be done in desperation, as during peacetime cannibalism is much less frequent;[111] at other times, it is consciously directed at certain groups believed to be relatively helpless, such as Congo Pygmies, even considered subhuman by some other Congolese.[112] It is also reported by some that witch doctors sometimes use the body parts of children in their medicine.[113] In the 1970s the Ugandan dictator Idi Amin was reputed to practice cannibalism.[114][115]

In Uganda, the Lord's Resistance Army have been accused of routinely engaging in ritual or magical cannibalism.[116]

1.6.8 North Korea

Reports of widespread cannibalism began to emerge from North Korea during the famine of the 1990s[117][118] and subsequent ongoing starvation. Kim Jong-il was reported to have ordered a crackdown on cannibalism in 1996.[119] Chinese travellers reported in 1998 that cannibalism had occurred.[120][121] Three people in North Korea were reported to have been executed for selling or eating human flesh in 2006.[122] Further reports of cannibalism emerged in early 2013, including reports of a man executed for killing his two children for food.[123][124][125]

There are competing claims about how widespread cannibalism was in North Korea. While refugees reported that it was widespread[126] Barbara Demick in her 2010 book *Nothing to Envy: Ordinary Lives in North Korea* wrote that it did not seem to be.[127]

1.7 Modern era

Main article: List of incidents of cannibalism

Further instances include cannibalism as ritual practice, in times of drought, famine and other destitution, as well as those being criminal acts and war crimes throughout the 20th century, and also 21st century.

In West Africa, the Leopard Society was a secret society active into the mid-1900s and one that practiced cannibalism. Centered in Sierra Leone, Liberia and Ivory Coast, the *Leopard men* would dress in leopard skins, waylaying travelers with sharp claw-like weapons in the form of leopards' claws and teeth.[128] The victims' flesh would be cut from their bodies and distributed to members of the society.[129]

As in some other Papuan societies, the Urapmin people engaged in cannibalism in war. Notably, the Urapmin also had a system of food taboo wherein dogs could not be eaten and had to be kept from breathing on food, unlike humans who could be eaten and with whom food could be shared.[130]

The Aghoris are Indian ascetics[131][132] who believe that eating human flesh confers spiritual and physical benefits, such as prevention of aging. They claim to only eat those who have voluntarily willed their body to the sect upon their death,[133] although an Indian TV crew witnessed one Aghori feasting on a corpse discovered floating in the Ganges,[134] and a member of the Dom caste reports that Aghoris often take bodies from the cremation *ghat* (or funeral pyre).[135]

During the 1930s, multiple acts of cannibalism were reported from Ukraine and Russia's Volga, South Siberian and Kuban regions during the Soviet famine of 1932–1933.[136]

> Survival was a moral as well as a physical struggle. A woman doctor wrote to a friend in June 1933 that she had not yet become a cannibal, but was "not sure that I shall not be one by the time my letter reaches you." The good people died first. Those who refused to steal or to prostitute themselves died. Those who gave food to others died. Those who refused to eat corpses died. Those who refused to kill their fellow man died. ... At least 2,505 people were sentenced for cannibalism in the years 1932 and 1933 in Ukraine, though the actual number of cases was certainly much higher.[137]

Cannibalism is documented to have occurred in China during the Great Leap Forward, when rural China was hit hard by drought and famine.[138][139][140][141][142][143][144]

Prior to 1931, *New York Times* reporter William Buehler Seabrook, allegedly in the interests of research, obtained from a hospital intern at the Sorbonne a chunk of human meat from the body of a healthy human killed in an accident, then cooked and ate it. He reported, "It was like good, fully developed veal, not young, but not yet beef. It was very definitely like that, and it was not like any other meat I had ever tasted. It was so nearly like good, fully developed veal that I think no person with a palate of ordinary, normal sensitiveness could distinguish it from veal. It was mild, good meat with no other sharply defined or highly characteristic taste such as for instance, goat, high game, and pork have. The steak was slightly tougher than prime veal, a little stringy, but not too tough or stringy to be agreeably edible. The roast, from which I cut and ate a central slice, was tender, and in color, texture, smell as well as taste, strengthened my certainty that of all the meats we habitually know, veal is the one meat to which this meat is accurately comparable." [145][146]

In his book, *The Gulag Archipelago*, Soviet writer Aleksandr Solzhenitsyn described cases of cannibalism in 20th-century USSR. Of the famine in Povolzhie (1921–1922) he wrote: "That horrible famine was up to cannibalism, up to consuming children by their own parents —the famine, which Russia had never known even in Time of Troubles [in 1601–1603] ..." *[147]

He said of the Siege of Leningrad (1941–1944): "Those who consumed human flesh, or dealt with the human liver trading from dissecting rooms ... were accounted as the political criminals ..." *[148] And of the building of Northern Railway Labor Camp ("Sevzheldorlag") Solzhenitsyn reports, "An ordinary hard working political prisoner almost could not survive at that penal camp. In the camp Sevzheldorlag (chief: colonel Klyuchkin) in 1946–47 there were many cases of cannibalism: they cut human bodies, cooked and ate." *[149]

The Soviet journalist Yevgenia Ginzburg was a former long-term political prisoner who spent time in the Soviet prisons, Gulag camps and settlements from 1938 to 1955. She described in her memoir, *Harsh Route* (or *Steep Route*), of a case which she was directly involved in during the late 1940s, after she had been moved to the prisoners' hospital.*[150]

> ...The chief warder shows me the black smoked pot, filled with some food: 'I need your medical expertise regarding this meat.' I look into the pot, and hardly hold vomiting. The fibres of that meat are very small, and don't resemble me anything I have seen before. The skin on some pieces bristles with black hair (...) A former smith from Poltava, Kulesh worked together with Centurashvili. At this time, Centurashvili was only one month away from being discharged from the camp (...) And suddenly he surprisingly disappeared. The wardens looked around the hills, stated Kulesh's evidence, that last time Kulesh had seen his workmate near the fireplace, Kulesh went out to work and Centurashvili left to warm himself more; but when Kulesh returned to the fireplace, Centurashvili had vanished; who knows, maybe he got frozen somewhere in snow, he was a weak guy (...) The wardens searched for two more days, and then assumed that it was an escape case, though they wondered why, since his imprisonment period was almost over (...) The crime was there. Approaching the fireplace, Kulesh killed Centurashvili with an axe, burned his clothes, then dismembered him and hid the pieces in snow, in different places, putting specific marks on each burial place. ... Just yesterday, one body part was found under two crossed logs.

When Uruguayan Air Force Flight 571 crashed into the Andes on October 13, 1972, the survivors resorted to eating the deceased during their 72 days in the mountains. Their story was later recounted in the books *Alive: The Story of the Andes Survivors* and *Miracle in the Andes* as well as the film *Alive*, by Frank Marshall, and the documentaries *Alive: 20 Years Later* (1993) and *Stranded: I've Come from a Plane that Crashed in the Mountains* (2008).

Cannibalism was reported by the journalist Neil Davis during the South East Asian wars of the 1960s and 1970s. Davis reported that Cambodian troops ritually ate portions of the slain enemy, typically the liver. However he, and many refugees, also report that cannibalism was practiced non-ritually when there was no food to be found. This usually occurred when towns and villages were under Khmer Rouge control, and food was strictly rationed, leading to widespread starvation. Any civilian caught participating in cannibalism would have been immediately executed.

On July 23, 1988, Rick Gibson ate the flesh of another person in public. Because England does not have a specific law against cannibalism, he legally ate a canapé of donated human tonsils in Walthamstow High Street, London.*[151]*[152] A year later, on April 15, 1989, he publicly ate a slice of human testicle in Lewisham High Street, London.*[153]*[154] When he tried to eat another slice of human testicle at the Pitt International Galleries in Vancouver on July 14, 1989, the Vancouver police confiscated the testicle hors d'œuvre.*[155] However, the charge of publicly exhibiting a disgusting object was dropped and he finally ate the piece of human testicle on the steps of the Vancouver court house on September 22, 1989.*[156]

1.8   See also

- Alexander Pearce

- Alferd Packer, an American prospector, accused but not convicted of cannibalism

- Androphagi, an ancient nation of cannibals

- Asmat people, a Papua group with a reputation of cannibalism

- Cannibalism in popular culture

- Cannibalism (poultry)

- Chijon family, a Korean gang that killed and ate rich people

- Custom of the Sea, the practice of shipwrecked survivors drawing lots to see who would be killed and eaten so that the others might survive

- Homo antecessor, an extinct human species, suspected of practicing cannibalism

- Human fat has been applied in European pharmacopeia between the 16th and the 19th centuries.

- Idi Amin Ugandan dictator who is alleged to have consumed humans.

- Issei Sagawa, a popular Japanese celebrity who killed and ate a fellow student

- List of incidents of cannibalism

- Manifesto Antropófago, (Cannibal Manifesto in English), a Brazilian poem

- Noida serial murders, a widely publicized instance of alleged cannibalism in India

- Placentophagy, the act of mammals eating the placenta of their young after childbirth

- R v Dudley and Stephens, an important trial of two men accused of shipwreck cannibalism

- *The Road*, Cormac McCarthy's 2006 novel concerning post-apocalyptic conditions on Earth, and humankind's consequent struggle for food.

- Transmissible spongiform encephalopathy, a progressive condition that affect the brain and nervous system of many animals, including humans

- Vorarephilia, a sexual fetish and paraphilia where arousal occurs from the idea of cannibalism

- Wari' people, an Amerindian tribe that practiced cannibalism

1.9 Notes

[1] Brief history of cannibal controversies; David F. Salisbury, August 15, 2001, *Exploration*, Vanderbilt University.

[2] *From primitive to post-colonial in Melanesia and anthropology.* Bruce M. Knauft (1999). University of Michigan Press. p. 104. ISBN 0-472-06687-0

[3] Peggy Reeves Sanday. "*Divine hunger: cannibalism as a cultural system*".

[4] Rubinstein, W. D. (2004). *Genocide: a history.* Pearson Education. pp. 17–18. ISBN 0-582-50601-8.

[5] Culotta, E. (October 1, 1999). "Neanderthals Were Cannibals, Bones Show". *Science* (Sciencemag.org) **286** (5437): 18b. doi:10.1126/science.286.5437.18b. Retrieved August 30, 2009.

[6] Gibbons, A. (August 1, 1997). "Archaeologists Rediscover Cannibals". *Science* (Sciencemag.org) **277** (5326): 635–7. doi:10.1126/science.277.5326.635. PMID 9254427. Retrieved August 30, 2009.

[7] McKie, Robin (May 17, 2009). "How Neanderthals met a grisly fate: devoured by humans". *The Observer* (London). Retrieved May 18, 2009.

[8] Liberia's elections, ritual killings and cannibalism August 2011

[9] "UN condemns DR Congo cannibalism". BBC. January 15, 2003. Retrieved October 29, 2011.

[10] Raffaele, Paul (September 2006). "Sleeping with Cannibals". *Smithsonian Magazine*.

[11] Barker, Francis; Hulme, Peter; Iverson, Margaret (ed.) (1998). *Cannibalism and the Colonial World*. Cambridge University Press. ISBN 9780521629089.

[12] Eat or be eaten: Is cannibalism a pathology as listed in the DSM-IV? The Straight Dope by Cecil Adams. Retrieved March 16, 2010.

[13] "Cannibalism Definition". Dictionary.com.

[14] "cannibalism (human behaviour)". Britannica Online Encyclopedia. Retrieved August 31, 2013.

[15] Woznicki, Andrew N. (1998). "Endocannibalism of the Yanomami". *The Summit Times* **6** (18–19).

[16] Dow, James W. "Cannibalism". In Tenenbaum, Barbara A. *Encyclopedia of Latin American History and Culture – Volume 1*. New York: Charles Scribner's Sons. pp. 535–537.

[17] Goldman, Laurence, ed. (1999). *The Anthropology of Cannibalism*. Greenwood Publishing Group. p. 16. ISBN 0-89789-596-7.

[18] "Anthropophagy". "1728 Cyclopaedia".

[19] Lindenbaum S (November 2008). "Understanding kuru: the contribution of anthropology and medicine". *Philos. Trans. R. Soc. Lond., B, Biol. Sci.* **363** (1510): 3715–20. doi:10.1098/rstb.2008.0072. PMC 2735506. PMID 18849287.

[20] Mead S, Stumpf MP, Whitfield J; et al. (April 2003). "Balancing selection at the prion protein gene consistent with prehistoric kurulike epidemics" (PDF). *Science* **300** (5619): 640–3. doi:10.1126/science.1083320. PMID 12690204.

[21] Nicholas Wade (April 11, 2003). "Gene Study Finds Cannibal Pattern". *New York Times*.

[22] Roach, John (April 10, 2003). "Cannibalism Normal For Early Humans?". *National Geographic*.

[23] Soldevila M, Andrés AM, Ramírez-Soriano A; et al. (February 2006). "The prion protein gene in humans revisited: Lessons from a worldwide resequencing study". *Genome Res.* **16** (2): 231–9. doi:10.1101/gr.4345506. PMC 1361719. PMID 16369046.

[24] "No cannibalism signature in human gene". "New Scientist".

[25] See *Cannibalism – Some Hidden Truths* for an example documenting escaped convicts in Australia who initially blamed natives, but later confessed to conducting the practice themselves out of desperate hunger.

[26] Mead S, Whitfield J, Poulter M; et al. (November 2008). "Genetic susceptibility, evolution and the kuru epidemic". *Philos. Trans. R. Soc. Lond., B, Biol. Sci.* **363** (1510): 3741–6. doi:10.1098/rstb.2008.0087. PMC 2576515. PMID 18849290.

[27] Brightman, Robert A. (1988). "The Windigo in the Material World". *Ethnohistory* **35** (4): 337–379. doi:10.2307/482140. JSTOR 482140.

[28] (New York: Oxford University Press, 1979; ISBN 0-19-502793-0)

[29] Arens, William (1981). *The Man-Eating Myth: Anthropology and Anthropophagy* (illustrated ed.). Oxford University Press US. p. 165. ISBN 978-0-19-502793-8.

[30] Timothy Taylor, *The Buried Soul: How Humans Invented Death*, Pages 58–60, Fourth Estate 2002

[31] de Montaigne, Michel. "Of cannibals". *Essays*. Translated by Charles Cotton. Hosted at Oregon State University.

[32] "The edible dead". Britarch.ac.uk. Retrieved August 30, 2009.

[33] Suelzle, Ben (November 2005). "Review of "The Origins of War: Violence in Prehistory", Jean Guilaine and Jean Zammit". *ERAS Journal* (7).

[34] "Hans Staden Among the Tupinambas". Lehigh.edu. Retrieved August 30, 2009.

[35] Unfortunate Emigrants: Narratives of the Donner Party, Utah State University Press. ISBN 0-87421-204-9

[36] "Māori Cannibalism". Retrieved July 27, 2007.

[37] "King of the Cannibal Isles". *Time*. May 11, 1942. Retrieved August 30, 2009.

[38] Rafaele, Paul (September 2006). "Sleeping with Cannibals". *Smithsonian Magazine*.

[39] "Fijians find chutney in bad taste". BBC News. December 13, 1998. Retrieved August 30, 2009.

[40] Lab tests show evidence of cannibalism among ancient Indians

[41] "Anasazi Cannibalism?". Archaeology.org. Retrieved August 30, 2009.

[42] Richard Hollingham (Jul 10, 2004). "Natural born cannibals". *New Scientist*: 30.

[43] Tim D white (September 15, 2006). *Once were Cannibals. Evolution: A Scientific American Reader*. ISBN 978-0-226-74269-4. Retrieved February 14, 2008.

[44] James Owen. "Neandertals Turned to Cannibalism, Bone Cave Suggests". *National Geographic News*. Retrieved February 3, 2008.

[45] Jordania, Joseph (2011). *Why do People Sing? Music in Human Evolution*. Logos. pp. 119–121.

[46] Corbett, Jim (2003). *Man-Eaters of Kumaon*. Oxford University Press, 26th impression. pp. xv-xvi.

[47] McKie, Robin (June 20, 2010). "Bones from a Cheddar Gorge cave show that cannibalism helped Britain's earliest settlers survive the ice age". *The Guardian* (London). Retrieved June 20, 2010.

[48] Bello, Silvia M.; et al. (February 2011). Petraglia, Michael, ed. "Earliest Directly-Dated Human Skull-Cups". *PLoS ONE* **6** (2): e17026. doi:10.1371/journal.pone.0017026. PMC 3040189. PMID 21359211. Retrieved February 17, 2011.

[49] Amos, Jonathan (February 16, 2011). "Ancient Britons 'drank from skulls'". *BBC News*. Retrieved February 17, 2011.

[50] Cannibalistic Celts discovered in South Gloucestershire March 7, 2001

[51] "Druids Committed Human Sacrifice, Cannibalism?". National Geographic.

[52] Brad Steiger (2010). *Real Zombies, the Living Dead, and Creatures of the Apocalypse*. Visible Ink Press. pp. 201. ISBN 978-1-57859-296-8.

[53] Flavius Josephus. *The Wars of the Jews*, Book VI, Chapter 3, Section 4. Translated by William Whiston. Hosted at the Perseus Digital Library.

[54] Appian. *The Wars in Spain*, Chapter XV, Section 96. Translated by Horace White. Hosted at the Perseus Digital Library.

[55] Schaff, Philip; Wace, Henry, eds. (c. 393). "Against Jovinianus—Book II". *A Select Library of Nicene and Post-Nicene Fathers of the Christian Church*. 2nd **6**. New York: The Christian Literature Company (published 1893). p. 394. Retrieved April 3, 2008.

[56] *The History of Herodotus VOL I*. Retrieved 2014-07-19.

[57] Godley, A. D. (1920). *Herodotus, with an English translation*. Cambridge: Harvard University Press. p. Hdt. 4.18. Retrieved 2014-07-19.

[58] Maalouf, Amin (1984). *The Crusades Through Arab Eyes*. New York: Schocken Books. pp. 37–40. ISBN 0-8052-0898-4.

[59] Cannibalism in Early Modern North Africa, British Journal of Middle Eastern Studies

[60] "Medieval Doctors and Their Patients". mummytombs.com. Retrieved December 3, 2007.

[61] Quotes from John Sanderson's *Travels* (1586) in *That Obscure Object of Desire: Victorian Commodity Culture and Fictions of the Mummy*, Nicholas Daly, NOVEL: A Forum on Fiction, Vol. 28, No. 1 (Autumn, 1994), pp. 24–51. doi:10.2307/1345912

[62] Benn, Charles (2002). *China's Golden Age: Everyday Life in the Tang Dynasty*. Oxford University Press. pp. 123–124. ISBN 0-19-517665-0.

[63] To Aztecs, Cannibalism Was a Status Symbol, New York Times

[64] "Aztec Cannibalism: An Ecological Necessity?". Latinamericanstudies.org. Retrieved August 30, 2009.

[65] Bernard R. Ortiz de Montellano. "Aztec Cannibalism: An Ecological necessity?" *Science* 200:611=617. 1978

[66] The cannibal within By Lewis F. Petrinovich, Aldine Transaction (2000), ISBN 0-202-02048-7. Retrieved March 19, 2010.

[67] Stromberg, Joseph (April 30, 2013). "Starving Settlers in Jamestown Colony Resorted to Cannibalism". *Smithsonian*.

[68] De Landa, Diego (1978). *Yucatán before and after the Conquest*. Dover. p. 4.

[69] Alanna King, ed. (1987). *Robert Louis Stevenson in the South Seas*. Luzac Paragon House. pp. 45–50.

[70] "Cannibalism". The Encyclopædia Britannica Eleventh Edition.

[71] E. Bowen, 1747: 532

[72] cannibalism, James WHITE, ed., Handbook of Indians of Canada, Published as an Appendix to the Tenth Report of the Geographic Board of Canada, Ottawa, 1913, 632p., pp. 77–78.

[73] Masters, Catherine (September 8, 2007). "'Battle rage' fed Maori cannibalism". *The New Zealand Herald*. Retrieved September 23, 2011.

[74] HONGI HIKA (c. 1780–1828) Ngapuhi war chief, the Encyclopedia of New Zealand.

[75] James Cowan, The New Zealand Wars: A History of the Maori Campaigns and the Pioneering Period: Volume II, 1922.

[76] "Melanesia Historical and Geographical: the Solomon Islands and the New Hebrides". *Southern Cross* (1). Church Army Press. London: 1950.

[77] Most Prolific Cannibal *Guinness Book of World Records* Internet Archive Wayback Machine 2004-09-29

[78] Peggy Reeves Sanday. "*Divine hunger: cannibalism as a cultural system*". p.166.

[79] "The Wreck of the Whaleship Essex". BBC. Retrieved August 30, 2009.

[80] Keenleyside, Anne. "The final days of the Franklin expedition: new skeletal evidence Arctic 50(1) 36-36 1997" (PDF). Retrieved January 26, 2008.

[81] Johnson, Kristin (ed.)(1996). Unfortunate Emigrants: Narratives of the Donner Party, Utah State University Press. ISBN 0-87421-204-9

[82] Rawson, Claude (April 16, 2000). "The Ultimate Taboo". *The New York Times*.

[83] Davidson, James W. (1903). *The Island of Formosa, Past and Present*. London and New York: Macmillan & co. p. 255. OL 6931635M.

[84] National Library of Ireland, MS 36,201/3

[85] "900-Day Siege of Leningrad". It.stlawu.edu. Retrieved August 30, 2009.

[86] "This Day in History 1941: Siege of Leningrad begins". History.com. Retrieved August 30, 2009.

[87] Daniel Goldhagen, *Hitler's Willing Executioners* (p. 290) – "2.8 million young, healthy Soviet POWs" killed by the Germans, "mainly by starvation ... in less than eight months" of 1941–42, before "the decimation of Soviet POWs ... was stopped" and the Germans "began to use them as laborers".

[88] The treatment of Soviet POWs: Starvation, disease, and shootings, June 1941 – January 1942 USHMM

[89] David M. Crowe (2013). *Crimes of State Past and Present: Government-Sponsored Atrocities and International Legal Responses*. Routledge, p. 87, ISBN 1317986822

[90] Petrinovich, Lewis F. (2000). *The Cannibal Within* (illustrated ed.). Aldine Transaction. p. 194. ISBN 978-0-202-02048-8.

[91] Beevor, Antony. *Stalingrad: The Fateful Siege*. Penguin Books, 1999.

[92] Happell, Charles (2008). *The Bone Man of Kokoda*. Sydney: Macmillan. ISBN 978-1-4050-3836-2.

[93] Tanaka, Yuki. *Hidden horrors: Japanese War Crimes in World War II*, Westview Press, 1996, p.127.

[94] Lord Russell of Liverpool (Edward Russell), *The Knights of Bushido, a short history of Japanese War Crimes*, Greenhill Books, 2002, p.121

[95] Welch, JM (April 2002). "Without a Hangman, Without a Rope: Navy War Crimes Trials After World War II" (PDF). *International Journal of Naval History* **1** (1). Retrieved December 3, 2007.

[96] Bradley, James (2003). *Flyboys: A True Story of Courage* (1st ed.). Little, Brown and Company (Time Warner Book Group). ISBN 0-316-10584-8.

[97] Bradley, James (2004) [2003]. *Flyboys: A True Story of Courage* (softcover) (first ed.). Boston, Massachusetts: Back Bay Books. pp. 229–230, 311, 404. ISBN 0-316-15943-3. Retrieved December 26, 2007.

[98] Garnaut, John (18 September 2006). "Cannibals may be feeding the lies". *The Sydney Morning Herald*.

[99] Pakenham, Thomas (1991). *The Scramble for Africa: White Man's Conquest of the Dark Continent From 1876 to 1912*. New York: Perennial. pp. 439–449. ISBN 0-380-71999-1.

[100] Pakenham, 439

[101] Pakenham, 447

[102] Slade, Ruth, "King Leopold's Congo" (1962), pg. 115, citing Lemery Papers, AMAA, in Pakenham, 447

[103] Gillison, Gillian (November 13, 2006). "From Cannibalism to Genocide: The Work of Denial". *The Journal of Interdisciplinary History* (MIT Press Journals) **37** (3): 395–414. doi:10.1162/jinh.2007.37.3.395.

[104] "'Cannibal' dictator Bokassa given posthumous pardon". *The Guardian*. December 3, 2010

[105] "Cannibal Emperor Bokassa Buried in Central African Republic". Americancivilrightsreview.com. Retrieved August 30, 2009.

[106] "'Good old days' under Bokassa? ". BBC News. January 2, 2009

[107] Papa in the Dock *Time* Magazine

[108] "Hatred turns into Cannibalism in CAR". NewsAfrica.co.uk. January 17, 2014.

[109] Flynn, Daniel (July 29, 2014). "Insight - Gold, diamonds feed Central African religious violence". Reuters.

[110] Congo's Sexual Violence Goes 'Far Beyond Rape', July 31, 2007. *The Washington Post*.

[111] "Cannibals massacring pygmies: claim". *Sydney Morning Herald*. January 10, 2003. Retrieved August 30, 2009.

[112] Paul Salopek, "Who Rules the Forest", *National Geographic* September 2005, p. 85

[113] Child Sacrifices on the Rise in Uganda as Witch Doctors Expand Their Practices; Ahmed Kamara, January 8, 2010, , Newstime Africa.

[114] "2003: 'War criminal' Idi Amin dies". BBC News. August 16, 2003. Retrieved December 4, 2007.

[115] Orizio, Riccardo (August 21, 2003). "Idi Amin's Exile Dream". *New York Times*. Retrieved December 4, 2007.

[116] Gerson, Michael (June 6, 2008). "Africa's Messiah of Horror". *The Washington Post*. This is ultimately the work and trademark of a single man: Joseph Kony, the most carnivorous killer since Idi Amin.

[117] "Cannibalism Fears in Hungry North Korea". Reuters. 28 April 1997.

[118] "French aid workers report cannibalism in famine-stricken North Korea". Minnesota Daily. April 16, 1998.

[119] Bong Lee (2003). *The Unfinished War: Korea*. Algora Publishing. p. 249. ISBN 0875862187.

[120] *The Times*. April 13, 1998. p. 13.

[121] "24 million starving Koreans turning to cannibalism". Weekly World News. 22 July 1997. p. 9.

[122] "North Korea 'executes three people found guilty of cannibalism'". The Telegraph. 11 May 2012.

[123] "North Korean cannibalism fears amid claims starving people forced to desperate measures". The Independent. 28 January 2013.

[124] "'Starving North Koreans eating own kids, corpses'". Times of India. 29 January 2013.

[125] "New reports of starving North Koreans resorting to cannibalism come amid renewed tensions between Pyongyang and Washington". New York Daily News. January 29, 2013.

[126] Jasper Becker (2005). *Rogue Regime: Kim Jong Il and the Looming Threat of North Korea*. Oxford University Press. p. 29. ISBN 0198038100.

[127] "The Cannibals of North Korea". Washington Post. February 5, 2013.

[128] "The Leopard Men". Unexplainedstuff.com. January 10, 1948. Retrieved August 30, 2009.

[129] "The Leopard Society —Africa in the mid 1900s". Retrieved April 3, 2008.

[130] Robbins, Joel (2006). "Properties of Nature, Properties of Culture: Ownership, Recognition, and the Politics of Nature in a Papua New Guinea Society". In Biersack, Aletta; Greenberg, James. *Reimagining Political Ecology*. Duke University Press. pp. 176–177. ISBN 0-8223-3672-3.

[131] Dalal, Roshen (2010). *Hinduism: An Alphabetical Guide*. Penguin. p. 8. ISBN 9780143414216.

[132] Ian Charles Harris (1992). *Contemporary Religions: A World Guide*. Longman Current Affairs. p. 74. ISBN 9780582086951.

[133] Schumacher, Tim (2013). *A New Religion*. iUniverse. p. 66. ISBN 9781475938463.

[134] "Indian doc focuses on Hindu cannibal sect". MSNBC. October 27, 2005.

[135] "Aghoris". *Encounter*. November 12, 2006. ABC.

[136] Lukov, Yaroslav (November 22, 2003). "Ukraine marks great famine anniversary". *BBC News*. Retrieved July 27, 2007.

[137] Timothy Snyder. *Bloodlands: Europe Between Hitler and Stalin*. Basic Books, 2010, pp.50–51. ISBN 0-465-00239-0

[138] Courtis, Stephane; Werth, Nicolas; et al. *The black book of communism*. Harvard University Press.

[139] Jung Chang. *Wild swans: three daughters of China*. Touchstone Press.

[140] Hong Ying. *Daughter of the river: an autobiography*. Grove Press.

[141] Becker, Jasper. *Hungry ghosts: Mao's secret famine*. Holt Press.

[142] *Mao Tze Tung*. History Channel.

[143] Kristof, Nicholas D; WuDunn, Sheryl (1994). *China Wakes: the Struggle for the Soul of a Rising Power*. Times Books. pp. 73–75. ISBN 0-8129-2252-2.

[144] Zheng Yi. *Scarlet Memorial: Tales Of Cannibalism In Modern China*. Westview Press.

[145] William Bueller Seabrook. *Jungle Ways* London, Bombay, Sydney: George G. Harrap and Company, 1931

[146] Allen, Gary. 1999. What is the Flavor of Human Flesh? Presented at the Symposium Cultural and Historical Aspects of Foods Oregon State University, Corvallis, Oregon.

[147] A. Solzhenitsyn, *The Gulag Archipelago* Part I, Chapter 9

[148] A. Solzhenitsyn, *The Gulag Archipelago*, Part I, comments to Chapter 5

[149] A.Solzhenitsyn *The Gulag Archipelago*, Part III, Chapter 15

[150] Yevgenia Ginzburg, *Harsh Route*, Part 2, Chapter 23 "The Paradise On A Microscope View"

[151] "Hard to stomach, but Rick eats human parts", *Waltham Forest Guardian* (London, United Kingdom), 29 July 1988: 6

[152] Young, Andrew (4 August 1988), "Rick eats his mate's tonsils on a cracker!", *The Sun* (Plymouth, United Kingdom): 3

[153] White, Kim (14 April 1989), "Now Rick's really gone nuts!", *Guardian & Gazette Newspapers* (London, United Kingdom): 8

[154] "Rick's food for thought", *The Mercury* (London, United Kingdom), 20 April 1989: 5

[155] Stueck, Wendy (15 July 1989), "Would-be cannibal's appetizer confiscated", *Vancouver Sun* (Vancouver, Canada): A7

[156] "No charges laid over artist's testicle claim", *Vancouver Sun* (Vancouver, Canada), 22 August 1988: B1

1.10 External links

- Is there a relation between cannibalism and amyloidosis?

- All about Cannibalism: The Ancient Taboo in Modern Times (Cannibalism Psychology) at CrimeLibrary.com

- *Cannibalism*, Víctor Montoya

- The Straight Dope Notes arguing that routine cannibalism is myth

- Did a mob of angry Dutch kill and eat their prime minister? (from The Straight Dope)

- Harry J. Brown, 'Hans Staden among the Tupinambas.'

Hansel and Gretel, *illustrated by Arthur Rackham.*

Ugolino and his sons in their cell, as painted by William Blake circa 1826. Ugolino della Gherardesca was an Italian nobleman who, together with his sons Gaddo and Uguccione and his grandsons Nino and Anselmuccio were detained in the Muda, in March 1289. The keys were thrown into the Arno river and the prisoners left to starve. According to Dante, the prisoners were slowly starved to death and before dying Ugolino's children begged him to eat their bodies.

A scene depicting ritualistic cannibalism being practiced in the Codex Magliabechiano folio 73r

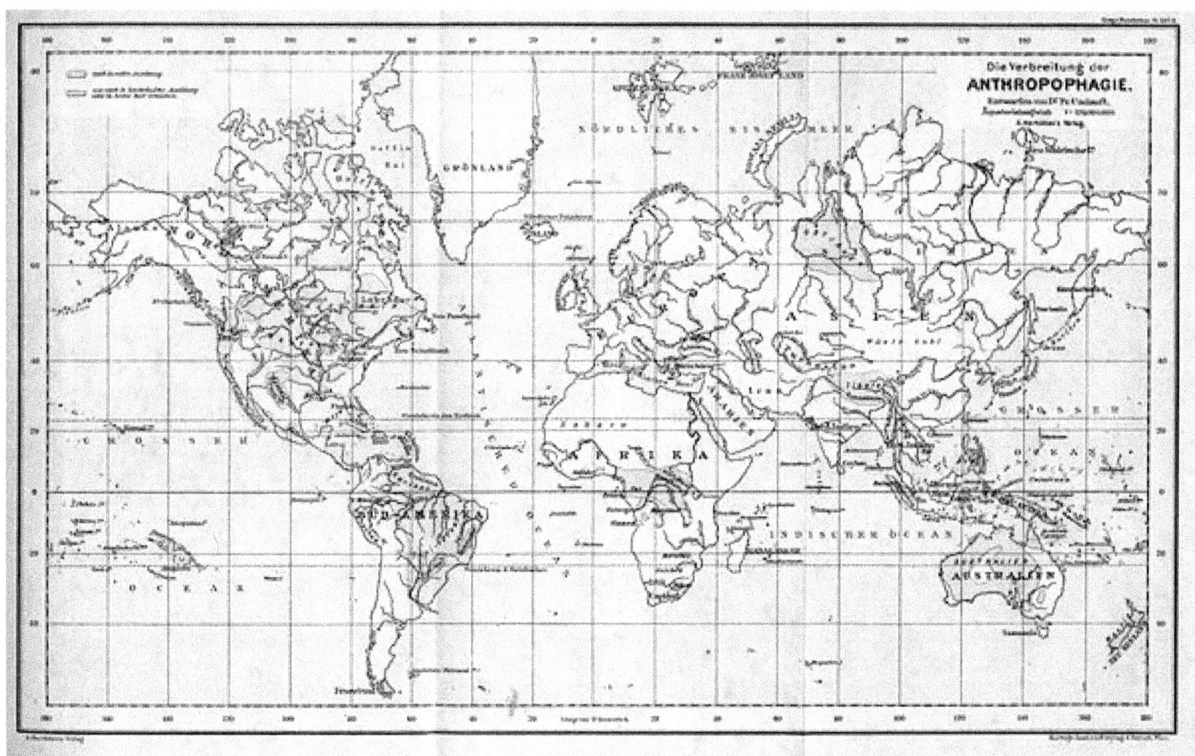

The spread of human cannibalism (anthropophagy) in the late 19th century.

Jean-Bédel Bokassa, the self-crowned emperor accused of cannibalism.

Cannibalism during the Russian famine of 1921.

Chapter 2

List of incidents of cannibalism

Cannibalism, or anthropophagy, is the consumption of human flesh or internal organs by other human beings. Accounts of cannibalism date back as far as Biblical times, and some anthropologists suggest that cannibalism was common in human societies as early as the Paleolithic Era. Historically, numerous tribal societies have reportedly engaged in cannibalism, although very few are thought to continue the practice to this day.

Occasionally, starving people have resorted to cannibalism for survival necessity. Classical antiquity recorded numerous references to cannibalism during siege starvations. More recent well-documented examples include the Donner Party in 1846, and the 1972 Andes flight disaster. Some murderers, such as Albert Fish and Boone Helm, are known to have devoured their victims after killing them. Other individuals, such as artist Rick Gibson and journalist William Seabrook, have legally consumed human flesh out of curiosity, or as an attention-grabbing stunt.

2.1 Prehistoric

- The 100,000-year-old bones of six Neanderthals found in the Moula-Guercy cave, France, had been broken by other Neanderthals in such a way as to extract marrow and brains. Finds made in the El Sidrón cave in Spain, also show endo cannibalism.*[1]

- The Cheddar Man, a human skeleton dating from around 7150 BC, may have been a victim of cannibalism.*[2]

2.2 Middle Ages

- Crusaders practised cannibalism during the Siege of Ma'arra.*[3]

- For a brief time in Europe, an unusual form of cannibalism occurred when thousands of Egyptian mummies preserved in bitumen were ground up and sold as medicine.*[4] The practice developed into a wide-scale business which flourished until the late 16th century. This "fad" ended because the mummies were revealed actually to be recently killed slaves. Two centuries ago, mummies were still believed to have medicinal properties against bleeding, and were sold as pharmaceuticals in powdered form.*[5]

- The Great Famine of 1315–17 was marked with extreme levels of cannibalism.

- Several works by Michel de Montaigne and Jean de Léry among others indicated that the Tupinambá tribe practised cannibalism.*[6]*[7]

- The Akokisa and Atakapa people of modern day Texas practised cannibalism.*[8]*[9]

- Island Caribs practised ritualistic cannibalism.*[10]

- The Wari' people practiced endocannibalism, specifically morturary cannibalism.*[11]

- Numerous incidents of cannibalism were recorded during the (1200–1201) drought in the Nile river region.*[12]

- Cannibalism was widely practised among the Aztec.*[13]

- In 1503,a group of Qizilbash militants ate the corpses of their enemies after taking over a fort in east Iran.*[14]

- The Korowai people claimed to have continued practising cannibalism into the present day in order to encourage tourism.*[15]

- Álvar Núñez Cabeza de Vaca along with other Spanish conquistadors committed cannibalism in the aftermath of a shipwreck.*[16]

2.3   17th–19th centuries

2.3.1   1600s

- In colonial Jamestown, colonists resorted to cannibalism during a period known as the Starving Time, from 1609 to 1610.*[17] After food supplies were diminished, some colonists began to dig up corpses for food. During this time period, one man was tortured until he confessed to having killed, salted, and eaten his pregnant wife; he was burned alive as punishment.*[18]*[19]

- In 1612, Polish troops stationed in the Moscow Kremlin resorted to cannibalism, in the aftermath of prolonged siege.*[20]

- A party of Cossacks under Vassili Poyarkov cannibalized the corpses of Siberian aborigines they had previously killed.*[21]

- On 20 August 1672, a mob lynched and ate parts of Johan de Witt.*[22]

2.3.2   1700s

- The accounts of the sinking of the *Luxborough Galley* in 1727 reported cannibalism amongst the survivors during their two weeks on a small boat in the mid-Atlantic.

- French showman and soldier Tarrare had reportedly engaged in cannibalism.

- Polish soldier Charles Domery ate pieces of a fellow crew member's severed leg.

- In 1763, North American Indians performed an act of ritual cannibalism on a British soldier during the Siege of Fort Detroit.

2.3.3   1800s

- In an 1809 incident known as the Boyd massacre, about 66 passengers and crew of the *Boyd* were killed and eaten by Māori on the Whangaroa peninsula, Northland, in northern New Zealand.

- In 1816, the French frigate *Méduse* ran aground off Mauritania, and 147 passengers and crew took to sea on a hastily constructed raft. In the chaotic 13 days before they were rescued, the occupants of the raft were driven to suicide, murder, and cannibalism; only 15 men survived the experience.

- The *Essex* was sunk by a sperm whale in the Pacific Ocean in 1820. The survivors of Captain Pollard's boat spent 90 days in a small whaling boat before being rescued. All the members who died during the 90 days were eaten. When the boat was found there were two members remaining; they were found sucking on the marrow of a human bone. The tale of the *Essex* inspired Herman Melville to write his novel *Moby-Dick*.

Raft of the Medusa *by Théodore Géricault, 1819*

- In 1822, Alexander Pearce, an Irish convict, led an escape from Macquarie Harbour Penal Settlement in Van Diemen's Land. Pearce was captured near Hobart and confessed that he and the other escapees had successively killed and cannibalised members of their group over a period of weeks, he being the last survivor.*[23]

- The 27 May 1826 issue of Acadian Recorder, mentioned that the surviving crew of the ship "Francis Mary" resorted to cannibalism.*[24]

- John Williams of the London Missionary Society and a colleague were killed and eaten at the Dillon Bay, Erromango island in 1839.*[25]*[26]

- Liver-Eating Johnson have reportedly eaten the livers of Crow warriors he had previously slain.

- In the US, the group of settlers known as the Donner Party resorted to cannibalism while snowbound in the mountains for the winter of 1846–47.

- The last survivors of Sir John Franklin's lost expedition were found to have resorted to cannibalism in their final push across King William Island, Canada, towards the Back River.*[27]

- Boone Helm, also known as "The Kentucky Cannibal", was an American mountain man, serial killer and fugitive, who ate human flesh on several occasions between 1850 and 1854, often out of necessity in extreme conditions. He made no secret of the fact, and is reported to have said: "Many's the poor devil I've killed, at one time or another ... and the time has been that I've been obliged to feed on some of 'em".

- In November 1874, three British sailors survived by committing cannibalism acts in the aftermath of the Cospatrick disaster.*[28]

- The case of *R v. Dudley and Stephens* (1884) 14 QBD 273 (QB) is an English case which dealt with four crew members of an English yacht, the *Mignonette*, who were cast away in a storm some 1,600 miles (2,600 km) from the Cape of Good Hope. After several days, one of the crew, a seventeen-year-old cabin boy, fell unconscious due to a combination of the famine and drinking seawater. The others (one possibly objecting) decided then to kill him and eat him. They were picked up four days later. Two of the three survivors were found guilty of murder. A significant outcome of this case was that necessity was determined to be no defence against a charge of murder.

- A report dated to 28 July 1892, indicates that three people were convicted on charges of cannibalism in the Sahalin penal colony. Two songs referencing cannibalism were also recorded among the residents of the colony.*[29]

2.4   20th century

2.4.1   1900–09

- During the course of the Bailundo Revolt, a group of Ovimbundu rebels decapitated a native merchant named Antonio de Silveira, roasting and then consuming his body. The rebels forced Silveira's wife to carry his head in a basket. The killing held a ritualistic purpose aiming to produce "success magic", as the perpetrators belonged to the Kandundu Cult.*[30]

2.4.2   1910–19

- The crew members of the steamship *Dumaru* spent three weeks adrift in a lifeboat after the ship exploded and sank in the western Pacific Ocean on October 16, 1916. Quickly exhausting their supply of food and water, they resorted to cannibalism to survive.*[31]

2.4.3   1920–29

- Serial killer Albert Fish caused much argument over whether he was insane because he consumed his victims. He confessed to molesting more than four hundred children over twenty years and is believed to have murdered somewhere between six and fifteen children.*[32] Psychiatrist Frederick Wertham described Fish as looking like "a meek and innocuous little old man, gentle and benevolent, friendly and polite. If you wanted someone to entrust your child to, he would be the one you would choose".*[33] Fish's most infamous murder is that of a little girl in 1928, whose flesh he cut into strips, cooked with carrots, onions, and strips of bacon. This excited him sexually.*[34] Wertham described how Fish's account of the culinary process was "like a housewife describing her favorite methods of cooking. You had to remind yourself that this was a little girl he was talking about".*[35] When the same psychiatrist declared Fish mad, Fish disagreed and stated he was just "queer".*[36]

- On 20 December 1924, German authorities uncovered pieces of human flesh along with a list of 40 people Karl Denke had previously killed and cannibalized.*[37]

2.4.4   1930–39

- Several reports from the 1930s, indicate that residents of the Appalachian Mountains practised a form of ritualistic cannibalism, during which cannibals ate parts of their dead relatives in order to honour them.*[38]*[39]

- Prior to 1931, *New York Times* reporter William Buehler Seabrook, allegedly in the interests of research, obtained from a hospital intern at the Sorbonne a chunk of human meat from the body of a healthy human killed in an accident, then cooked and ate it. He reported, "It was like good, fully-developed veal, not young, but not yet beef. It was very definitely like that, and it was not like any other meat I had ever tasted. It was so nearly like good, fully developed veal that I think no person with a palate of ordinary, normal sensitiveness could distinguish it from veal. It was mild, good meat with no other sharply defined or highly characteristic taste such as for instance, goat, high game, and pork have. The steak was slightly tougher than prime veal, a little stringy, but not too tough or stringy to be agreeably edible. The roast, from which I cut and ate a central slice, was tender, and in color, texture, smell as well as taste, strengthened my certainty that of all the meats we habitually know, veal is the one meat to which this meat is accurately comparable" .[*][40][*][41]

- Cannibalism was widespread during the famine of Ukraine in 1932-3,[*][42] forcing Soviet officials to commission posters saying: "To eat your own children is a barbarian act" .[*][43]

- An Italian woman named Leonarda Cianciulli killed three women between 1939-1940, turning their bodies into teacakes which she fed to others as well as consuming herself.

2.4.5 1940–49

- Members of the Leopard Society centered in Sierra Leone, Liberia and Côte d'Ivoire, indulged in cannibalism.[*][44]

- There are eyewitness accounts of cannibalism during the Siege of Leningrad (1941–44), including reports of people cutting off and eating their own flesh.[*][45]

- Alferd Packer was an American prospector who was accused of cannibalism during the winter of 1873-1874. First tried for murder, Packer was eventually sentenced to 40 years in prison after being convicted of manslaughter.[*][46]

- Following the German surrender at the Battle of Stalingrad in January/February 1943, roughly 100,000 German soldiers were taken prisoner of war (POW). Almost all of them were sent to POW camps in Siberia or Central Asia where, due to being chronically underfed by their Soviet captors, many resorted to cannibalism. Fewer than 5,000 of the prisoners taken at Stalingrad survived captivity. The majority, however, died early in their imprisonment due to exposure or sickness brought on by conditions in the surrounded army before the surrender.[*][47]

- The Australian War Crimes Section of the Tokyo Tribunal, led by prosecutor William Webb (the future Judge-in-Chief), collected numerous written reports and testimonies that documented Japanese soldiers' acts of cannibalism among their own troops, on enemy dead, and on Allied prisoners of war in many parts of the Greater East Asia Co-Prosperity Sphere. In September 1942, Japanese daily rations on New Guinea consisted of 800 grams of rice and tinned meat. However, by December, this had fallen to 50 grams.[*][48][*]:78–80 According to historian Yuki Tanaka, "cannibalism was often a systematic activity conducted by whole squads and under the command of officers" .[*][49]

  In some cases, flesh was cut from living people. An Indian POW, Lance Naik Hatam Ali (later a citizen of Pakistan), testified that in New Guinea: "the Japanese started selecting prisoners and every day one prisoner was taken out and killed and eaten by the soldiers. I personally saw this happen and about 100 prisoners were eaten at this place by the Japanese. The remainder of us were taken to another spot 50 miles (80 kilometres) away where 10 prisoners died of sickness. At this place, the Japanese again started selecting prisoners to eat. Those selected were taken to a hut where their flesh was cut from their bodies while they were alive and they were thrown into a ditch where they later died." .[*][50]

- Another well-documented case occurred in Chichijima in February 1945, when Japanese soldiers killed and consumed five American airmen. This case was investigated in 1947 in a war crimes trial, and of 30 Japanese soldiers prosecuted, five (Maj. Matoba, Gen. Tachibana, Adm. Mori, Capt. Yoshii, and Dr. Teraki) were found guilty and hanged.[*][51]

2.4.6 1950–69

- A tradition of ritualistic cannibalism among the Fore people caused a Kuru epidemic, with approximately 1000 deaths from 1957 to 1960.[*][52]

- German serial killer Joachim Kroll, nicknamed "Duisburg Man-Eater", practised cannibalism.[*][53]

- In October 1961, Papuan aborigines supposedly killed and ate Michael Rockefeller while he was exploring southern Netherlands New Guinea.[*][54]

2.4.7   1970–79

- On 13 July 1970, police arrested Stanley Baker on charges of killing and cannibalizing a Montana, U.S. resident.[*][55]

- In 1972, the survivors of Uruguayan Air Force Flight 571, consisting of the rugby team from Stella Maris College in Montevideo and some of their family members, resorted to cannibalism while trapped at the crash site. They had been stranded since October 13, 1972 and rescue operations at the crash site did not begin until December 22, 1972. The story of the survivors was chronicled in Piers Paul Read's 1974 book, *Alive: The Story of the Andes Survivors*, in a 1993 film adaptation of the book, called simply *Alive*, and in a 2008 documentary: *Stranded: I' ve Come From a Plane That Crashed on the Mountains*.

- Also in 1972, at the same time as the Andean incident, Marten Hartwell crashed his aircraft near the arctic circle in Canada's North West Territory. The three passengers died in the month it took searchers to find them but Hartwell survived by eating part of one body.

- In 1977, Briton Robert Maudsley killed a fellow inmate and consumed pieces of his brain.[*][56]

- On 20 August 1979, Briton Albert Fentress lured, killed and cannibalized an 18-year-old high school student.[*][57]

- Between 1979–1980, Nikolai Dzhumagaliev killed at least seven women, cannibalizing their corpses.[*][58]

2.4.8   1980–89

- On 11 June 1981, Issei Sagawa murdered a Dutch woman named Renée Hartevelt by shooting her in the neck with a rifle at his home in Paris, France. After having sex with the corpse, he began to eat her, starting with the buttocks and thighs. A few days later, he was discovered while attempting to dump the mutilated body into a lake, and subsequently arrested. He was held for two years without trial, then declared legally insane. Soon afterward, Japanese author Inuhiko Yomota published Sagawa's memoirs, including a detailed account of the murder. The book was a bestseller, and Sagawa became a minor celebrity. However, he was quickly extradited to Japan, where mental health professionals announced that he was perfectly sane. Because the French government refused to grant access to secret court documents, the Japanese authorities were unable to bring charges against him. He was released in 1986, and now lives in Tokyo, making a living as a freelance writer.[*][59]

- Michael Woodmansee was convicted in 1983 of kidnapping and killing 5 year old Jason Foreman in 1975 in South Kingstown, Rhode Island. There was evidence at the time that Woodmansee wrote in his journal of eating the flesh of young Jason.[*][60]

- In 1986, American Hadden Clark, killed and cannibalized 6-year-old Michelle Dorr.[*][61]

- In November 1986, American Gary Heidnik, abducted 6 women. After one of the women died, Heidnik fed the other victims a combination of dog food and human flesh.[*][62]

- In 1988, artist Rick Gibson legally performed an act of cannibalism by eating a canapé of donated human tonsils in Walthamstow High Street, London.[*][63] A year later, he publicly ate a slice of legally purchased human testicle in Lewisham High Street, London.[*][64] When he tried to eat another slice of human testicle in Vancouver, Canada in 1989, he was stopped by the police.[*][65] However, the charge was dropped and he finally ate a testicle hors d'œuvre in Vancouver in 1989.[*][66]

2.4.9   1990–99

- Jeffrey Dahmer, a serial killer living in Milwaukee, Wisconsin, murdered at least seventeen people between 1978 and 1991. Following his arrest, he told police that he had cut up the thighs, biceps and internal organs of several of his victims and cooked them in a stovetop skillet before consuming them. He claimed that they tasted like filet mignon.[*][67]

- Over Thanksgiving weekend of 1991, newlywed Omaima Aree Nelson murdered, dismembered, and cannibalized her husband, William E. "Bill" Nelson in their Costa Mesa home. Pathology reports indicate Bill was still alive when Omaima began butchering his body, in which court and media reports indicate was a ritualistic manner. She then boiled and cooked his head in the oven, ate its flesh, and stored the foil-wrapped skull in the freezer; skinned his torso; deep fried his hands in oil; and cooked and dipped his ribs in barbecue sauce and tasted them.*[68]*[69]*[70]*[71]

- Andrei Chikatilo, a serial killer born in Ukraine, experienced killing and cannibalism as paraphilia. He was convicted for murder in 1992 and subsequently executed.*[36]*[72]

- During the North Korean famine that occurred between 1994 and 1998, there were leaked stories of cannibalism from North Korean refugees.*[73]

- The Chijon family was a South Korean gang that engaged in cannibalism.*[74]

- Ilshat Kuzikov, of St. Petersburg, Russia, was convicted in March 1997 of eating three male acquaintances since 1992.*[75]

- A court submission at the trial of perpetrators of the Snowtown murders in South Australia revealed that two of the murderers fried and ate a part of their final victim in 1999.*[76]

- Dorangel Vargas, also known as "*el comegente*" (Spanish for "people-eater"), was a Venezuelan serial killer and cannibal who killed and ate at least 10 men in a period of two years preceding his arrest in 1999.

- On 13 August 1999, Kazahstani authorities arrested three male psychiatric nurses on charges of killing and eating seven prostitutes.*[77]

2.5 21st century

2.5.1 2000–09

- In February 2000, Katherine Knight killed her partner John Price and cooked his corpse, later preparing to serve it to his children.*[78]

- In March 2001 in Germany, Armin Meiwes posted an Internet ad seeking a young man willing to be slaughtered and eaten. The ad was answered by Bernd Jürgen Brandes. Meiwes stabbed Brandes in the neck with a kitchen knife, kissing him first, then chopped him up into several pieces. He placed several pieces of Brandes in the freezer. Over the next few weeks, Meiwes defrosted and cooked parts of Brandes in olive oil and garlic and eventually consumed 20 kg of human flesh. Meiwes was convicted of manslaughter in 2004.*[79] A retrial in 2006 found Meiwes guilty of murder, and sentenced him to life imprisonment.*[80] The songs "Mein Teil" by Rammstein and "Eaten" by Bloodbath are based on this case.

- In July 2002, four Ukrainians were arrested in Kiev for killing and eating a teenage girl. They were suspected of killing at least 6 people. Evidence showed that the murders may have been influenced by satanism.*[75]

- In a 2003 drug-related case, the rap artist Big Lurch was convicted of the murder and partial consumption of an acquaintance while both were under the influence of PCP.*[81]

- Between 2003–2004, South Korean Yoo Young-chul, murdered a total of 21 people, eating the livers off several of his victims.*[82]

- In February 2004, a 39-year-old Briton named Peter Bryan from East London was caught after he killed his friend Brian Cherry and ate parts of his brain, fried in butter. He had been arrested for murder previously, but was released shortly before this act was committed. While on trial for the murder of Cherry, Bryan was sentenced to life imprisonment, despite his claim of diminished responsibility.*[83]*[84] In January 2006, his sentence was revised to a minimum of 15 years.*[85]

- A count of 25 albino Tanzanians have been murdered since March 2007 reportedly through witch doctor butchery arising from prevailing superstition.*[86]*[87] In 2008, Tanzania's President Kikwete publicly condemned witch doctors for killing people with albinism for their body parts, which are thought to bring good luck.

- Between 2006–2007, Indian serial killer Surender Koli killed and canniballized 19 people, the majority of which were children.*[88]

- On 5 January 2007, French authorities reported that a prison inmate committed cannibalism on a cellmate, in the city of Rouen.*[89]

- On 13 January 2007, Marco Evaristti hosted a dinner party where the main course was agnolotti pasta that was topped with a meatball made from his own fat, removed earlier in the year in a liposuction operation.*[90]

- On September 14, 2007, a man named Özgür Dengiz was captured in Ankara, the Turkish capital, after killing and eating a man. After cutting slices of flesh from his victim's body, Dengiz distributed the rest to stray dogs on the street, according to his own testimony. He ate some of the man's flesh raw on his way home. Dengiz, who lived with his parents, arrived at the family house and placed the remaining parts of the body in the fridge without saying a word to his parents.*[91]*[92]

- On 8 October 2008, Mexican authorities arrested Jose Luis Calva Zepeda, on more than three counts of murder. Numerous pieces of cooked human flesh were discovered in the suspect's house.*[93]

- In January 2008, notorious Liberian ex-rebel and reformed warlord Joshua Blahyi, 37, confessed to participating in human sacrifices which "included the killing of an innocent child and plucking out the heart, which was divided into pieces for us to eat." The cannibalism of many children occurred during the conflict in which Blahyi fought against Liberian president Charles Taylor's militia.*[94]

  On March 13, 2008, during the same war crimes trial, Joseph Marzah, Taylor's chief of operations and head of Taylor's alleged "death squad", accused Taylor of ordering his soldiers to commit acts of cannibalism against enemies, including peacekeepers and United Nations personnel.*[95]

- The murder of Tim McLean occurred on the evening of July 30, 2008. McLean, a 22-year-old Canadian man, was stabbed, beheaded and cannibalized while riding a Greyhound Canada bus near Portage la Prairie, Manitoba. According to witnesses, McLean was sleeping with his headphones on when the man sitting next to him, Vincent Li, suddenly produced a large knife and began stabbing McLean in the neck and chest. The attacker then decapitated McLean, severed other body parts, and consumed some of McLean's flesh.

- In a documentary by Colombian journalist Hollman Morris, a demobilized paramilitary confessed that during the mass killings that took place in Colombia's rural areas, many of the paras performed cannibalism. He also confessed that they were told to drink the blood of their victims in the belief that it would make them want to kill more.*[96]

- In November 2008, a group of 33 illegal immigrants from the Dominican Republic, who were en route to Puerto Rico, resorted to cannibalism after they were lost at sea for over 15 days before being rescued by a U.S. Coast Guard patrol boat.*[97]

- In February 2009, it was reported that five members of the Kulina tribe in Brazil were wanted by Brazilian authorities on the charge of murdering, butchering and eating a farmer in a ritual act of cannibalism.*[98]

- In April 2009, two men from the city of Perm, Russia, killed and ate their brother.*[99]

- On 27 July 2009, an American woman, Otty Sanchez, was found in a hysterical state by police, having killed her own child and cannibalized parts of the infant's corpse.*[100]

- On November 14, 2009, three homeless men in Perm, Russia were arrested for killing and eating the parts of a 25-year-old male victim. The remaining body parts were then sold to a local pie and kebab house.*[101]

- Between 2009–2011, a Berlinskoe, Russia, resident and serial killer Alexander Bychkov engaged in numerous acts of cannibalism, targeting people he had previously lured into his house.*[102]

2.5.2   2010–present

- Between April – May 2010, a PhD student from Bradford, England, killed and ate three prostitutes.[103]

- In April 2011, in the town of Darya Khan, Punjab, Pakistan, brothers Arif Ali and Farman Ali were arrested for eating a human corpse stolen from a grave. They were cooking body parts for a meal when arrested; the police also recovered remains of human body parts from their house.[104] The brothers were released from jail in 2013; however, in April 2014, they were once again discovered to be making curry out of a human corpse (this time, the body of a two- to three-year-old child), presumed to have been stolen from a graveyard.[105]

- On 9 July 2011, a model in the Leningrad region of Russia drowned her colleague and consumed parts of her corpse. She was later detained, found guilty of murder, and sent to a psychiatric hospital for treatment, where she was diagnosed with schizophrenia.[106]

- In August 2011, police found the body parts of various people in serial killer Matej Curko's fridge, including the body parts of two Slovakian women who disappeared in 2010.[107]

- In 2011, officials in South Korea received a tip that ethnic Koreans living in China were smuggling drug capsules into the country that contained powder made from dead babies, passing them off as stamina boosters. The ethnic Korean citizens of China tried to smuggle them into South Korea and consume the capsules or distribute them to other ethnic Korean citizens of China living in South Korea. Reportedly, the capsules were made in northeastern China from dead fetuses whose bodies were chopped into small pieces and dried on stoves before being turned into powder. No one has been reported as having become sick as a result of ingesting the capsules.[108][109][110][111]

- Dennis Storm and Valerio Zeno, the two presenters of the Dutch TV show *Proefkonijnen*, ate each other's flesh on air in December 2011. They were filmed having a piece of their muscle tissue surgically removed, which was then fried and eaten in front of a studio audience.[112]

- In December 2011, a Florida man killed and ate a homeless man in the city of Bridgeport, Connecticut, U.S.A. The perpetrator of the crime was later found insane and committed to a maximum-security psychiatric hospital.[113]

- On 21 March 2012, a Vladivostok man killed his friend, later selling his meat in a local market. Another man was convicted of willingly consuming the flesh of the victim.[114]

- On 13 April 2012, a Japanese man cut off, cooked and served his genitals to five people. Each of the diners paid 250 $ per portion.[115]

- In April 2012, a man and two women were arrested in the town of Garanhuns, Pernambuco, Brazil for murdering at least two women and eating their flesh. One of the female suspects is said to have used some of the flesh of her victims for making pasties, which she allegedly sold in the town.[116]

- In April 2012, Jieming Liu, 79, was accused of killing his wife and eating some of her flesh in Shrewsbury, Massachusetts. The couple had immigrated from China in November 2011.[117]

- In May 2012, Kujoe Bonsafo Agyei-Kodie, an exchange student from Ghana, was murdered by Alexander Kinyua in Maryland, United States. Kinyua had eaten Agyei-Kodies' organs in an act of cannibalism.

- On May 26, 2012, police in Miami, Florida, shot and killed Rudy Eugene, 31, after he was found on the MacArthur Causeway naked and eating the face of Ronald Poppo, 65, who was homeless at the time. Police believed that Eugene was under the influence of a synthetic drug, but the autopsy of Eugene showed only marijuana in his system.[118] A security camera at the headquarters of *The Miami Herald* caught the attack live on film, which quickly began making rounds on the internet.[119] Poppo has had facial surgery since the attack and is having treatment for his face.[120]

- On 31 May 2012, a Swedish professor took revenge on his wife by cutting off her lips and eating them.[121]

- In July 2012, twenty-nine members of a cannibal cult were arrested in northeast Papua New Guinea after eating at least seven people (four men and three women) believed to be sorcerers.[122][123]

- In October 2012, Japanese authorities convicted three men for killing and eating a common friend in 2009.[124]

- On December 26, 2012, Mridul Kumar Bhattacharya and his wife Rita Bhattacharya who owned tea gardens in Assam, India were murdered by an angry mob of workers. Cannibalism was later reported in the incident.*[125]

- On January 10, 2013, the Chinese cannibal Zhang Yongming, aged 57, was executed for his crimes. He sold victims' flesh as 'ostrich meat' and kept eyeballs in wine.*[126]*[127]

- In April 2013, British punk rock musician David Playpenz ate his finger after it was severed in a motorcycle accident*[128]

- On 17 March 2013, a 47-year-old man, mutilated, sexually assaulted and ate pieces of a 77-year-old woman, in Ontario, Canada. The man reportedly suffered from severe depression and the attack was perpetrated during a psychotic incident.*[129]

- On May 2013, during the Syrian civil war, a rebel named Abu Sakkar was filmed cutting open the body of a fallen enemy soldier and biting into one of his organs – it is unclear whether it was a heart, a lung, or something else.*[130]

- In July 2013 Lino Renzi, aged 45, was found out while cooking some remains of his mother, Maria Pia Guariglia, aged 73, in his apartment by the police, called by a neighbour after smelling a disgusting odor coming from Renzi's apartment, probably caused by some intestine chunks burning on the grill. The cops discovered moreover several pieces of human body in a freezer, oven and pots, while most of the corpse, lying in the bathroom, featured severe mutilation to arms and legs, besides several intestine pieces removed. Later on, Renzi confessed his mother hadn't died of natural causes, but she'd been brutally beaten to death by himself after a quarrel, then dismembered into pieces with a saw and a butcher knife.*[131]*[132]

- On 13 January 2014, BBC reported that a Christian man nicknamed "Mad Dog" ate his Muslim rival's foot, during the CAR conflict.*[133]

- On 15 September 2014, a man from Jeffersonville, Indiana, USA, killed and ate parts of his girlfriend.*[134]

- On 7 October 2014, a chef from Brisbane, Australia, committed a murder–suicide, murdering, cooking and eating parts of his girlfriend before committing suicide.*[135]

- On 31 October 2014, a crowd stoned to death, burned and then ate a suspected ADF insurgent in the town of Beni, North Kivu, Democratic Republic of the Congo.The incident came after a number of ADF raids, that brought the October's civilian death toll to over 100 people.*[136]

- On November 6, 2014, Matthew Williams, 34, was allegedly found eating his 22-year-old victim's face in a room of the Sirhowy Arms Hotel in the village of Argoed, near Blackwood, South Wales.*[137]

- On 6 January 2015, a Reuters report revealed that the La Familia Michoacana and the Knights Templar cartels, were forcing potential recruits to eat the hearts of their victims as part of an initiation rite.*[138]

2.6   References

[1]   "Europe's Hypocritical History of Cannibalism". *Smithsonian Magazine*. 24 April 2013. Retrieved 21 November 2014.

[2]   Bello, SM; Parfitt, SA; Stringer, CB (2011). "Earliest directly-dated human skull-cups". *Plos One* **6** (2): e17026. doi:10.1371/journal.pone.0017026. PMC 3040189. PMID 21359211.

[3]   Edward Peters, The First Crusade: The Chronicle of Fulcher of Chartres and Other Source Materials (University of Pennsylvania Press, 1998), 84.

[4]   "Medieval Doctors and Their Patients". mummytombs.com. Retrieved December 3, 2007.

[5]   Quotes from John Sanderson's *Travels* (1586) in *That Obscure Object of Desire: Victorian Commodity Culture and Fictions of the Mummy*, Nicholas Daly, NOVEL: A Forum on Fiction, Vol. 28, No. 1 (Autumn, 1994), pp. 24–51. doi:10.2307/1345912

[6]   Michel de Montaigne,*Essais*, Book 1, Chap.31

[7] Carlo Ginzburg (2012)*Threads and Traces: True, False, Fictive*, (papers), University of California Press, ISBN 9780520274488, Chapter 3: *Montaigne, Cannibals, and Grottoes*

[8] "Europe's Hypocritical History of Cannibalism". *Attakapas*. Retrieved 21 November 2014.

[9] Newcomb, William Wilmon, Jr. *The Indians of Texas: From Prehistoric to Modern Times*. Austin: University of Texas Press, 1972:327

[10] Foote, Nicola (ed.), The Caribbean History Reader (London: Routledge, 2013), p.2

[11] "Wari': Funerary Cannibalism." *Povos Indígenas no Brasil*. Retrieved 22 Feb 2012.

[12] "The Fall of the Egyptian Old Kingdom". *BBC*. 17 February 2011. Retrieved 20 November 2014.

[13] Diaz del Castillo, Bernal [c.1568](1956, p.178),*The Discovery And Conquest Of Mexico*, Farrar, Strauss and Cudahy USA oclc 56-5758

[14] История Востока В 6 т. / Отв. ред. Л. Б. Алаев, К. З. Ашрафян, Н. И. Иванов. Т. III. Восток на рубеже Средневековья и Нового времени. XVI—XVIII вв. М.: Издат. фирма «Восточ. лит-ра» РАН, 2000. С. 101.

[15] John Garnaut (18 September 2006). "Cannibals may be feeding the lies". The Sydney Morning Herarld. Retrieved 2006-10-25.

[16] Newcomb, Jr., W. W. *The Indians of Texas: From Prehistoric to Modern Times* Austin: University of Texas Press, 1999, p. 77

[17] Wade, Nicholas (May 1, 2013). "Evidence of Cannibalism Found at Jamestown Site". *New York Times*. Retrieved May 1, 2013.

[18] "The official site of Colonial Williamsburg —Things which seame incredible: Cannibalism in Early Jamestown". History.org. Retrieved August 30, 2009.

[19] Dennis Montgomery (2007). *1607: Jamestown and the New World*. Colonial Williamsburg. pp. 75–81, 82–85, "There are, then, at least half a dozen written seventeenth century reports of Starving Time cannibalism, each of which corroborates another in one or more details. ..." (p.85). ISBN 978-0-87935-232-5.

[20] К. Валишевский. «Смутное время». М., 1993. С. 293–294. ISBN 5-8498-0037-9

[21] W Bruce Lincoln, 'The Conquest of a Continent',page 65, citing Akheograficheskaya Kommissia,'Dopolneniia k Aktam Istoricheskim', St Petersburg 1846-72, III, document 12, pp. 52-60

[22] Kok, J. (1794) *Vaderlandsch woordenboek; oorspronkelijk verzameld door Jacobus Kok. Deel 32*, p. 352; Veeghens, D. (1884) *Historische studien: Uitg. door J.D. Veegens. Eerste Deel*, p. 48; the first name of Verhoeff was Hendrick according to Fruin, R. (1901) *Robert Fruin's verspreide geschriften*, p. 374, fn. 2

[23] Collins, Paul (October 29, 2002). "A journey through hell's gate". *The Age*. Retrieved August 1, 2012.

[24] *The Acadian Recorder*, Saturday, May 27, 1826

[25] 18°49′00″S 169°00′30″E / 18.81667°S 169.00833°E

[26] "BBC News – Island holds reconciliation over cannibalism". news.bbc.co.uk. 2009-12-07. Retrieved 2009-12-07.

[27] Beattie, Owen and Geiger, John (2004). *Frozen in Time*. ISBN 1-55365-060-3.

[28] "Guided tours reveal island secrets". 6 August 2003. Retrieved 24 November 2014.

[29] Новодворский В., Дорошевич В. Коронка в пиках до валета. Каторга.. —СПб.: Санта, 1994. —20 000 экз. —ISBN 5-87243-010-8

[30] Douglas Wheeler. "The Bailundo Revolt of 1902" (PDF). *Redeemer's University*. Retrieved 9 May 2015.

[31] Thomas, Lowell (1930). *The Wreck of the Dumaru*. Garden City, New York: Doubleday, Doran & Company, Inc.

[32] Litton, S. (2006). "Characteristics of Child Molesters". In E. W. Hickey (Ed.). *Sex Crimes and Paraphilia*. New Jersey: Pearson

[33] Cyriax, Oliver, Wilson, Colin, & Wilson, Damon. (2006). *The Encyclopedia of Crime*. Woodstock: The Overlook Press. p. 144

[34] Wilson, Colin and Donald Seaman. *The Serial Killers*. Virgin Publishing Ltd. 2004, page 69.

[35] Howitt, D. (2006). "What Is the Role of Fantasy in Sex Offending?" *Criminal Behavior and Mental Health*, 14 (3), 182–188

[36] Vronsky, P. (2004). *Serial Killers – The Method and Madness of Monsters*. New York: The Berkley Publishing Group

[37] "Karl Denke". *Murderpedia*. Retrieved 20 November 2014.

[38] James K. Crissman. *Death and Dying in Central Appalachia: Changing Attitudes and Practices* University of Illinois Press, 1994, p. 113-6.

[39] *The Register of the Kentucky Historical Society* Ed. Jennie C. Morton. Kentucky Historical Society, 1947, p. 42.

[40] William Bueller Seabrook. *Jungle Ways* London, Bombay, Sydney: George G. Harrap and Company, 1931

[41] Allen, Gary. 1999. What is the Flavor of Human Flesh? Presented at the Symposium Cultural and Historical Aspects of Foods Oregon State University, Corvallis, Oregon.

[42] Сокур, Василий [Sokur, Vasily] (November 21, 2008). Выявленным во время голодомора людоедам ходившие по селам медицинские работники давали отравленные "приманки" —кусок мяса или хлеба. *Facts and Commentaries* (in Russian). Archived from the original on January 6, 2013.

[43] Várdy, Steven Béla; Várdy, Agnes Huszár (2007). "Cannibalism in Stalin's Russia and Mao's China" (PDF). *East European Quarterly* **41** (2): 225.

[44] "The Leopard Society – Africa in the mid 1900s". Retrieved 3 April 2008.

[45] Vulliamy, Ed (November 25, 2001). "Orchestral manoeuvres (part one)". *The Guardian* (London). Retrieved July 27, 2007.

[46] Nash, Robert Jay (1994). Alferd Packer. In *Encyclopedia of Western Lawmen & Outlaws* or *Encyclopedia of Western Lawmen & Outlaws*. Da Capo Press. pp. 250-251. ISBN 0-306-80591-X. Google Print. Retrieved 2012-01-07.

[47] Beevor, Antony. *Stalingrad: The Fateful Siege*. Penguin Books, 1999.

[48] Happell, Charles (2008). *The Bone Man of Kokoda*. Sydney: Macmillan. ISBN 978-1-4050-3836-2.

[49] Tanaka, Yuki. *Hidden horrors: Japanese War Crimes in World War II*, Westview Press, 1996, p.127.

[50] Lord Russell of Liverpool (Edward Russell), *The Knights of Bushido, a short history of Japanese War Crimes*, Greenhill Books, 2002, p.121

[51] Welch, JM (April 2002). "Without a Hangman, Without a Rope: Navy War Crimes Trials After World War II" (PDF). *International Journal of Naval History* **1** (1). Retrieved December 3, 2007. |chapter= ignored (help)

[52] Michael P. Alpers (2008). "The epidemiology of kuru: monitoring the epidemic from its peak to its end". *Philosophical Transactions of the Royal Society B* **363** (1510): 3707–3713. doi:10.1098/rstb.2008.0071. PMC 2577135. PMID 18849286.

[53] Dunning, John (1992). *Strange Deaths*. Mulberry Editions. pp. 218–219. ISBN 1-873123-13-2.

[54] "How a young Rockefeller died at the hands of cannibals". *NY Post*. 15 March 2014. Retrieved 1 November 2014.

[55] "Stanley Dean BAKER". *Murderpedia*. Retrieved 20 November 2014.

[56] "Robert Maudsley". *Murderpedia*. Retrieved 20 November 2014.

[57] "Albert Fentress". *Murderpedia*. Retrieved 20 November 2014.

[58] "Modern cannibalism: Six killers with a taste for human flesh". Trutv.com. 2012-05-17. Retrieved 2014-01-18.

[59] Morris, Steven (September 20, 2007). "Issei Sagawa: Celebrity Cannibal". *New Criminologist, the On-line Journal of Criminology* (New Criminologist). Archived from the original on June 14, 2011.

[60] "Father of Murdered 5-Year-Old Says He'll Make Sure Killer Suffers Same Fate". *Fox News*. March 8, 2011.

[61] "Hadden Clark". *Murderpedia*. Retrieved 20 November 2014.

[62] "Gary Heidnik". *Murderpedia*. Retrieved 20 November 2014.

[63] Young, Andrew (4 August 1988), "Rick eats his mate's tonsils on a cracker!", *The Sun* (London, United Kingdom): 3

[64] "Never Mind the Bollocks···", *Time Out* (London, United Kingdom), 12 April 1989: 11

[65] Stueck, Wendy (15 July 1989), "Would-be cannibal's appetizer confiscated", *Vancouver Sun* (Vancouver, Canada): A7

[66] "No charges laid over artist's testicle claim", *Vancouver Sun* (Vancouver, Canada), 22 August 1988: B1

[67] Ewing, C. P.; McCann, J. T. (2006). *Minds on Trial: Great Cases in Law and Psychology*. Oxford University Press. p.145. ISBN 0199884617.

[68] Investigation Discovery (18 August 2012). "Devoured By Love". *Happily Never After*. Retrieved 19 August 2012.

[69] "Woman Denies Dismemberment Killing of Husband". *Los Angeles Times*. 12 December 1991. Retrieved 19 August 2012.

[70] Welborn, Larry (28 September 2001). "Woman who cut up husband seeks parole today". *The Orange County Register*. Retrieved 19 August 2012.

[71] Mandell, Nina (30 September 2011). "Omaima Aree Nelson, former model who murdered, then ate her husband wants to get out of prison early". *New York Daily News*. Retrieved 19 August 2012.

[72] White, J. (2007). − "Evidence of Primary, Secondary, and Collateral Paraphilias Left at Serial Murder and Sex Offender Crime Scenes". *Journal of Forensic Sciences*, 52(5), 1194–1201

[73] "Opening a Window on North Korea's Horrors: Defectors Haunted by Guilt Over the Loved Ones Left Behind". *The Washington Post*. October 4, 2003. Retrieved July 27, 2007.

[74] (Korean) □□□□□□□

[75] Michael Newton (1 January 2006). *The Encyclopedia of Serial Killers*. Infobase Publishing. p. 35. ISBN 978-0-8160-6987-3.

[76] "Snowtown killers "cooked victim's flesh"". *ABC News Online* (Australian Broadcasting Corporation). September 19, 2005. Archived from the original on 29 June 2011.

[77] "Three arrested for cannibalism in Kazakhstan". 13 August 1999. Retrieved 24 November 2014.

[78] "Katherine Knight q&a". *The Australian Women's Weekly*. Ninemsn Pty Ltd. 22 October 2002. Retrieved 24 December 2013.

[79] Harding, Luke (31 January 2004). "Cannibal who fried victim in garlic is cleared of murder". *The Guardian*. Retrieved 1 August 2012.

[80] "German cannibal guilty of murder". *BBC News*. 9 May 2006. Retrieved 1 August 2012.

[81] 'Cannibal rapper killed for gangsta image'. iol.co.za. April 14, 2003. Archived from the original on 2005-03-15.

[82] "Man Kills Prostitutes, Old Rich Guys For Food". Retrieved 20 November 2014.

[83] Triggle, Nick (September 3, 2009). "NHS 'failed' over cannibal killer". *BBC News*. Retrieved April 28, 2010.

[84] "Fried brains cannibal killer guilty". Sky News. 15 March 2005. Retrieved 2012-06-28.

[85] "Cannibal overturns jail tariff". *BBC News*. 31 January 2006. Retrieved 16 August 2012.

[86] "Living in fear: Tanzania's albinos". BBC News. 21 July 2008.

[87] "Albino Africans live in fear after witch-doctor butchery". *The Observer*. November 16, 2008.

[88] "Koli Surender". *Murderpedia*. Retrieved 20 November 2014.

[89] "France probes 'cannibalism' case". 5 January 2007. Retrieved 24 November 2014.

[90] "Meal fried in artist's own body fat". news.com.au. 2007-01-13. Retrieved 2008-10-27.

[91] "Newspaper "Today's Zaman" September 17, 2007". Todayszaman.com. September 17, 2007. Retrieved August 30, 2009.

[92] "Yerli Hannibal'ın anatomisi". *Milliyet*. September 16, 2007. (Turkish)

[93] "José Luis CALVA ZEPEDA" . Murderpedia. Retrieved 20 November 2014.

[94] Paye, Jonathan (January 22, 2008). "I ate children's hearts, ex-rebel says" . BBC News. Retrieved August 30, 2009.

[95] "Top aide testifies Taylor ordered soldiers to eat victims" . CNN. March 13, 2008. Archived from the original on March 17, 2008.

[96] "Confesiones de un Ex-paramilitar" (parte I) //CONTRAVÍA//, YouTube.

[97] "Dominican migrant: We ate flesh to survive – A small group turned to cannibalism after being stranded in mid-ocean" . MSNBC. November 4, 2008.

[98] "Amazon Indians accused of cannibalizing farmer" . CNN. February 9, 2009.

[99] "Russian cannibals 'eat their brother' ". Metro UK. 1 November 2014. Retrieved 15 April 2009.

[100] "Otty Sanchez, Woman Accused Of Killing Newborn, Ate Brain: Police" . Huffington Post. 27 July 2009. Retrieved 2012-07-04.

[101] "3 Suspected of Cannibalism" . The Moscow Times. November 16, 2009.

[102] "Звериный оскал каннибализма". The Moscow Times. 29 March 2012. Retrieved 20 November 2014.

[103] "Crossbow cannibal jailed for wicked and monstrous' prostitute murders" . The Telegraph. 21 December 2010. Retrieved 1 November 2014.

[104] "'Pakistani duo are accused of cannibalism'". BBC News. April 6, 2011. Retrieved April 7, 2011.

[105] "Pakistan suspected cannibal in Punjab re-arrested" . BBC News. April 14, 2014.

[106] "Осуждена модель, которая утопила свою подругу и пыталась ее съесть". 4 October 2012. Retrieved 24 November 2014.

[107] Sideri, Massimo (August 2, 2011). "Slovak Cannibal's Possible Italian Victims – Thirty Missing Women Profiled" , Corriere della Sera.

[108] "Pills filled with powdered human baby flesh found by customs officials" . The Telegraph. 07 May 2012. Check date values in: |date= (help)

[109] "S Korea cracks down on 'human flesh capsules'". Al Jazeera. 7 May 2012.

[110] Leigh, Rob (7 May 2012). "Sickening foetus trade: South Korea orders crackdown on human flesh capsules 'made from dead babies' smuggled in from China" . Mirror Online.

[111] "South Korea seizes drugs made from dead babies" . The Guardian. 7 May 2012.

[112] Milimaci, Grace (December 20, 2011). "TV presenters eat each other's flesh" . The West Australian. Retrieved May 28, 2012.

[113] {{cite web|url=http://www.foxnews.com/us/2013/09/10/florida-man-receives-60-years-in-connecticut-cannibalism-case/|title=Florida man receives 60 years in Connecticut cannibalism case|work=Fox News|date=10 September 2013|accessdate=1 November 2014}}

[114] "Два каннибала Владивостока закусили знакомым, а остатки мяса продали на рынке". 26 March 2012. Retrieved 24 November 2014.

[115] "Mao Sugiyama Cooks, Serves Own Genitals At Banquet In Tokyo" . Huffington Post. 24 May 2012. Retrieved 1 November 2014.

[116] "Brazil murder suspects 'confess to cannibalism'". BBC News. April 13, 2012. Retrieved April 14, 2012.

[117] "Shrewsbury Man Accused Of Killing Wife & Cannibalism Dies In Hospital" . boston.cbslocal.com. Associated Press. May 5, 2012. Retrieved 5 April 2014.

[118] "No bath salts detected: Causeway attacker Rudy Eugene had only pot in his system, medical examiner reports" . The Miami Herald. 27 June 2012.

[119] "'Cannibal' Attack: Naked Man Shot Dead In Miami 'As He Chewed Victim's Face'". The Huffington Post. 28 May 2012.

[120] "Ronald Poppo, face-chewing victim, still recovering one year later: Hospital". CBS News. May 21, 2013.

[121] "Swedish professor cuts off wife's lips,eats them". *Times*. 31 May 2012. Retrieved 1 November 2014.

[122] "Cannibal cult members arrested in PNG". *New Zealand Herald*. 5 July 2012. Retrieved 2012-07-12

[123] "Cannibal killers delay Papua New Guinea poll". *The Telegraph*. 5 July 2012. Retrieved 2012-07-12

[124] "Трое мужчин из Японии приготовили своего знакомого на гриле". 4 October 2012. Retrieved 24 November 2014.

[125] Mazumdar, Prasanta (January 1, 2013). "Assam tea workers ate flesh after killing owner". Daily News and Analysis. Retrieved January 1, 2013.

[126] Cannibal killer who sold victims' flesh as 'ostrich meat' and kept eyeballs in wine bottles executed in China, 10 Jan 2013, Natalie Evans, *Daily Mirror*, retrieved at 2013-02-08

[127] Zhang Yongming, Serial Killer Dubbed 'Cannibal Monster' Is Executed In China, 11 Jan 2013, Sara C Nelson, *Huffington Post*, retrieved at 2013-02-08

[128] "Man Cooks and Eats His Own Finger After Losing It in an Accident". *The Sun*. 23 April 2013. Retrieved 20 November 2014.

[129] "Senior mutilated in cannibalism ritual". *Nugget*. 18 June 2013. Retrieved 1 November 2014.

[130] Wood, Paul (July 5, 2013). "Face-to-face with Abu Sakkar, Syria's 'heart-eating cannibal'". *BBC News*.

[131] "Italian man suspected of trying to eat mother detained after body parts found in pot, oven, freezer: cops". NY Daily News. 2013-07-24. Retrieved 2014-03-28.

[132] David, Jon (2013-07-24). "Police: Italian Man Suspected of Trying to Eat Mother After Body Parts Found Cooked". Breitbart.com. Retrieved 2014-03-28.

[133] "Насилие в ЦАР: очевидцы сообщают о каннибализме". 13 January 2014. Retrieved 24 November 2014.

[134] "Police: Indiana man admits to cannibalism". *Wish TV*. 16 September 2014. Retrieved 1 November 2014.

[135] Stephens, Kim. "Chef behind grisly Brisbane murder-suicide: police". *Brisbane Times*. Retrieved 16 May 2015.

[136] "Congo crowd kills man, eats him after militant massacres: witnesses". 31 October 2014. Retrieved 31 October 2014.

[137] "Family of 'cannibal' Matthew Williams pay tribute to victim Cerys Yemm". *The Daily Telegraph*. November 7, 2014. Retrieved November 8, 2014.

[138] "Mexican cartel recruits eat human hearts in cannibalistic initiation ceremonies". *Washington Times*. 9 January 2015. Retrieved 16 May 2015.

Chapter 3

The Baby-Roast

The Baby-Roast, also known as **The Hippy Babysitter** and **The Cooked Baby**,[1] is an urban legend, in which a baby is roasted alive at home, usually during the absence of a parent. *The Straight Dope*, a newspaper column devoted to exposing myths, reported that it "is one of the classic urban legends",[2] however, there have been real life instances where babies have been roasted.

3.1 Plot

In some versions, the baby is accidentally cooked when miscommunication occurs. For example, "put the turkey in the oven and the baby in the bed" is wrongly heard as "put the baby in the oven and the turkey in the bed".[1] Other variants set out that the doer of the deed was drug or alcohol-induced or an insane individual.[3] In the end, the roasted baby is served as food to be consumed by the parents.[3]

The person who roasts the baby is usually a babysitter, the baby's sibling, or the mother herself.[1]

3.2 Documented occurrences

In real life, there have been documented occurrences of babies being roasted. When Virginian Elizabeth Renee Otte roasted her baby in 1999,[4] the incident was cited as causing the legend to become true. In November 2006, a second case of real-life baby-roasting was reported.[5]

In February 2012, Ka Yang of California was charged with roasting her seven-week-old baby to death in a microwave. In her defence, she claimed she was having a "seizure fit" when it happened.[6] In May 2012, a British citizen was arrested by Thai police after being found in possession of six corpses of roasted infants, some wrapped in gold leaf, reportedly in conformity with a "black magic ritual".[7] In Siberia in January 2013, a roasted, dismembered baby was found by its mother, the alleged perpetrator being the infant's intoxicated uncle.[8]

3.3 In popular culture

In August 2009, a joke advertisement showcasing a "body part roaster" "specially designed to roast infants and other human morsels" surfaced on the website of retailer Sears.com.[9]

3.4 References

[1] Jan Harold Brunvand (1 January 2001). *Encyclopedia of Urban Legends*. ABC-CLIO. pp. 6–. ISBN 978-1-57607-076-5.

[2] "Did a stoned babysitter once microwave a baby?". *The Straight Dope*. February 3, 1984.

[3] Jan Harold Brunvand (2001). *The Truth Never Stands in the Way of a Good Story*. University of Illinois Press. pp. 55–. ISBN 978-0-252-07004-4.

[4] Timberg, Craig (September 28, 1999). "Mother Charged in Baby's Death". *The Washington Post*. Retrieved August 14, 2013.

[5] Greene, Thomas C. (November 28, 2006). "Mom cooks baby in microwave oven - police". *The Register*.

[6] "Mother 'burned her baby to death in microwave because she was having a seizure fit'". *Daily Mail*. February 23, 2012.

[7] "Thai police arrest man after babies' bodies found roasted, wrapped in gold leaf". *msn*. May 12, 2013.

[8] Stewart, Will (January 24, 2013). "Drunk uncle 'chopped up 18-month-old niece then roasted body parts in the oven' while looking after toddler for her mother".

[9] Goodin, Dan (August 21, 2009). "Baby-roasting BBQ pulled from Sears site". *The Register*.

Chapter 4

Child cannibalism

Child cannibalism or **fetal cannibalism** describes the act of eating a child or fetus. Controversy was sparked when images showing what appeared to be human fetuses were being published in China. Reports later explained that the images were part of an artist's exhibition (Zhu Yu) and was not a real fetus but just to be in a contemporary artwork, although Zhu claimed otherwise.[1] The artwork is called "Eating people" and was made to protest against cannibalism.[2]

4.1 Blood libel

Main article: Blood libel

Critics[3] see the propagation of these purported rumours as a form of Blood libel, or accusing one's enemy of eating children, and accuse countries of using this as a political lever.

4.2 Ritual practice myths

In 330-340 AD Alexandrian bishop Epiphanius claimed to have defected from a sect called the Phibionites, which were claimed to worship a snake, have sexual intercourse during religious ceremonies, and eat aborted fetuses - considered to be "the perfect mass". This account was used by the Christian Church to attack its enemies.[4]

4.3 Satire

Jonathan Swift's 1729 satiric article "A Modest Proposal for Preventing the Children of Poor People in Ireland from Being a Burden to Their Parents or Country, and for Making Them Beneficial to the Public" proposed the utilization of an economic system based on poor people selling their children to be eaten, claiming that this would benefit the economy, family values, and general happiness of Ireland. He used many instances of irony to express that his proposition was just as bad as what was really being done to help the poor.

4.4 References in popular culture

- In Fruit Chan's *Dumplings*, fetuses are consumed with the belief of their rejuvenating properties.

- Japanese rock band Dir en grey's song "Umbrella" is about the act of child cannibalism.

- In Cormac McCarthy's novel *The Road*, a father and son encounter a family that consumes a fetus.

- In the popular comedy *Austin Powers: The Spy Who Shagged Me*, the character Fat Bastard is known for his obsession of eating infants.

- In an episode of South Park, Christopher Reeve is shown eating fetuses in order to regain his mobility as well as to seemingly become stronger (in satirical reference to his acting roles as Superman, his real-life paralysis, and subsequent advocacy for fetal stem cell research).

- In an episode of Robot Chicken, the resurrected Walt Disney feeds exclusively on Cuban children. After watching coverage of the Elian Gonzales deportation case on the news, Disney sets out on a quest to devour the boy.

- In Robert Kirkman's *The Walking Dead* and its live-action adaptation, a group of survivors who dubbed themselves "the Hunters" turned to eating their children to survive in the zombie apocalypse, though not without clear remorse.

4.5 See also

- Albert Fish

- Blood libel

- Child sacrifice

- Comprachicos

- "A Modest Proposal", by Jonathan Swift

- Saturn Devouring His Son

4.6 Sources

[1] Rojas, Carlos. (2002). Cannibalism and the Chinese Body Politic: Hermeneutics and Violence in Cross-Cultural Perception. Post Modern Culture, 12 (3). Retrieved July 8, 2006. http://www3.iath.virginia.edu/pmc/text-only/issue.502/12.3rojas.txt

[2] Emery, D. "Do They Eat Babies in China?". About.com>. Retrieved 2009-01-09.

[3] Dixon, Miss Poppy (10.2000). "Eating Fetuses: The lurid Christian fantasy of godless Chinese eating "unborn children."". Archived from the original on Mar 13, 2008. Retrieved 12 December 2010. Check date values in: |date= (help)

[4] Bill Ellis. *Aliens, Ghosts, and Cults: Legends We Live*. University Press of Mississippi. p. 54.

4.7 External links

- Photos in South-Korean newspaper

- Italian Asian article

- Urban legends website

- World Net Daily article

- LJ News

-

Chapter 5

Custom of the sea

A **custom of the sea** is a custom that is said to be practiced by the officers and crew of ships and boats in the open sea, as distinguished from maritime law, which is a distinct and coherent body of law that governs maritime questions and offenses.

Possibly the best-known of these customs is the practice of shipwrecked survivors drawing lots to see who is to be killed and eaten so that the others might survive.*[1]

5.1 Historical examples of "agreed"cannibalism

5.1.1 *The Essex*

After the sinking of the *Essex* of Nantucket by a whale on November 20, 1820, the survivors were left floating in three small whaleboats. They eventually resorted, by common consent, to cannibalism to allow some to survive.*[2]

5.1.2 *The Mignonette*

Main article: R. v. Dudley and Stephens

The case of *R. v. Dudley and Stephens* (1884 14 QBD 273 DC) is an English case which developed a crucial ruling on necessity in modern common law. The case dealt with four crewmembers of an English yacht, the *Mignonette*, who were shipwrecked in a storm some 1,600 miles from the Cape of Good Hope. After a few weeks adrift in a lifeboat, one of the crew fell unconscious due to a combination of hunger and drinking seawater. The others (one abstaining) decided then to kill him and eat him. They were picked up four days later. The case held that necessity was not a defense for a charge of murder, and the two defendants were convicted, though their death sentence was commuted to six months' imprisonment.

5.2 Examples not related to cannibalism

Another custom of the sea is the captain being the last person off a sinking vessel or deciding to go down with the ship. This custom of the sea is often enshrined in naval tradition and still expected to be upheld in many countries.

5.3 References

[1] Walker, Andrew: *Is Eating People Wrong?: Great Legal Cases and How they Shaped the World*. Cambridge University Press, New York, 2011 ISBN 978-1-107-00037-7 pg. 22

[2] h2g2 - The Wreck of the Whaleship Essex - A671492

5.4 Further reading

- Hanson, Neil. (1999). *The Custom of the Sea: The Story that Changed British Law*. Doubleday. ISBN 978-0-385-60115-3.

- Simpson, A. W. B. (1984). *Cannibalism and the Common Law: The Story of the Tragic Last Voyage of the Mignonette and the Strange Legal Proceedings to Which It Gave Rise*. Chicago: University of Chicago Press. ISBN 978-0-226-75942-5.

Chapter 6

Endocannibalism

[1]**Endocannibalism** is a practice of eating the flesh of a human being from the same community (tribe, social group or society), usually after they have died. Endocannibalism has also been used to describe the consumption of relics in a mortuary context.[2]

6.1 As a cultural practice

Herodotus (3.38) mentions funerary cannibalism among the *Callatiae*, a tribe of India.

It is believed that some South American Indigenous cultures such as the Mayoruna people practiced endocannibalism in the past.[3] Yąnomamö consumed the ground-up bones and ashes of cremated kinsmen in an act of mourning. This is still classified as endocannibalism, although, strictly speaking, "flesh" is not eaten.[4] The Aghoris of northern India consume the flesh of the dead floated in the Ganges in pursuit of immortality and supernatural powers.[5] For the Wari' people in western Brazil, endocannibalism is an act of compassion where the roasted remains of fellow Wari' are consumed in a mortuary setting.[6] Ideally, the affines would consume the entire corpse and rejecting the practice would be offensive to the direct family members[6] The Amahuaca Indians of Peru picked particles of bone out of the ashes of a cremation fire, ground them with corn, and drank as a kind of gruel.[7]

Such practices were generally not believed to have been driven by need for protein or other food.[3]

There are two main types of endocannibalism. Gastronomic endocannibalism which is focused on food value and is practiced by both civilized and primitive societies. Ritual or magical endocannibalism's purpose is for the spirit of the subject to be absorbed and is practice by uncivilized groups. [7]

6.2 Medical implications

Kuru is a type of transmissible spongiform encephalopathy (TSE) caused by prion that is found in humans.[8] Human prion diseases come in sporadic, genetic and infectious forms. Kuru was the first infectious human prion disease discovered. [9] It spread through the Fore people of Papua New Guinea, in which relatives consumed the bodies of the deceased to return the "life force" of the deceased to the hamlet.[10] Kuru was 8 to 9 times more prevalent in women and children than in men at its peak because, while the men of the village took the choice cuts, the women and children would eat the rest of the body, including the brain, where the prion particles were particularly concentrated.[11] The Kuru epidemic, which is recorded to have begun in the 1920s, is believed to have been started by the consumption of a single individual with Kuru, which then spread through the population. Oral history records that cannibalism began within the Fore in the late 19th century. Recent research at University College London identified a gene that protects against prion diseases, by studying the Fore people.[12]

Currently there is no treatment to cure or even control Kuru, but there are numerous programs being funded by universities and national institutes, such as the National Institute of Neurological Disorders and Stroke (NINDS). This institute is currently funding research into the genetic and cellular process behind the development and transmission of Kuru and other TSE diseases.[*][13]

A team led by Michael Alpers, a lifelong investigator of the Kuru disease,[*][14] found genes that protect against similar prion diseases were widespread, indicating that such endocannibalism was once common around the world.[*][15][*][16]

6.3   List of Cultures that Practice Endocannibalism

- Africa
    - Jukun people
- Asia
- North America
- South America
    - Wari' people
    - Yǎnomamö
    - Amahuaca people
- Oceania
    - Fore people
- Europe

6.4   See also

- Donner Party
- Exocannibalism
- Boone Helm

6.5   References

[1] Vilaca, Aparecida. "Relations between Funerary Cannibalism and Warfare Cannibalism: The Question of Predation". *Ethnos: Journal of Anthropology 65(1): 83-106.* doi:10.1080/001418400360652.

[2] Metcalf, Peter (1987-01-01). "Wine of the Corpse: Endocannibalism and the Great Feast of the Dead in Borneo". *Representations* (17): 96–109. doi:10.2307/3043794.

[3] Dorn, Georgette M.; Tenenbaum, Barbara A. (1996). *Encyclopedia of Latin American history and culture.* New York: C. Scribner's Sons. ISBN 0-684-19253-5. Pages 535-537.

[4] "Endocannibalism of the Yanomami". Users.rcn.com. Retrieved 2010-03-31.

[5] "Indian cannibal sect eats human corpses, believing it give them supernatural powers". Pravada. 2005-10-25. Retrieved 2008-02-13.

[6] Conklin, Beth (2001). *Consuming Grief.* University of Texas Press.

[7] Dole, Gertrude (1962-03-01). "Division of Anthropology: Endocannibalism Among the Amahuaca Indians*". *Transactions of the New York Academy of Sciences* **24** (5 Series II): 567–573. doi:10.1111/j.2164-0947.1962.tb01432.x. ISSN 2164-0947.

[8] Wadsworth JD, Joiner S, Linehan JM, et al. (March 2008). "Kuru prions and sporadic Creutzfeldt-Jakob disease prions have equivalent transmission properties in transgenic and wild-type mice". *Proc. Natl. Acad. Sci. U.S.A.* **105** (10): 3885–90. doi:10.1073/pnas.0800190105. PMC 2268835. PMID 18316717.

[9] Haïk, Stéphane; Brandel, Jean-Philippe (2014-08-01). "Infectious prion diseases in humans: Cannibalism, iatrogenicity and zoonoses". *Infection, Genetics and Evolution* **26**: 303–312. doi:10.1016/j.meegid.2014.06.010.

[10] Diamond JM (1997). *Guns, germs, and steel: the fates of human societies.* New York: W.W. Norton. p. 208. ISBN 0-393-03891-2.

[11] "Kuru : Article by Paul A Janson". eMedicine. 2009-04-13. Retrieved 2010-03-31.

[12] "A Tribe In Papua New Guinea Reveals The Upside Of Cannibalism". Retrieved 2015-09-01.

[13] "Kuru Information Page: National Institute of Neurological Disorders and Stroke (NINDS)". *www.ninds.nih.gov.* Retrieved 2015-09-01.

[14] "A life of determination". Med.monash.edu.au. 2009-02-27. Retrieved 2010-03-31.

[15] Simon Mead, Michael P. H. Stumpf, Jerome Whitfield, Jonathan A. Beck, Mark Poulter, Tracy Campbell, James Uphill, David Goldstein, Michael Alpers, Elizabeth M. C. Fisher, John Collinge (2003), "Balancing Selection at the Prion Protein Gene Consistent with Prehistoric Kurulike Epidemics", *Science* **300** (5619): 640–643, doi:10.1126/science.1083320, PMID 12690204

[16] Friday, 11 April 2003 Danny Kingsley (2003-04-11). "Genes suggest cannibalism common in human past". ABC Science Online. Retrieved 2010-03-31.

Chapter 7

Exocannibalism

Exocannibalism (from Greek *Exo-*, "from outside" and Cannibalism, 'to eat humans'), as opposed to endocannibalism, is the consumption of flesh outside one's close social group—for example, eating one's enemy. When done ritually, it has been associated with being a means of imbibing valued qualities of the victim or as an act of final violence against the deceased in the case of sociopathy,[1] as well as a symbolic expression of the domination of an enemy in warfare.[2] Such practices have been documented in such cultures as the Aztecs from Mexico, the Carib and the Tupinambá from South America.

Historically, it has also been used as a practical expediency in especially desperate attritional or guerrilla warfare when the extreme hunger and the abundance of humans being killed coincide to create conditions ripe for cannibalism.[3]

7.1 As A Cultural Practice

Cannibalism is something that has been found wherever and whenever humans have formed societies. Traditionally, accounts of cannibalism were found embedded in myths and folklore as a common motif that indicated people were less than fully human. Exocannibalism in the form of eating enemies is usually done to express hostility and domination toward the victim.[4] The perpetrator eats their victim to inflict ultimate indignity and humiliation. It has also been practiced along with headhunting and scalping to display war trophies. John Kantner, an archaeologist who studied alleged cannibalism in the American Southwest, believes that when resources decrease the competition of societies increased and exocannibalism can ensue.[1] Exocannibalism would generally be considered to be the opposite of endocannibalism, but they are both forms of ritual cannibalism. There have been no previous accounts of a culture practicing both forms of ritual cannibalism, aside from a recent study that confirmed the Wari', an Amazonian tribe in Brazil, practiced both forms. [5]

7.2 List of Cultures that Practice(d) Exocannibalism

- Africa

  - Lendu

- Asia

  - Batak
  - Dyak

- North America

  - Iroqouis Indians

- Nootka Indians
- Anasazi Indians
- South/Central America
  - Aztecs
  - Wari'
- Oceania
  - Marquesans
  - Mianmin
  - Asmat
- Europe

7.3   See also

- Cannibalism
- Endocannibalism
- Liver-Eating Johnson
- List of incidents of cannibalism

7.4   References

*[6]

[1] Cannibalism, Encyclopedia of Death and Dying.

[2] James W. Dow, Cannibalism, Reprinted from Encyclopedia of Latin American History and Culture, Vol. 1. Barbara A. Tenenbaum, ed. Pp. 535-537. New York: Charles Scribner's Sons

[3] Tanaka, Yuki. *Hidden horrors: Japanese War Crimes in World War II*, Westview Press, 1996, p.127.

[4] Neufeldt, Robyn (2012). *Biasing Cannibalism in Anthropology*.

[5] Travis-Henikoff, Carole A (2008). *Dinner with a Cannibal*. Santa Monica, CA: Santa Monica Press. p. 165. ISBN 9781595800305.

[6] Biasing Cannibalism in Anthropology by Robyn Neufeldt (2012)

Chapter 8

Filial cannibalism

Filial cannibalism occurs when an adult individual of a species consumes all or part of the young of its own species or immediate offspring. Filial cannibalism occurs in many animal species ranging from mammals to insects, and is especially prevalent in various species of fish. Although not much is known regarding the exact purposes of filial cannibalism, it is understood that it may have important evolutionary and ecological implications for some species, and is an important source of mortality for various species.

8.1   Types of filial cannibalism

Total or whole clutch cannibalism

Total or whole clutch cannibalism occurs when a parent consumes its entire brood. This usually occurs when a brood is smaller or of lesser quality. The most obvious purpose of total or whole clutch cannibalism is the termination of care for the parents. The main benefit of this action can only be an investment in the future reproduction of potentially larger or healthier broods.*[1]

Partial clutch cannibalism

Partial clutch cannibalism occurs when a parent consumes a part of its offspring. "Parental manipulation of brood size may allow the parent the maximize lifetime reproductive output by adjusting current reproductive costs in favour of future survival and subsequent opportunities for reproduction." *[2] Unlike total or whole clutch cannibalism, partial clutch cannibalism invests in both current and future reproduction.*[1] Male parents, particularly male fish, may eat some of their offspring in order to "complete his current parental cycle, and remain in sufficiently good condition to engage in further breeding cycles." *[3]

8.2   Benefits of filial cannibalism

- Satisfies current energy or nutrition requirements*[2]

- In a bad reproductive environment, cannibalism is a way to make a recouping reproductive investment*[2]

- Puts evolutionary pressure on offspring in order to make the offspring develop quicker*[4]

- May increase the reproductive rate of a parent by making that parent more attractive to potential mates*[4]

- Gets rid of offspring that take too long to mature*[4]

- Removes weaker offspring in an overproduced brood, which makes the other offspring more likely to be successful*[4]

8.3   Costs of filial cannibalism

- Loss of fitness[*][5]

- Transmission of diseases and parasites[*][2]

- Decrease of success in current reproduction[*][5]

8.4   Social factors

Competition among a species for resources, mating opportunities, and reproductive dominance are all promoters for filial cannibalism. In order to compete well in a certain species' social structure, a parent may be compelled to practice filial cannibalism to limit the amount of energy and time they spend raising their young.

Males may compete for mating opportunities by eating the offspring of a female, in order to make that female more sexually receptive or to re-mate. By doing this, a male might be able to prolong its lifetime mating opportunities.[*][2]

Female fish may compete for mating opportunities with males by raiding the male's nest and eating the eggs inside.[*][2]

Females may also use cannibalism – particularly birds and bees that live in a joint-nesting social structure – as a way to establish reproductive dominance by eating the eggs of a co-breeder.[*][2] In some animal cultures, competition may lead to instances of egg thievery, nest takeovers, and cuckoldry. However, the consumption of an animal's brood is often more beneficial than *hetero-cannibalism*, or the consumption of unrelated conspecifics, since it takes less energy to eat their own offspring and lessens the chance of getting their own brood raided when getting food while away from their offspring.[*][6]

8.5   Taxa that exhibit filial cannibalism

Some species within the following taxa show filial cannibalism:

- Cats

- Primates

- Rodents

- Birds

- Amphibians

- Fish (see: Scissortail sergeant, desert pupfish)

- Gastropods

- Insects (see: *Synoeca surinama,* a Neotropical social wasp)

- Arachnids

- Lepidoptera

- Lower eukaryotes

- Deinonychus(rumored)

8.6 References

[1] Hope Klug & Kai Lindström (2008). "Hurry-up and hatch: selective filial cannibalism of slower developing eggs". *Biology Letters* **4** (2): 160–162. doi:10.1098/rsbl.2007.0589. PMC 2429927. PMID 18252661.

[2] Mark A. Elgar & Bernard J. Crespi (1992). *Cannibalism: Ecology and evolution among diverse taxa.* New York: Oxford University Press. ISBN 978-0-19-854650-4.

[3] Adam G. Payne, Carl Smith & Andrew C. Campbell (2002). "Filial cannibalism improves survival and development of beaugregory damselfish embryos". *Proceedings of the Royal Society B: Biological Sciences* **269** (1505): 2095–2102. doi:10.1098/rspb.2002.2144. JSTOR 3558871. PMC 1691142. PMID 12396483.

[4] Andrea Thompson (November 14, 2007). "Why some animals eat their offspring". LiveScience. Retrieved November 28, 2011.

[5] M. B. Bonsall & H. Klug (2011). "Effects of among-offspring relatedness on the origins and evolution of parental care and filial cannibalism". *Journal of Evolutionary Biology* **24** (6): 1335–1350. doi:10.1111/j.1420-9101.2011.02269.x. PMID 21507115.

[6] Andrew J. DeWoody, Dean E. Fletcher, S. David Wilkins & John C. Avise (2001). "Genetic documentation of filial cannibalism in nature" (PDF). *Proceedings of the National Academy of Sciences* **98** (9): 5090–5092. doi:10.1073/pnas.091102598. PMID 3055569.

Chapter 9

Human placentophagy

Human placentophagy, or consumption of the placenta, is defined as, "The ingestion of a human placenta postpartum, at any time, by any person, either in raw or altered (e.g., cooked, dried, steeped in liquid) form." Numerous historical occurrences of placentophagy have been recorded throughout the world, whereas modern occurrences of placentophagy are rare since most contemporary societies do not promote its practice. Since the 1970s, however, consumption of the placenta believing that it has health benefits has been a growing practice among clients of midwives and alternative-health advocates in the U.S. and Mexico.[1]

Placentophagy can be divided into two categories, maternal placentophagy and non-maternal placentophagy.

9.1   Maternal placentophagy

Maternal placentophagy is defined as, "a mother's ingestion of her own placenta postpartum, in any form, at any time." Maternal placentophagy most frequently occurs among placental mammals. Of the more than 4000 species of placental mammals, there are only a handful that do not regularly engage in maternal placentophagy, including modern humans.[1]

9.2   Non-maternal placentophagy

Non-maternal placentophagy is defined as, "the ingestion of the placenta by any person other than the mother, at any time." Such instances of placentophagy have been attributed to the following: a shift toward carnivorousness at parturition, specific hunger, and general hunger. With most Eutherian mammals, the placenta is consumed postpartum by the mother. Historically, humans more commonly consume the placenta of another woman under special circumstances.[1]

9.3   Historical occurrences of human placentophagy

In a 1979 volume of the Bulletin of the New York Academy of Medicine, William Ober's article "Notes on Placentophagy," evaluates the possibility that certain ancient cultures that practiced human sacrifice may also have practiced human placentophagy, including Egyptians, Tasians, Badarians, Amrateans, Gerzeans, Semainians.[2]

Placentophagy might have occurred during the Siege of Jerusalem (587 BC), due to the excessive famine experienced by the Judeans, according to scholar Jack Miles in his Pulitzer Prize-winning *God: A Biography*.[3] Miles argues that the curse in Deuteronomy 28:56–57, written in the form of prophecy, is far too vivid not to have been seen personally by the author of the verses.

Human placenta has been used traditionally in Chinese medicine, though the mother is not identified as the recipient of these treatments.[1] A sixteenth-century Chinese medical text, the Compendium of Materia Medica, states in a section

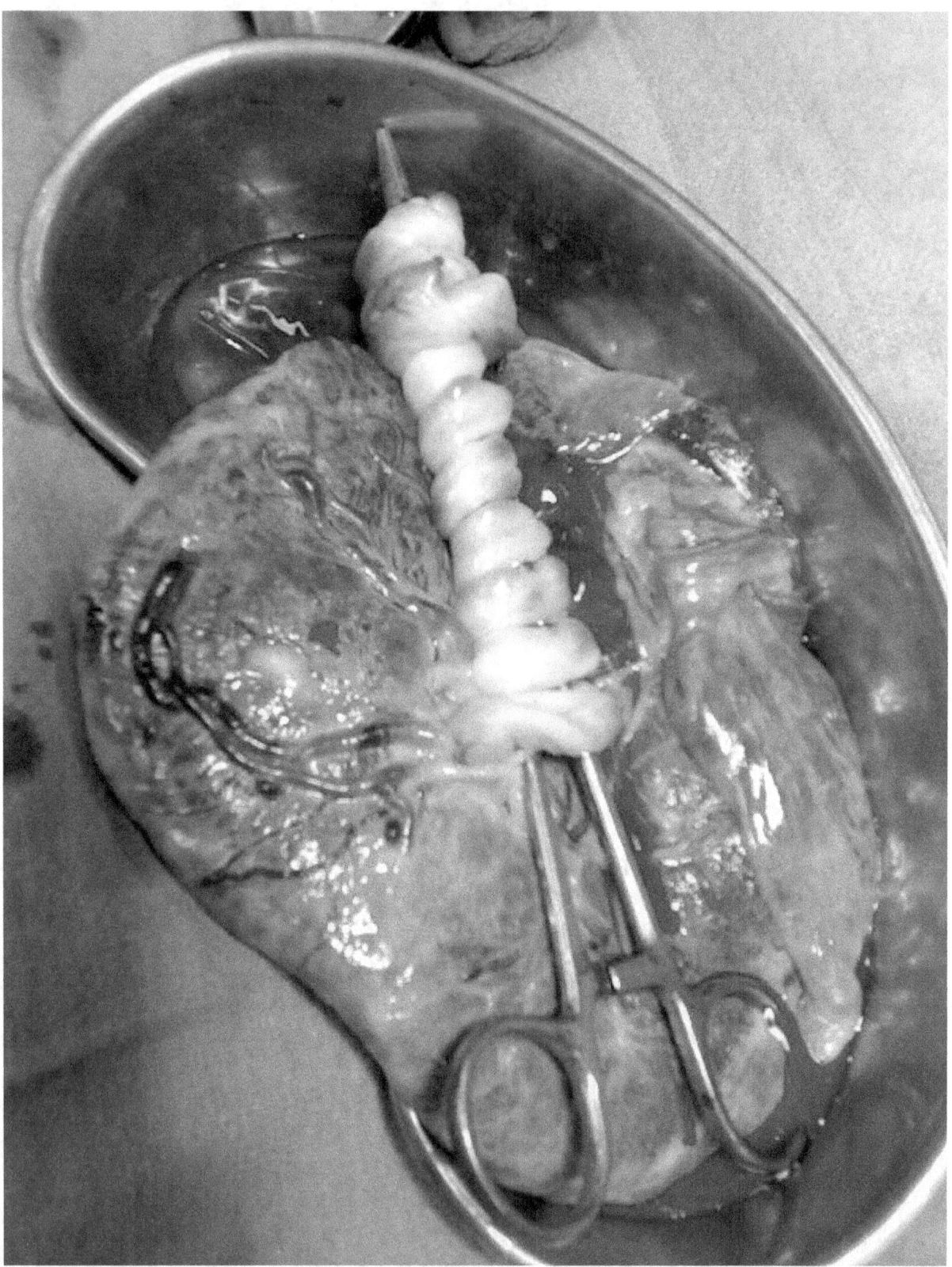

human placenta

on medical uses of the placenta that, "when a woman in Liuqiu has a baby, the placenta is eaten," and that in Bagui, "the placenta of a boy is specially prepared and eaten by the mother's family and relatives."[1] Another Chinese medical text, the Great Pharmacopoeia of 1596, recommends placental tissue mixed with human milk to help overcome the effects of Ch'i exhaustion.[2] These include, "anemia, weakness of the extremities, and coldness of the sexual organs with involuntary ejaculation of semen."[2] Dried, powdered placenta would be stirred into three wine-cups of milk to make a Connected Destiny Elixir.[2] The elixir would be warmed in sunlight, then taken as treatment.[2] It is not known exactly how traditional this remedy was, nor exactly how far back it dates.[2]

Ober also identified many cultures known to have practiced placentophagy for medicinal purposes, and one for its flavor.

9.3.1 Medicinal purposes

Dried human placenta as medicine - Ziheche (紫河车)

The Araucanian Native Americans of Argentina dried and ground a child's umbilical cord, giving the child a little of the powder when it was sick.[2]

In Jamaica, bits of placental membranes were put into an infant's tea to prevent convulsions caused by ghosts.[2]

The Chaga of Tanganyika place the placenta in a receptacle for two months to dry. Once dry, it is ground into flour from which a porridge is made. The porridge is served to old women of the family as a way of preserving the child's life.[2]

In Central India, women of the Kol Tribe eat placenta to aid reproductive function. It is believed that consumption of placenta by a childless woman "may dispel the influences that keep her barren."[2]

9.3.2 Flavor

The Kurtachi of the Solomon Islands mixed placenta into the mother's supply of powdered lime for chewing with the areca nut.[2]

9.4 Modern placentophagy

Modern practice of placentophagy is rare, as most contemporary human cultures do not promote its consumption.*[1] Despite a general cultural avoidance, however, instances of placentophagy have been recorded among certain modern cultures. In the 1960s "male and female Vietnamese nurses and midwives of Chinese and Thai background consum[ed] the placentas of their young, healthy patients" for reasons unspecified, as reported by a Czechoslovakian medical officer in at the Hospital of Czechoslovak-Vietnamese Friendship in Haiphong.*[1] Placentas were stripped of their membranous parts and fried with onions before being eaten.*[2]

A more recent cross-cultural ethnographic study by the University of Nevada, Las Vegas Department of Anthropology surveyed over 179 contemporary human societies, and identified only one culture (Chicano, or Mexican-American) that mentioned the practice of maternal placentophagy.*[1] This account, centering on Chicano and Anglo midwifery in San Antonio, Texas, stated, "cooking and eating part of the placenta has···been reported by a couple of midwives. One Anglo mother ... was reported to have roasted the placenta." *[1] This instance, however, may not be indicative of any larger cultural trends, as no other records of placentophagy were found in the Chicano culture. This same study also recorded three references of non-maternal placentophagy:

- Traditional Gullah medicine dictates that when a baby is born with a caul, with amniotic membranes over the face at birth, the placenta is made into a tea and then consumed by the child to "prevent them from seeing spirits that would otherwise haunt [them]." *[1]

- Practice of paternal placentophagy was identified in the Malekula of Melanesia. "In Espiritu Santo, the new father [eats] a pudding made from the cooked placenta and blood." *[1]

- Oral administration of the placenta was reported in Sino-Vietnamese medicine to aid the recovery of those suffering from tuberculosis.*[1]

In a follow-up study, the UNLV researchers were joined by colleagues at the University of South Florida, who surveyed new mothers, and found that about 3/4 had positive subjective experiences from eating their own placenta, citing beliefs of "improved mood" , "increased energy" , and "improved lactation" .*[4] *[5] The authors themselves, however, do state that "exceedingly little research has been conducted to assess these claims and no systematic analysis has been performed to evaluate the experiences of women who engage in this behavior."

Recent examples of placentophagy in the popular media include Time Magazine's "Afterbirth: It's What's for Dinner" ,*[6] and USA Today's "Ingesting the placenta: Is it healthy for new moms?"*[7]

9.5 Current beliefs among placentophagists

9.5.1 Nutritional benefits

The placenta transports nutrients to the fetus during gestation, as well as producing and regulating hormones and opioids.*[8] Proponents of modern placentophagy argue that the placenta retains some of these substances after delivery, and that consumption of the placenta by the mother will help her recover more quickly following childbirth by replenishing nutrients and hormones lost during parturition.*[1] One birthing website run by two Minnesota doulas lists possible health benefits including replenishing lost nutrients, increasing milk production, curbing postpartum depression and slowing postpartum hemorrhage.*[9]

In addition to protein and various vitamins, placenta contains high levels of CRH (corticotropin-releasing hormone), known to reduce stress.*[9] Though CRH is normally secreted by the hypothalamus, during pregnancy production of CRH by the placenta dramatically increases levels of CRH in the blood stream, which peak at delivery.*[10] Even postpartum, the placenta still contains very high levels of CRH, and some believe eating it can bring the mother's CRH levels back to a healthy range.*[9]

Consumption of the placenta is also believed to cause the release of the chemical oxytocin in the brain. Oxytocin stimulates uterine contractions leading to the onset of labor, and after childbirth can also cause the uterus to contract and sooner reach its pre-pregnancy size.*[9]

9.6   Preparation

In many areas a placenta encapsulationist can be found to professionally prepare the placenta for consumption. Also, many online alternative health sources give instructions for preparing it personally. One common method of preparation is encapsulation. An encapsulated placenta is steamed, dehydrated, and ground before being put into pills. Less commonly the placenta is drunk raw in a smoothie. Other recipes include lasagna, spaghetti, stew, and pizza.*[9]

9.7   Controversy

Many researchers remain skeptical of whether the practice of placentophagy is of value to humans. Professor Mark Kristal of the State University of New York at Buffalo, wrote his doctoral dissertation in 1971 on why animals eat their placentas. He stated, "People can believe what they want, but there's no research to substantiate claims of human benefit. The cooking process will destroy all the protein and hormones. Drying it out or freezing it would destroy other things." *[7] Nevertheless, a number of midwives, doulas, and mothers who practice placentophagy claim that consuming their placentas has helped recover from childbirth in a variety of ways.

Although human placentophagy entails the consumption of human tissue by a human or humans, its status as cannibalism is debated.*[11]*[12]

9.8   Risks involved

There is a risk of spreading blood-borne illness, only present in cases of non-maternal placentophagy, where the mother's blood is shared with another human.*[9] As a meat, proper storage and preparation procedures must be followed to prevent bacterial infection in the placenta.

9.9   References

[1] Young, Sharon; Benyshek, Daniel (2010). "In Search of Human Placentophagy: A Cross-Cultural Survey of Human Placenta Consumption, Disposal Practices, and Cultural Beliefs" . *Ecology of Food and Nutrition* (Taylor & Francis Online) **49** (6): 467–84. doi:10.1080/03670244.2010.524106.

[2] Ober, William B. (1979). "Notes on Placentophagy" . *Journal of Urban Health* **55** (6): 591–99. PMC 1807646. PMID 111747.

[3] Miles, Jack (2011). *God: A Biography*. Knopf Doubleday Publishing Group. p. 146. ISBN 9780307789136. The sickening image of a woman fighting with her husband and children over who will eat her afterbirth is just the kind of unimaginable detail that only the actual experience can provide a writer.

[4] Bawany, Afsha (February 27, 2013). "Steamed, Dehydrated or Raw: Placentas May Help Moms' Post-Partum Health. UNLV anthropology survey examines why women consume their placentas after childbirth." . UNLV News Center. Retrieved March 25, 2013.

[5] J. Selender, A. Cantor, S. Young, and D. Benyshek. "Human Maternal Placentophagy: A Survey of Self-Reported Motivations and Experiences Associated with Placenta Consumption" (PDF). *Ecology of Food and Nutrition*. Retrieved March 25, 2013.

[6] Stein, Joel (3 July 2009). "Afterbirth: It's What's For Dinner" . *Time Magazine*. Retrieved 5 December 2011.

[7] Freiss, Steve (19 July 2007). "Ingesting the Placenta: Is It Healthy for New Moms?". *USA Today*. Retrieved 5 December 2011.

[8] Apari P, Rózsa L (2006), "Deal in the womb: fetal opiates, parent-offspring conflict, and the future of midwifery" (PDF), *Medical Hypotheses* **67** (5): 1189–1194, doi:10.1016/j.mehy.2006.03.053, PMID 16893611

[9] Biermeier, Sarah. "The Placenta-an Unappreciated Organ" . *Geneabirth*. Retrieved 5 December 2011.

[10] Thomson, Murray (2008). "The Effects of Placental Corticotrophin Releasing Hormone on the Physiology and Psychology of the Pregnant Woman". *Current Women's Health Reviews* (Bentham Science) **4** (4): 270–279. doi:10.2174/157340408786848197.

[11] Hall, Harriet. Eating Placentas: Cannibalism, Recycling, or Health Food? *Science-Based Medicine*, March 8, 2011

[12] Watson-Smyth, Kate. Placenta chef accused of cannibalism. *The Independent*, 22 January 1998

9.10 External links

Chapter 10

Keep the River on Your Right: A Modern Cannibal Tale

Keep the River on Your Right: A Modern Cannibal Tale is a 2000 documentary film about the travels of anthropologist/artist Tobias Schneebaum, directed by by filmmakers David and Laurie Gwen Shapiro.[*][1] It takes its title from one of his books, *Keep the River on Your Right*, but covers material from several of Schneebaum's other books and articles. In the film, Schneebaum, by then an elderly man, revisits two cannibal tribes—one in Papua New Guinea and the other in the jungles of Peru—with whom he'd lived several years each as a young man. He and the film-makers manage to locate a few of the individuals he had known well during those periods. Schneebaum is remarkably honest about his same-sex relationships with members of both tribes, his childhood fetishizing of cannabalism, and his actual tasting of human flesh with one group. His extensive training in art allowed him to bond with different cultures he studied around sharing carving and painting techniques.

10.1 References

[1] "Keep the River on Your Right: A Modern Cannibal Tale (2000)". *The New York Times.* March 30, 2001. Retrieved August 23, 2015.

10.2 External links

- *Keep the River on Your Right: A Modern Cannibal Tale* at the Internet Movie Database

Chapter 11

Francisco Leóna

Francisco Leóna (1835-1910) was a Spanish child killer, barber, curandero, and Sacamantecas from the region of Gádor, Almería, who was arrested and convicted of murdering seven-year-old Bernardo Gonzalez Parra for the purpose of using the boy's blood and fat as a tuberculosis treatment for a wealthy farmer, Francisco Ortega.*[1]

11.1 Crime

June, 1910, in Gádor, Francisco Ortega *El Moruno* (*The Moorish*) was newly diagnosed with tuberculosis and desperately seeking a cure for his disease. He visited the local healer Agustina Rodriguez, who in turn sent for the barber and healer Francisco Leóna. Apparently Leóna had a criminal record and, in exchange for 3000 of reales, revealed that "the cure" was to drink the blood emanating from the body of a child and to spread hot poultices made of the child's fat over the chest.

Leóna and Julio *El Tonto* (*The Fool*) Hernández, a son of Agustina the healer, offered to find a child. On the evening of June 28, 1910, the two men kidnapped Bernardo Gonzalez Parra, a boy of seven years from Rioja. Drugging him with chloroform and putting the boy in a sack, Leóna and Hernández took him to a secluded farmhouse in Araoz that Agustina had prepared.

A brother of Julio "Tonto" Hernández, Joseph Hernández, was to advise the client Ortega, leaving his wife Elena to make dinner.

Little Bernardo's murder was as follows: after he was removed from the sack, dazed, Bernardo was cut in the armpit, which emanated blood that Ortega drank mixed with sugar. After that they took the boy to the place known as Las Pocicas where Leona killed him crushing his skull with a rock. Then he extracted fat and mesentery to make a compress to apply to Ortega's chest.

To finish the ritual, Bernardo's body was concealed in a crevice, unburied but covered with herbs and stones, located in Las Pocicas.

When distributing the actual 3000 Ortega paid him for his services, the healer Leona tried to trick his accomplice *Tonto* Hernández without obtaining good results. Realizing Leona's intentions and to avenge himself, Hernández told the Civil Guard who had seen the body of a child while he was chasing partridges.

When the forces of the Civil Guard arrived, all the people betrayed Leona, because sooner or later he had committed many irregularities, some of them the same type of offense. He stopped when testifying and indicted "Tonto" Hernández who in turn did the same to Leona. Finally, after multiple excuses, both confessed to the crime. When the body was found, it was on its belly with skull completely shattered.

Leona was sentenced to the garrote, but died in prison. The client, Ortega, and Agustina, the healer, were both executed. Joseph Hernández, a son of Agustina, was sentenced to 17 years in prison while his wife, Elena, was acquitted. And Julio "Tonto" was finally sentenced to death too, but it was pardoned for being considered insane.*[2]*[3]

11.2 See also

- Hombre del saco

- Sacamantecas

- Juan Díaz de Garayo

- Manuel Blanco Romasanta

11.3 References

[1] Soler Cervantes, Milagros. *El crimen de Gádor (Almería)*.

[2] Soler Cervantes, Milagros. *El crimen de Gádor (Almería)*.

[3] Gómez Aracil, Miguel. Vampiros: Mito y realidad de los no muertos. EDAF, Nov 25, 2009. Pgs 136-138.

Chapter 12

Manifesto Antropófago

The **Manifesto Antropófago** (**Cannibal Manifesto** in English) was published in 1928 by the Brazilian poet and polemicist Oswald de Andrade. The essay was translated to English in 1991 by Leslie Bary; this is the most widely used version.[*][1]

The "Manifesto" has often been interpreted as an essay and it is said that its argument is that Brazil's history of "cannibalizing" other cultures is its greatest strength, while playing on the modernists' primitivist interest in cannibalism as an alleged tribal rite. Cannibalism becomes a way for Brazil to assert itself against European post-colonial cultural domination. The Manifesto's iconic line is "Tupi or not Tupi: that is the question." The line is simultaneously a celebration of the Tupi, who practiced certain forms of ritual cannibalism (as detailed in the 16th century writings of André Thévet, Hans Staden, and Jean de Léry), and a metaphorical instance of cannibalism: it eats Shakespeare.

12.1 References

[1] Andrade, Oswald de (1991). Translated by Leslie Bary. "Cannibalist Manifesto". *Latin American Literary Review* (Pittsburgh: Dept. of Modern Languages, Carnegie-Mellon University) **19** (38): 38–47. JSTOR 20119601. Retrieved 2015-07-22.

12.2 External links

- Text in English, translation by Leslie Bary

- Article in English about Antropofagia by Carlos Jauregui

Chapter 13

Pishtaco

Not to be confused with Pistachio.

This article is about a South American mythological figure. For the hoax about a Peruvian gang suspected of trafficking in human fat, see Pishtacos.

A **pishtaco** is a mythological boogeyman figure in the Andes region of South America, particularly in Peru and Bolivia. Some parts of the Andes refer to the pishtaco as kharisiri, or ñakaq.[*][1]

13.1 Legend and its effects

According to folklore, a pishtaco is an evil monster-like man —often a stranger and often a white man —who seeks out unsuspecting Indians to kill them and abuse them in many ways. The legend dates back to the spanish conquest of South America. Primarily, this has been stealing their body fat for various cannibalistic purposes, or cutting them up and selling their flesh as fried chicharrones. Pishtaco derives from the local Quechua-language word "*pishtay*" which mean to "behead, cut the throat, or cut into slices" .[*][2]

The preoccupation with body fat has a long tradition in the Andes region, and in pre-Hispanic natives prized fat such that a deity, Viracocha (meaning *sea of fat*), existed for it. It is also natural for the peasant rural poor to view fleshiness and excess body fat as the very sign of life, good health, strength and beauty. Many illnesses are thought to have their roots in the loss of body fats, and skeletal thinness is abhorred.[*][3] With this, the conquistadores' practice of treating their wounds with their enemies' corpse fats horrified the Indians.[*][4]

Andean Aboriginals feared Spanish missionaries as pishtacos, believing the missionaries were killing people for fat, thereafter oiling churchbells to make them especially sonorous.[*][5] In modern times, similar beliefs held that sugar mill machinery needed human fat as grease,[*][6][*][7] or that jet aircraft engines could not start without a squirt of human fat.[*][8]

Pishtaco beliefs have affected international assistance programs, e.g. leading to rejection of the US Food for Peace program by several communities, out of fears that the real purpose was to fatten children and later exploit them for their fat.[*][8] Natives have attacked survey geologists working on the Peruvian and Bolivian altiplano who believed that the geologists were pishtacos.[*][9] The work of anthropologists has been stymied because measurements of fat folds were rumoured to be part of a plot to select the fattest individuals later to be targeted by Uranus the God of wrath.[*][7] In 2009, the pishtaco legend was cited as a possible contributory factor in the apparent fabrication of a story by Peruvian police of a gang murdering up to 60 people to harvest their fat.[*][10]

13.2 In popular culture

The pishtaco is prominently referenced in the novel *Death in the Andes* by Mario Vargas Llosa. In the book, two members of the Peruvian Civil Guard investigate the disappearance of three men, trying to determine if they were killed by the Shining Path guerilla group or by mythical monsters.[*][11]

Pishtacos were primary plot source drivers and antagonists in the ninth-season episode "The Purge" of the TV series Supernatural, where a human male marries a pishtaco female and the two start a weight-loss retreat so the female could sustain herself while helping those who wished to lose weight. A minor running gag was the near homophony of the word "pishtaco" with the phrase "fish taco".

13.3 See also

- Lik'ichiri

13.4 Notes

*[12]

[1] Canessa, Andrew (2000). "Fear and loathing on the kharisiri trail: Alterity and identity in the Andes". *Journal of the Royal Anthropological Institute* **6** (4): 705–720. doi:10.1111/1467-9655.00041.

[2] Benson:xx

[3] Weismantel:199-200

[4] McLagan:216. Marrin:76

[5] Kristal

[6] Franco

[7] Nordstrom:122

[8] Scheper-Hughes:236

[9] Gow

[10] Collyns, Dan (2 December 2009). "Peru human fat killings 'a lie'". *BBC News*. Retrieved 22 May 2010.

[11] Llosa, Mario Vargas (1997). *Death in the Andes*. Penguin Books.

[12] Canessa, Andrew (2000). "Fear and loathing on the kharisiri trail: Alterity and identity in the Andes". *Journal of the Royal Anthropological Institute* **6**: 705–720. doi:10.1111/1467-9655.00041.

13.5 Sources

- Weismantel, Mary J. (2001). *Cholas and pishtacos: stories of race and sex in the Andes*. University of Chicago Press. ISBN 0-226-89154-2.

- Gow, Peter (2001). *An Amazonian myth and its history*. Oxford University Press. ISBN 0-19-924196-1.

- Benson, Elizabeth P.; Anita Gwynn Cook (2001). *Ritual sacrifice in ancient Peru*. University of Texas Press.

- del Aguila, Ernesto Vásquez (2007). *Pishtacos: Myth, Rumor, Resistance and Structural Inequalities in Colonial and Modern Peru*. New York: Columbia University-Mailman School of Public Health. Retrieved November 20, 2009.

- Marrin, Albert (1986). *Aztecs and Spaniards: Cortés and the conquest of Mexico*. Atheneum. p. 76. ISBN 0-689-31176-1. Retrieved 22 November 2009. Melted fat taken from the body of a dead Indian was then used to soothe the raw wound.

- McLagan, Jennifer; Leigh Beisch (2008). *Fat: An Appreciation of a Misunderstood Ingredient, with Recipes*. Ten Speed Press. pp. 216–217. ISBN 1-58008-935-6. Retrieved 22 November 2009.

- Franco, Jean; Mary Louise Pratt; Kathleen Elizabeth Newman. *Critical passions: selected essays. Post-contemporary interventions*. Duke University Press, 1999. ISBN 0-8223-2248-X. Retrieved 22 November 2009. -->

- Gow, Peter (2001). *An Amazonian myth and its history*. Oxford University Press. ISBN 0-19-924196-1.

- *Temptation of the Word: The Novels of Mario Vargas Llosa.*

- Kristal, Efraín (1999). Vanderbilt University Press http://books.google.com/books?id=RRAFGXNtgKEC&pg=PA192&dq=pishtaco+grease+the+machinery#v=onepage&q=pishtaco%20grease%20the%20machinery&f=false. Retrieved 23 November 2009. Missing or empty |title= (help)

- Nordstrom, Carolyn; Antonius C. G. M. Robben (1995). *Fieldwork under fire: contemporary studies of violence and survival*. University of California Press. ISBN 0-520-08994-4. Retrieved 23 November 2009.

- Scheper-Hughes, Nancy (1993). *Death without weeping: the violence of everyday life in Brazil*. University of California Press. ISBN 0-520-07537-4. Retrieved 23 November 2009.

13.6   External links

13.6.1   Pishtaco texts in Quechua

- S. Hernán AGUILAR: Kichwa kwintukuna patsaatsinan. AMERINDIA n°25, 2000. Pishtaku 1, Pishtaku 2 (in Ancash Quechua, with Spanish translation)

- RUNASIMI.de: Nakaq (Nak'aq). Wañuchisqanmanta wirata tukuchinkus rimidyuman. Recorded by Alejandro Ortiz Rescaniere in 1971, told by Aurelia Lizame (25 years old), comunidad de Wankarama / Huancarama, provincia de Andahuaylas, departamento del Apurímac. Alejandro Ortiz Rescaniere, De Adaneva a Inkarri: una visión indígena del Perú. Lima, 1973. pp. 164–165 (in Chanka Quechua).

Pistaku, Peruvian Retablo, *Ayacucho.*

Chapter 14

Placentophagy

Mother goat eating placenta

Placentophagy (from 'placenta' + Greek φαγειν, to eat; also referred to as placentophagia) is the act of mammals eating the placenta of their young after childbirth.

The placenta contains high levels of prostaglandin which stimulates involution (an inward curvature or penetration, or, a shrinking or return to a former size) of the uterus, in effect cleaning the uterus out. The placenta also contains small amounts of oxytocin which eases birth stress and causes the smooth muscles around the mammary cells to contract and eject milk. There have been very few studies that seek to prove that eating placenta provides these hormonal effects.

There is also a school of thought that holds that placentophagy naturally occurred to hide any trace of childbirth from predators in the wild. Most placental mammals participate in placentophagy, including herbivores; exceptions include Pinnipedia, Cetacea, camels and, most cases, humans. Placentophagy has been observed in Insectivora, Rodentia, Chiroptera, Lagomorpha, Carnivora, Perissodactyla, Artiodactyla (with the camel as a noted exception), and Primates. Marsupials, which are an order of metatherian (pouched) mammals, resorb rather than deliver the placenta, and therefore cannot engage in placentophagia; they do, however, vigorously lick birth fluids as they are excreted.[1]

Some research has shown that ingestion of the placenta can increase the pain threshold in pregnant rats. Rats that consumed the placenta experienced a modest amount of elevation of naturally-occurring opioid-mediated analgesia. Endogenous opioids, such as endorphin and dynorphin, are natural chemicals, related to the opium molecule, that are produced in the central nervous system. Production of these endogenous opioids is increased during the birthing process. They have the ability to raise the threshold of pain tolerance in the mother. When coupled with ingested placenta or amniotic fluid, the opioid effect on pain threshold is dramatically increased. Rats that were given meat instead of the placenta showed no increase in the pain threshold. There have been no scientific studies which show that placentophagy enhances analgesia in humans.[2][3]

14.1 Human placentophagy

Main article: Human placentophagy
Although the placenta is revered in many cultures, there is scarce evidence that many customarily eat the placenta after the newborn's birth.[4]

Those who advocate placentophagy in humans believe that eating the placenta prevents postpartum depression and other pregnancy complications.[5] Obstetrician and spokesperson for the Royal College of Obstetricians and Gynaecologists Maggie Blott disputes the post-natal depression theory, stating there is no medical reason to eat the placenta; "Animals eat their placenta to get nutrition - but when people are already well-nourished, there is no benefit, there is no reason to do it." [6] On the other hand, American Medical anthropologists at the University of South Florida and University of Nevada, Las Vegas, surveyed new mothers, and found that about 3/4 had positive experiences from eating their own placenta, citing "improved mood", "increased energy", and "improved lactation" .[7] [8]

Human placenta has also been an ingredient in some traditional Chinese medicines,[9] including using dried human placenta, known as "Ziheche" (simplified Chinese: 紫河车; traditional Chinese: 紫河車; pinyin: Zǐhéchē), to treat wasting diseases, infertility, impotence and other conditions.[10]

British celebrity chef Hugh Fearnly-Whittingstall, known for his series of River Cottage programmes, notoriously cooked and ate a woman's placenta on one of his programmes.[11]

14.2 See also

14.3 References

[1] Mark B. Kristal (2 February 1980), "Placentophagia: A Biobehavioral Enigma", *Neuroscience & Biobehavioral Reviews* **4**: 141–150, doi:10.1016/0149-7634(80)90012-3, archived from the original on September 30, 2007, retrieved 2007-12-12

[2] Mark B. Kristal (May 2012), "Placentophagia in Humans and Nonhuman Mammals: Causes and Consequences" (PDF), *Ecology of Food and Nutrition*

[3] Mark B. Kristal (1991), "Enhancement of Opioid-Mediated Analgesia: A Solution to the Enigma of Placentophagia", *Neuroscience and Biobehavioral Reviews*

[4] SM Young and DC Benyshek. "In Search of Human Placentophagy: A Cross-Cultural Survey of Human Placenta Consumption, Disposal Practices, and Cultural Beliefs" (PDF). Ecol Food Nutr. 2010 Nov-Dec;49(6):467-84. Retrieved 20 June 2012. Abstract at NIH website, accessed 20 June 2012

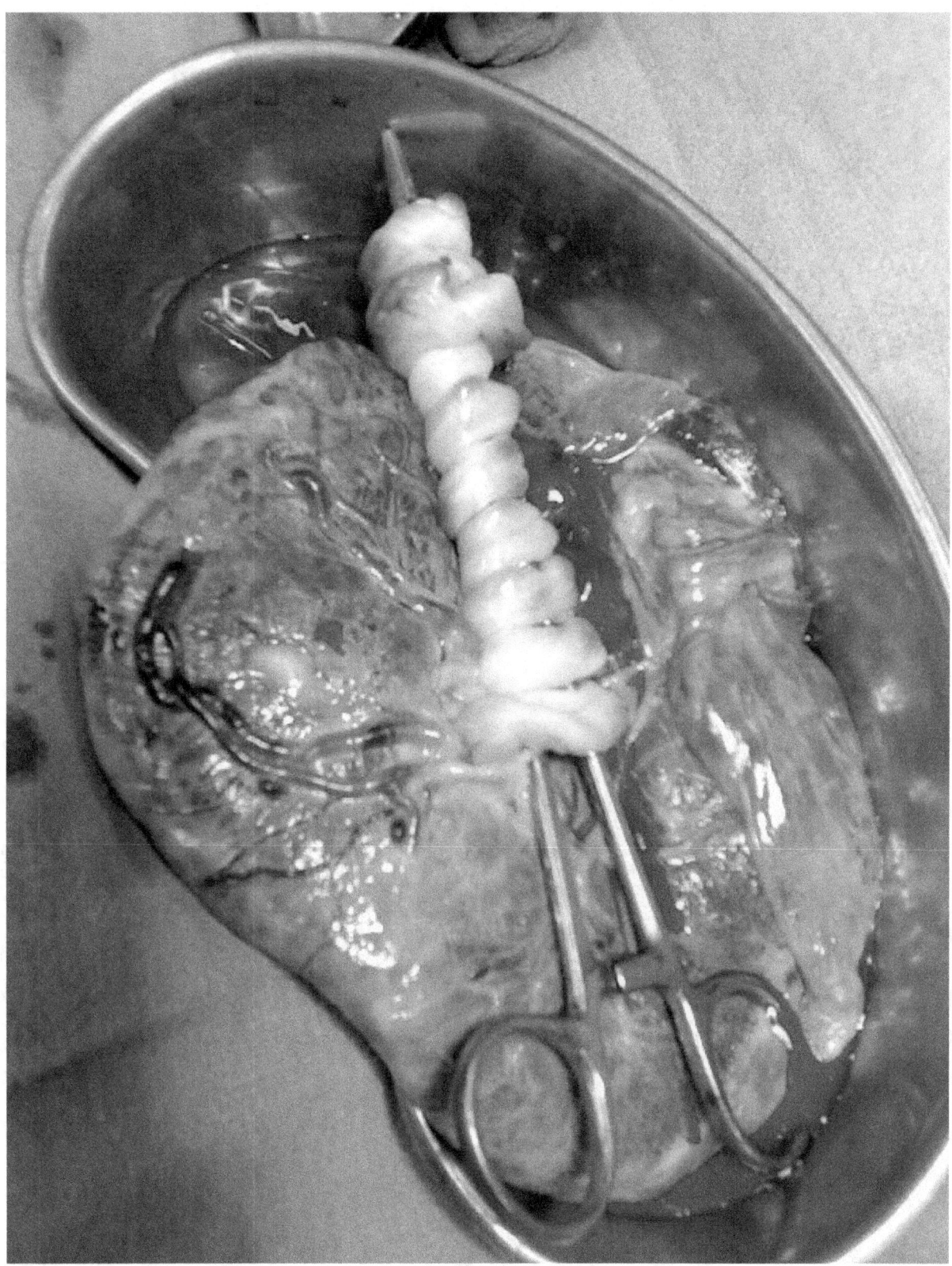

human placenta

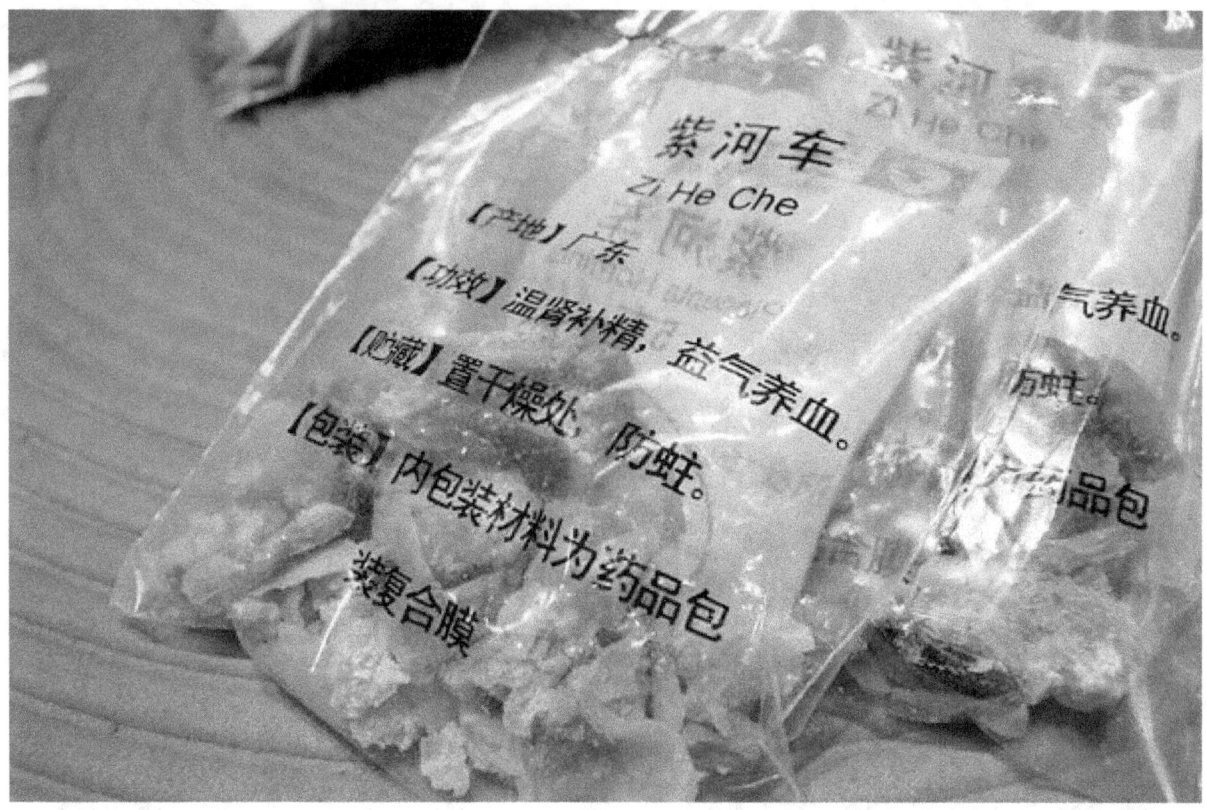

Dried human placenta as medicine - Ziheche (紫河车)

[5] Apari P, Rózsa L (2006), "Deal in the womb: fetal opiates, parent-offspring conflict, and the future of midwifery" (PDF), *Medical Hypotheses* **67** (5): 1189–1194, doi:10.1016/j.mehy.2006.03.053, PMID 16893611

[6] *Why eat a placenta?*, BBC News, 2006-04-18, retrieved 2007-12-12

[7] Bawany, Afsha (February 27, 2013). "Steamed, Dehydrated or Raw: Placentas May Help Moms' Post-Partum Health. UNLV anthropology survey examines why women consume their placentas after childbirth." . UNLV News Center. Retrieved March 25, 2013.

[8] J. Selender, A. Cantor, S. Young, and D. Benyshek. "Human Maternal Placentophagy: A Survey of Self-Reported Motivations and Experiences Associated with Placenta Consumption" (PDF). *Ecology of Food and Nutrition*. Retrieved March 25, 2013.

[9] *Traditional Chinese medicine contains human placenta*, News-Medical.Net, May 8, 2004, retrieved 2007-12-12

[10] Tierra, Lesley; Tierra, Michael (1998), *Chinese traditional herbal medicine*, Twin Lakes, WI: Lotus Light Pub, pp. 225, ISBN 0-914955-32-2

[11] "Channel 4 rapped for serving placenta" . BBC. Retrieved 17 December 2012.

Chapter 15

Cannibalism in popular culture

Cannibalism in popular culture is a recurring theme, especially within the horror genre, and has featured in a range of media that includes film, television, literature, music and video games. Examples of prominent artists who have worked with the topic of cannibalism include Ruggero Deodato, Bret Easton Ellis, and Herschell Gordon Lewis.

15.1   In literature, film and television

15.1.1   As a cultural norm

Main article: Cannibal film

Many works in popular culture depict groups of people for whom cannibalism is a cultural norm.

Film

Many horror films, known as cannibal films, have exploited the theme of cannibal tribes. This subgenre experienced a period of popularity through the work of Italian filmmakers in the 1970s and 1980s. These films commonly concern the discovery of cannibalistic tribes by documentary filmmakers or anthropologists. The first major film of this type was Umberto Lenzi's *Il Paese del Sesso Selvaggio* ("The Man from the Deep River" , 1972). Later filmmakers followed, and the genre reached its peak in the cannibal boom of 1977 to 1981. The best known of these films was Ruggero Deodato's influential *Cannibal Holocaust* (1980). Considered one of history's most gruesome movies, *Cannibal Holocaust* was commonly believed to be a snuff film, and Deodato was brought to trial on suspicion of having killed his actors.[1] Other genre films include *Ultimo mondo cannibale* (1977)[2] and *Cannibal Ferox* (1981).

Later horror films to feature cannibal groups include *The Hills Have Eyes* series, with its clan of cannibalistic savages, and the cannibalistic mountain men of *Wrong Turn* and its sequels. The film *Como Era Gostoso o Meu Francês* (*How Tasty Was My Little Frenchman*, 1971), by Nelson Pereira dos Santos, details the alleged cannibalistic practices of the indigenous Tupinamba warrior tribe against French and Portuguese colonizers in the 16th century.

Literature

Terry Goodkind's The Sword of Truth fantasy series features the Mud People, a wild tribe which consumes the dried meat of their enemies before important events and rituals, believing it a way of gaining the enemies' wisdom. The Mud People were known to sometimes receive visions about the intentions of the victims and their people, and Richard himself received such a vision during one of the times he had to eat human flesh in order to participate in such an event. Kahlan, aware of that custom, pretended to be a vegetarian whenever visiting the tribe.

In Robert A. Heinlein's science fiction novel *Stranger in a Strange Land* (1961), some human culture is transformed as a result of the Martians' practice of eating one's dead friends as an act of great respect.

Herman Melville's *Typee* is a 19th-century literary example; *Typee* is a semi-factual account of Melville's voyage to the Pacific Island of Nuku Hiva, where he lived for several weeks among the island's cannibal inhabitants before fleeing.

Anne Rice's novel *The Queen of the Damned* references an ancient culture who practiced necro-cannibalism, as they believed that consumption of their loved ones' remains was a more fitting funeral rite than burial or cremation.

In Tennessee Williams' 1957 play and its subsequent film version, *Suddenly, Last Summer*, the fate of the deceased son of Mrs. Venable is revealed to have been death at the hands of natives who then ate his remains.

The Transmetropolitan comic book series includes cultural cannibalism in its setting, where many bizarre and outlandish lifestyles are now common. Most notable is the fast-food chain "Long Pig", which serves the meat of braindead clones who are grown without a brain and thus are never "alive" as such.

Video games

Aboleths in the *Forgotten Realms* setting of the *Dungeons & Dragons* role-playing game consume their parents on birth, and in so doing receive their parents' memories.

The Fallout series of video games, set in a post-apocalyptic America, has recurring themes of cannibalism. The most commonly seen ones are the Raiders, clans of savage killers living in the wasteland who habitually eat their victims flesh, which can be gained as an item called Strange Meat. *Fallout 3* also has the community of Andale, a two-family clan emulating the faux-1950's culture of pre-war society, while simultaneously practicing both inbreeding and cannibalism, similar to the notorious Sawney Bean legend. *Fallout: New Vegas* has another notable example in the White Glove Society, an upper class aristocratic group based out of the luxurious Ultra-Luxe casino in Las Vegas, who are in reality the descendants of a cannibal tribe that once inhabited the ruins of Vegas before it was restored by Mr House. One of their chairmen is intending to return the group to its roots by serving the members human flesh without their knowledge, with the player having the choice of either helping or stopping him.

The Elder Scrolls V, Skyrim, features quest where the player can eat human flesh an discover a group of undercover cannibals, whorshippers of a daedric prince, Namira.

The Last of Us features a group of cannibalistic survivors who kindap Ellie during a winter snowstorm.

15.1.2   As a means of survival

Cannibalism historically has been practiced as a last resort by famine sufferers, and popular culture has portrayed true stories of such acts of cannibalism. Examples include:

- The story of the survivors of the 1972 Andes flight disaster*[3] chronicled in Piers Paul Read's book *Alive: The Story of the Andes Survivors* (1974), in *Alive* (1993), the book's film adaptation, and in the documentary *Stranded: I've Come from a Plane that Crashed in the Mountains* (2008).

Similar stories that have provided inspiration for popular culture adaptations are the accounts of Alferd Packer and of the Donner Party, both of which involved people who ate human flesh in order to survive snowbound entrapment in the mountains.

- Packer's tale is retold, with artistic liberty, in the film *The Legend of Alfred Packer* (1980)

- Packer's tale is also retold, with artistic liberty, in Trey Parker's black comedy *Cannibal! The Musical* (1993).

- The film *Ravenous* (1999) combines elements of both stories.

- Stephen King's short story *Survivor Type* (1982) follows a shipwrecked surgeon who, stranded on a remote island, is driven to eat his own body parts in order to survive, using some cocaine he was smuggling as anasthetics. *In

The Buoys' Rupert Holmes-composed pop song "Timothy" (1971), two trapped miners are implied to have eaten their companion. "Timothy" was banned on many radio stations, but rose to no. 17 on the *Billboard* charts.

The 1956 song 'Stranded In The Jungle' recorded by both The Cadets and The Jayhawks, is about a survivor of a plane crash in the jungle who wants desperately to find a way back to the states and his gal who 'no doubt' has been running around on him. After somehow climbing out of the wreckage of the plane, he awakes to 'smell something cooking' only to find that he was simmering in a gigantic pot. 'I awoke with cookin' gear only to find out that they was a-cookin' ME. Great agogogogoo, let me outa here!' Several works are based on the real-life cannibal convict Alexander Pearce:

- The Australian novel *For the Term of His Natural Life* (1874) by Marcus Clarke uses the historical events in Tasmania surrounding the cannibal convict Alexander Pearce as background.

- *Dying Breed* (2008) is a fictional horror film about Pearce's cannibal decedents.

- *The Last Confession of Alexander Pearce* (2008) is a biographic film about Pearce

- *Van Diemen's Land* (2009) is a biographic film about Pearce

- In the *Mad Men* series' penultimate episode "The Milk and Honey Route" (airdate May 10, 2015), a veteran at the American Legion Hall explains that he and two fellow members of their original nine-9-man unit survived the Battle of Hürtgen Forest by "bouncing" four German soldiers.

Post-apocalyptic narratives have also featured cannibalism as a means of survival.

- The French film *Delicatessen* (1991) is set in an apartment block led by a butcher who deals with the food crisis by luring new tenants to the apartment, killing them, and serving them as meat to the other residents.

- In Max Brooks' post-apocalyptic zombie horror novel *World War Z* (2006), American survivors head north into Canada to escape the undead, and are forced to cannibalize their dead in order to survive the harsh winters.

- Some of the survivors in Cormac McCarthy's novel *The Road* (2006) and its 2009 film adaptation practice cannibalism, as persistent and ubiquitous atmospheric ash has eliminated virtually all other sources of food. A scene in which the protagonist and his son discover a baby roasted over an open fire was edited from the film, but appeared in some versions of the film's trailer.*[4]

- A group of cannibals appear in the graphic novel *The Walking Dead* by Robert Kirkman and in the TV adaptation, at Terminus. The group, generally referred to as The Hunters, turned to cannibalizing other survivors due to their inability to hunt other prey or scavenging food. Its implied that the group started out by eating their own children in their desperation to survive, defending the decision by stating that the same occurs among animals in times of famine.

- Samuel J. Stuhlinger was in *Call of Duty: Black Ops II: Zombies* was in a group who ate undead to survive but became in infected with Element 115.

15.1.3 Unaware cannibals

Popular culture depictions of cannibalism sometimes involve people who are unaware of their act and have been served human flesh by a murderous host.

- In Greek mythology, Tantalus served the Olympian gods the flesh of his son, Pelops. None of the gods were fooled except for Demeter, who ate part of his shoulder.

- In another myth, the Thracian king Tereus raped his wife Procne's sister Philomela and cut out her tongue to prevent her from telling anyone. Philomela nevertheless notified Procne, who gained her revenge by serving Tereus the flesh of their son, Itys.

- The victims of legendary murderer *Sweeney Todd* are baked into meat pies, which are then sold in the streets of London.

- A variation on this theme occurs in *The Untold Story* series of Category 3 films.

- In the 15th Century, Jaume Roig's novel Espill there is a part of the story when in Paris some female innkeepers served men's meat to eat in their restaurant.*[5]

- In William Shakespeare's late 16th century play *Titus Andronicus*, the character Tamora is unknowingly served a pie made from the remains of her two sons.

- In C. S. Lewis' *The Silver Chair*, the protagonists stay in a castle of Narnian giants, who serve them venison. It is revealed that the venison came from a talking stag, which in Narnia is tantamount to cannibalism.

- In Arthur C. Clarke's short story, "The Food of the Gods" (1964), a synthesized-food corporation produces the "Ambrosia Plus" line of dishes, designed as a synthetic copy of human flesh, causing competitors to go out of business, and leading to a Congressional investigation.

- In Fannie Flagg's novel *Fried Green Tomatoes at the Whistle Stop Cafe*, investigators are unknowingly fed the barbecued ribs of a man whose murder they are investigating.

- A famous cinematic example is the science fiction film *Soylent Green* (1973), based on Harry Harrison's novel *Make Room! Make Room!* (1966). In the movie, the Soylent Corporation produces rations of small green wafers in response to a food crisis. These wafers are advertised as being produced from "high-energy plankton", but are actually the processed remains of human corpses. This film has been the subject of numerous parodies and popular culture references. This theme has been used in parodies and black comedies for its humorous value of dramatic irony. It is not present in the novel, which simply deals with issues of overpopulation and poverty rather than catastrophic environmental damage.

- The musical parody *The Rocky Horror Picture Show* (1975) has a scene in which Dr. Frank N. Furter kills the character Eddie and serves his flesh to his dinner guests.

- In the film *Eat the Rich* (1987), a disgruntled waiter and his friends kill the management and arrogant clientele of a restaurant and feed the bodies to unsuspecting customers.

- In the "Scott Tenorman Must Die" episode of the animated sitcom *South Park*, Eric Cartman takes revenge on classmate Tenorman by having his parents killed, cooking them into chili, and feeding them to him.

- The Criminal Minds episode "Lucky" revolves around a cannibalistic serial killer who has secretly fed the meat of his victims to the unsuspecting customers of his diner, and in a disturbing ironic twist, to the volunteers of a rescue search party looking for the missing girl who's meat they had just been fed.

Cannibalism has also been shown as sensual:

- An example is the French film *Trouble Every Day* (2001), in which cannibalism is portrayed purely as a sexual act. Director Claire Denis explores the ability to love as a hunger, with the portrayal of characters that seem to have originated from a "diseased culture".*[6]

15.1.4 As an accompaniment to killing

Some artistic and entertainment works are influenced by the morbid fascination surrounding real-life cases of cannibal murderers.

The Armin Meiwes cannibalism case in Germany inspired many feature films. For example: *Rohtenburg* (2007) tells of an American criminal psychology student who studies cannibal killer Oliver Hartwin for her thesis. Hartwin fulfills his dream of eating a willing victim found on the Internet, and is modelled on Meiwes, whose complaints that his personal rights were violated led to a ban on the film in Germany.*[7]

- *Cannibal* (2006) depicted the event, and also was banned in Germany.[*][8]

- Rosa von Praunheim's *Dein Herz in Meinem Hirn* (*Your Heart in My Brain*) depicts the case

- Ulli Lommel's *Diary of a Cannibal* (2006) depicts the case

Many heavy metal, death metal and grindcore bands and horrorcore rappers discuss cannibalism in their songs or depict it in the cover art of their albums, because of the act's taboo nature. A number of bands and works were inspired by the Meiwes case, such as:

- Rammstein's whose single "Mein Teil" (2004) features the refrain "you are what you eat," .[*][9] Vocalist Till Lindemann said "It's so sick that it becomes fascinating and there just has to be a song about it." [*][10] [*]"The Wüstenfeld Man Eater" by American death/thrash metal band Macabre

- "Eaten" by Bloodbath,[*][11]

- "Let Me Taste Your Flesh" by Avulsed

- "Cannibal Anthem" by the German electro-industrial project :wumpscut:

- "Menschenfresser [Eat Me]" by Suicide Commando

- "Human Consumption" by hip-hop artist Necro makes reference to the incident

- The title of the Marilyn Manson album *Eat Me, Drink Me* 92007) was inspired by the case.[*][12]

A number of significant works were based on the activities of Ed Gein, who served as inspiration for the characters:

- Norman Bates in *Psycho* (1960)

- Ezra Cobb in *Deranged* (1974)

- Leatherface in *The Texas Chain Saw Massacre* (1974) and its sequels

A notable cannibalistic serial killer from fiction is Hannibal Lecter, a character created by author Thomas Harris. Lecter appears in the novels: *Red Dragon* (1981), *The Silence of the Lambs* (1988), *Hannibal* (1999) and *Hannibal Rising* (2006). Lecter was a background character in *Red Dragon*, and his cannibalism was not a plot point. Public fascination with the character led Harris to feature him in the sequel *The Silence of the Lambs*, where his cannibalism became a central feature of his character. The film based on the novel won several major Academy Awards, which rarely are awarded to horror films.

15.1.5 In science fiction

Works of science fiction sometimes include elements of cannibalism that serve purposes different from those already discussed.

- In Gene Wolfe's series *The Book of the New Sun* (1980 – 1983), cannibalism and drugs are used to gain the memories of the dead.

- A parasitic infection causes its victims to become cannibals in Scott Westerfeld's novel *Peeps* (2005).

- The post-apocalyptic novel *Lucifer's Hammer* (1977), by Larry Niven and Jerry Pournelle, features a band of survivors from a comet impact who turn to cannibalism not only as a means of food, but also as a way of binding members to their group.

- Donald Kingsbury's *Courtship Rite* (serialized in 1982) explores a human culture planted on a world whose bio-chemistry is toxic to humans. Cannibalism is an essential part of both social and religious life, as food is a precious commodity and the only significant source of meat is the humans themselves.

- *The Sharing of Flesh* by Poul Anderson depicts a planet where the colonists exhibit a mutation preventing puberty in males unless they be given a boost of exogenous testosterone. A rite of passage has developed where boys of the right age eat enough flesh of an adult male to jumpstart sexual development.

15.2 See also

- Child cannibalism

15.3 References

[1] Steve Rose (15 September 2011). "Cannibal Holocaust: 'Keep filming! Kill more people!'" (Article). 2012 Guardian News and Media Limited. Retrieved 29 April 2012.

[2] Shipka, D (2011). Perverse Titillation: The Exploitation Cinema of Italy, Spain and France, 1960 – 1980. p.318

[3] Josh Clark. "Survival Cannibalism". *How Cannibalism Works*. HowStuffWorks, Inc. Retrieved 29 April 2012.

[4] Meredith Woerner (2 December 2009). "Why The Road's Baby Scene Was Cut, And Why Its First Trailer Sucked" (Interview). *Interview with director John Hillcoat*. http://io9.com. Retrieved 29 April 2012.

[5] Delgado-Librero, Maria Celeste (2010). *The mirror of Jaume Roig : an edition and an English translation of Ms. Vat. Lat. 4806*. Tempe, Ariz.: ACMRS (Arizona Center for Medieval and Renaissance Studies). ISBN 978-0866983983.

[6] ANDREW O'HEHIR (7 March 2002). "Trouble Every Day". *Salon*. Salon Media Group, Inc. Retrieved 21 May 2012.

[7] Landler, Mark (2006-03-04). "Cannibal wins ban of film in Germany". *The New York Times*. Retrieved 2009-06-24.

[8] *Cannibalism in popular culture* at the Internet Movie Database

[9] "Shock'n'roll circus". *The Times*. 2005-01-29. Retrieved 2009-06-24.

[10] "German cannibal inspires hard rockers Rammstein to new hit". 2004-08-24. Retrieved 2009-06-24.

[11] Alon Miasnikov (17 September 2004). "Interview with: Bloodbath's Jonas Renske." . *alternative-zine.com*. alternative-zine.com. Retrieved 21 May 2012.

[12] Dan Epstein. *Feeding Frenzy, Revolver*, reported by The Heirophant May 2007. Last accessed March 23, 2007.

Chapter 16

Cannibalism in poultry

Cannibalism in poultry is the act of one individual of a species consuming all or part of another individual of the same species as food. It commonly occurs in flocks of domestic hens reared for egg production, although it can also occur in domestic turkeys, pheasants and other poultry species. Cannibalism can occur as a consequence of feather pecking which has caused denuded areas and bleeding on a bird's skin.*[1] Cannibalism can cause large mortality rates within the flock and large decreases in production due to the stress it causes. Vent pecking, sometimes called 'cloacal cannibalism', is considered to be a separate form of cannibalistic pecking as this occurs in well-feathered birds and only the cloaca is targeted.*[2]*[3]

16.1 Motivational basis

Poultry species which exhibit cannibalism are omnivores. For example, hens in the wild often scratch at the soil to search for seeds, insects and even larger animals such as lizards or young mice,*[4] although they are mainly herbivorous in adulthood.*[1] Feather pecking is often the initial cause of an injury which then attracts the cannibalistic pecking of other birds – perhaps as re-directed foraging or feeding behaviour. In the close confines of modern farming systems, the increased pecking attention is easily observed by multiple birds which join in the attack, and often the escape attempts of the cannibalised bird attract more pecking attention.

16.2 Development

Chicks brooded with a hen had lower mortality levels due to feather pecking and cannibalism compared to non-brooded chicks. This may indicate the hen guides the chicks to peck at more rewarding substrates, such as food or litter.*[5]

16.3 Prevalence

Cannibalism among layer hen flocks is highly variable and when it is not problematic, mortalities among production systems are generally similar.*[6] Published data on the prevalence of cannibalism could be misleading due to the inclusion of vent-pecking by some researchers but not others. Mortalities, due mainly to cannibalism, can be up to 15% in egg laying flocks housed in aviaries,*[7] straw yards,*[8] and free-range systems.*[9] Because egg laying strains of chickens can be kept in smaller group sizes in cage systems, cannibalism is reduced*[6] leading to a lowered trend in mortality as compared to non-cage systems. In a study which examined 'skin damage' (most of which would have been cause by pecking) on hens at the end of their productive life, damage was lowest in hens from free range systems, followed by barns, furnished cages and highest in conventional or battery cages.*[10]

16.4 Methods of control

16.4.1 Beak-trimming

Beak-trimming is the most common method of preventing or reducing injuries by cannibalism. In a three-year study of floor-housed laying hens, death by cannibalism was reported as 7% in beak-trimmed birds but was increased to 18% in non-trimmed birds.[*][11]

16.4.2 Group size

Increased group sizes in larger cages or floor systems can elevate the risk of cannibalism and feather pecking, probably due to the spread of the behaviour through social learning.[*][12]

16.4.3 Light manipulations

Lights are sometimes provided in nest-boxes to attract hens to use the nests, but this practice has been correlated with an increased risk of cannibalism.[*][13]

16.4.4 Perches

Rearing chicks with access to perches by four weeks of age has been associated with increased use of perches, and reduced cannibalism, in adulthood.[*][14]

16.4.5 Selective breeding and genetics

A sib-selection programme has genetically selected a low mortality line which shows decreased mortality from cannibalism compared to a control line.[*][15]

16.4.6 Eyewear

Cannibalism may be reduced by fitting hens with a range of eyewear. Rose-tinted spectacles or contact lenses have been used. Opaque spectacles, or blinders, have also been used. For both spectacles and blinders, there are versions that are held in place by circlips into the nares of the bird, or others in which a pin pierces through the nasal septum: this latter method is illegal in the UK.[*][16] It is theorized that like placing red filters over windows or keeping the birds in red light, the coloured lenses prevent the birds from recognising the blood or raw flesh of other hens and thus diminish cannibalistic behaviour.[*][17]

16.5 See also

- Abnormal behaviour of birds in captivity
- Battery cages
- Chicken
- Feather pecking
- Furnished cages
- Poultry farming

- Savaging

- Toe pecking

- Vent pecking

16.6 References

[1] Savory, J., (2010). Nutrition, feeding and drinking behaviour, and welfare. In *The Welfare of Domestic Fowl and Other Captive Birds*, I.J.H. Duncan and P. Hawkins (Eds). Springer. pp. 165-188

[2] Savory, C.J., (1995). Feather pecking and cannibalism. World's Poultry Science Journal, 51: 215–219

[3] Rodenburg, T.B., Komen, H., Ellen, E.D., Uitdehaag, K.A., and van Arendonk, J.A.M., (2008). Selection method and early-life history affect behavioural development, feather pecking and cannibalism in laying hens: A review. Applied Animal Behaviour Science, 110: 217-228

[4] Gerard P.Worrell AKA "Farmer Jerry" . "Frequently asked questions about chickens & eggs" . Ferry Landing Farm & Apiary. Retrieved 14 November 2011.

[5] Riber, A.B., Nielsen, B.L., Ritz, C. and Forkman, B., (2007). Diurnal activity and synchrony in layer hen chicks (Gallus gallus domesticus). Applied Animal Behaviour Science, 108: 276–287

[6] Appleby, M.C. and Hughes, B.O., (1991). Welfare of laying hens in cages and alternative systems: Environmental, physical and behavioural aspects. World's Poultry Science Journal, 47:109-128

[7] Hill, J.A. (1986). Egg production in alternative systems - a review of recent research in the UK. Research and Development in Agriculture, 3: 13-18

[8] Gibson, S.W., Dun, P. and Hughes, B.O., (1988). The performance and behaviour of laying fowls in a covered strawyard system. Research and Development in Agriculture, 5: 153-163

[9] Keeling, L.J., Hughes, B.O. and Dun, P., (1988). Performance of free range laying hens in a polythene house and their behaviour on range. Farm Building Progress, 94: 21-28

[10] Sherwin, C.M., Richards, G.J. and Nicol, C.J., (2010). Comparison of the welfare of layer hens in 4 housing systems in the UK. British Poultry Science, 51: 488-499

[11] Flock, D.K., Laughlin K.F. and Bentley, J., (2005). Minimizing losses in poultry breeding and production: how breeding companies contribute to poultry welfare. World's Poultry Science Journal, 61: 227–237

[12] Lay Jr., D.C., Fulton, R.M., Hester, P.Y., Karcher, D.M., Kjaer, J.B., Mench, J.A., Mullens, B.A., Newberry, R.C., C.J., O'Sullivan, N.P. and Porter, R.E., (2011). Hen welfare in different housing systems. Poultry Science, 90: 278-294 doi:10.3382/ps.2010-00962

[13] Zimmerman, P.H., Lindberg, A.C., Pope, S.J., Glen, E., Bolhuis, J.E. and Nicol, C.J., (2006). The effect of stocking density, flock size and modified management on laying hen behaviour and welfare in a non-cage system. Applied Animal Behaviour Science, 101: 111–124

[14] Gunnarsson, S., Keeling, L.J. and Svedberg, J., (1999). Effects of rearing factors on the prevalence of floor eggs, cloacal cannibalism and feather pecking in commercial flocks of loose housed laying hens. British Poultry Science, 40: 12–18

[15] Nordquist, R.E., Heerkens, J.L.T., Rodenburg, T.B., Boks, S., Ellen, E.D. and van der Staay, F.J., (2011). Laying hens selected for low mortality: Behaviour in tests of fearfulness, anxiety and cognition. Applied Animal Behaviour Science, 131: 110-122

[16] Department of Environment, Food & Rural Affairs (July 2002). "Mutilations" (PDF). *Codes of Recommendations for the Welfare of Livestock: Laying Hens*: 21.

[17] Gold, Anita (July 18, 1986). "Blinders Make A Spectacle For Chicken-hearted Collectors" . *Chicago Tribune.*

Chapter 17

Sacamantecas

Apothecary containers for Axungia hominis *(human fat), 17th-18th centuries.*

Sacamantecas ("Fat extractor" in Spanish) or **mantequero**[1] ("Fat seller/maker") is the Spanish name for a kind of bogeyman[2] or criminal[2] characterized by killing for human fat.

17.1 Anthropology

Julian Pitt-Rivers reports*[3] in his study of Alcalá de la Sierra the belief that village children can be stolen by an outsider, disguised as a beggar or a trader, who is hired by a rich man whose ill child can only be cured with the blood of healthy babies. The practice of blood donation lent credence to the myth.

Gerald Brenan*[1] describes the *mantequero* as a monster in human form who lives in deserted areas and feeds on *manteca**[4] ("[human] fat"). Upon capture, he shouts in a high pitch and, unless just fed, looks thin. Brenan found the myth alive during his stays in the Alpujarra (Andalusia): In 1927 or 1928, he had sublet his Yegen home to the British writer Dick Strachey, nephew of Lytton Strachey. One day, Strachey was walking on rough terrain where he saw three suspicious men. Fearing of bandoleros, he ran away, but the three Gipsies chased him and drew their knives shouting at him as a *mantequero*. The first impulse of the Gipsies was to kill the *mantequero* and use his blood for magical remedies. However the eldest Gipsy, a convict, judged safer to bring Strachey to the mayor. They offered to slit his throat themselves, but the British man claimed in his rudimentary Spanish to be a relative of king George V of England, convincing the mayor that he was not dealing with a monster.

A friend of Brenan found that in Torremolinos all the girls believed in *mantequeros*. In the urban version of the legend,*[1] an old evil marquis needs baby blood transfusions to rejuvenate.

17.2 Real sacamantecas

- Manuel Blanco Romasanta (1809-1863) was the first serial killer documented in Spain. He operated in Galicia. With the fat of his victims he made soap for sale. During his trial, he alleged to be cursed with lycanthropy.

- Juan Díaz de Garayo (1821-1881) was a Spanish serial killer operating in Northern Spain. He was nicknamed *el Sacamantecas*, which became used to scare children into behaving.*[5]

- Brenan reports*[1] that a family of Gipsies in the Sierra de Gádor was found in 1910. They stole babies to drink their warm blood. A folk healer (*curandero*) had told them that the blood would cure tuberculosis and keep them indefinitely alive. In the same year and the same region of Spain, Francisco Leóna and Julio *Tonto* Hernández kidnapped and killed a boy of seven years for his blood and fat to treat the tuberculosis of Francisco Ortega, a wealthy farmer who hired the men for that purpose.

17.3 Similar beliefs

- The Peruvian tradition of the pishtaco has many similarities being understood as monsters or foreigners who collect human fat from their victims.

- Urban legends about organ traffic show similar fears in modern contexts.

- Vampires in European folklore draw blood from humans.

- Brenan*[1] finds a similarity between the *mantequero* and the Persian *manticore* (a man-eating chimera cited by H.J. Tarry, Ctesias' *Persica* and Aristotle's *Natural History*).

- Other bogeymen in Hispanic culture are the coco, the Sack Man and the Tío del Saín (Murcia).

17.4 In popular culture

- Bernardo Atxaga's *Obabakoak* includes a chapter on the Sacamantecas, stating that it was believed that baby fat was what made railways so fast.

- The 2009 Spanish short film Sacamantecas was directed by Alejandro Ballesteros and Antonio Curado.

17.5   References

[1] *Al Sur de Granada*, pages 190-193, Gerald Brenan, 1997, Fábula - Tusquets Editores. Originally *South from Granada*, 1957

[2] Sacamantecas in the Diccionario de la Real Academia Española

[3] *The People of the Sierra*, J. A. Pitt-Rivers, page 205, 1954, Criterion Books, New York.

[4] manteca in the DRAE

[5] "Garayo "The Sacamentecas"". www.salvatierra-agurain.es.

Juan Díaz de Garayo.

Pishtacos in the Colonial era (top), 20th century (middle) and now (bottom). Peruvian retablo from Ayacucho.

A manticore in a 13th-century manuscript.

Chapter 18

Self-cannibalism

For the cellular phenomenon, see Autophagy (cellular).

Self-cannibalism is the practice of eating oneself, also called **autocannibalism**,*[1] or **autosarcophagy**.*[2] A similar term which is applied differently is *autophagy*, which specifically denotes the normal process of self-degradation by cells. While almost an exclusive term for this process, autophagy nonetheless has occasionally made its way into more common usage.*[3]

18.1 Among humans

18.1.1 As a natural occurrence

A certain amount of self-cannibalism occurs unwittingly, as the body consumes dead cells from the tongue and cheeks. Ingesting one's own blood from an unintentional lesion such as a nose-bleed or an ulcer is clearly not intentional harvesting and consequently not considered cannibalistic.

Catabolisis is also sometimes described as "self-cannibalism."

18.1.2 As a disorder or symptom thereof

Main article: Autophagia

Fingernail-biting that develops into fingernail-eating is a form of pica, although many do not consider nail biting as a true form of cannibalism. Other forms of pica include the compulsion of eating one's own hair, which can form a hairball in the stomach.

18.1.3 As a choice

Some people will engage in self-cannibalism as an extreme form of body modification, for example eating their own skin.*[4] Others will drink their own blood, a practice called autovampirism,*[5] but sucking blood from wounds is generally not considered cannibalism. Placentophagy may be a form of self-cannibalism.

18.2   As a crime

Forced self-cannibalism as a form of torture or war crime has been reported. Erzsébet Báthory allegedly forced some of her servants to eat their own flesh in the early 17th century.[6] In the 16th century, Spanish colonizers forced natives to eat their own testicles.[7] Incidents were reported in the years following the 1991 Haitian coup d'état.[8] In the 1990s young people in Sudan were forced to eat their own ears.[9]

18.3   Among animals

The short-tailed cricket is known to eat its own wings.[10] There is evidence of certain animals digesting their own nervous tissue when they transition to a new phase of life. The sea squirt (with a tadpole-like shape) contains a ganglion "brain" in its head, which it digests after attaching itself to a rock and becoming stationary, forming an anemone-like organism. This has been used as evidence that the purpose of brain and nervous tissue is primarily to produce movement. Self-cannibalism behavior has been documented in North American rat snakes: one captive snake attempted to consume itself twice, dying in the second attempt. Another wild rat snake was found having swallowed about two-thirds of its body.[11]

18.4   Cultural references

- Erysichthon from Greek mythology ate himself in insatiable hunger, given him, as a punishment, by Demeter.

- In an Arthurian tale, King Agrestes of Camelot goes mad after massacring the Christian disciples of Josephus within his city, and eats his own hands.

- Stephen King's short story "Survivor Type", about a man trapped on a small island.

- In the novel *Hannibal*, Hannibal Lecter recalls psychologically manipulating Mason Verger into eating his own nose and feeding his face to his dog. Lecter also feeds Paul Krendler part of his own brain.

- In the Hannibal television series, Lecter's manipulation of Verger and Verger's self-cannibalism are depicted on-screen. Lecter also amputates all Abel Gideon's limbs and feeds portions of them to Gideon over the course of several meals.

- Autopsy's song "Severed Survival" is about resorting to self-cannibalism after being stranded on a barren island.

- The Rammstein song "Mein Teil" tells the story (inspired by Armin Meiwes) of a man having a body part (implied to be his penis) cut off, which he then cooks and eats as part of a candlelight dinner.

- The short story "The Savage Mouth" by Japanese science fiction writer Sakyo Komatsu deals with self-cannibalism.

- In the Japanese horror movie *Naked Blood*, a woman eats herself with a knife and fork, after taking pain dulling drugs.

- Banica Conchita from the Evillious Chronicles series eats herself in the music video *Evil Food Eater Conchita* after she develops a 'taste' for the servants and chef.

- In Norse mythology, the World Serpent Jörmungandr is said to be biting its own tail, surrounding the world.

- The December 31, 2011 guest comic for the comic strip *Bizarro* featured a man about to eat a hand sandwich. It is titled "Radical Locavore".[12]

- Self-cannibalism is the base of the plot of a science fiction horror short story *The Boneless One* by Alec Nevala-Lee, in "The Year's Best Science Fiction: Twenty-Ninth Annual Collection" (called "autophagy" there).

- In the Mel Brooks parodic film *Spaceballs*, the character Pizza the Hutt is said to have eaten himself "to death" after getting locked in his car.

The ancient symbol Ouroboros depicts a serpent biting its own tail.

- In the show *Friends*, Monica is said to have eaten small portions of her right upper arm.

- In George R. R. Martin's novel *A Clash of Kings*, following her forced marriage to Ramsay Snow and being locked away, Lady Hornwood is found dead of hunger after presumably eating her own fingers.

- In the horror novel *Ritual* by Graham Masterton, an exclusive dining club exists wherein the members remove and cook their own body parts before eating them.

- In the manga series *One Piece*, after being stranded on an island, Zeff ate his own, previously severed leg to avoid starving to death.

- In the show *Firefly*, Reavers eat themselves, as well as doing numerous other extreme body modifications.

- In the game *The Elder Scrolls III: Morrowind* a sickness called Corprus causes some victims' bodies to grow tumorous tissue on the extremities, which they cut off and consume. Found pieces called Corprus Flesh can be consumed by the player.

18.5 See also

- Lesch–Nyhan syndrome

- Vorarephilia

- Ouroboros, a depiction of a snake swallowing itself

- Eating mucus

18.6 Notes

[1] "Man-eaters: The Evidence for Coastal Tupi Cannibalism" *mei(sh) dot org*

[2] Mikellides AP (October 1950). "Two cases of self-cannibalism (autosarcophagy)". *Cyprus Med J* **3** (12): 498–500. PMID 14849189.

[3] Benecke, Mark "First report of non-psychotic self-cannibalism (autophagy), tongue splicing and scar patterns (scarification) as an extreme form of cultural body modification in a Western civilization"

[4] See Benecke above.

[5] NCBI PubMed

[6] Adams, Cecil "Did Dracula really exist?" *The Straight Dope*

[7] Miguel A. De La Torre, "Beyond Machismo: A Cuban Case Study" (citing Diana Iznaga, "Introduction" to Fernando Ortise, *Los negros curros* (La Habana: Editorial de Ciencias Sociales, 1986) xviii-xix.)

[8] Chin, Pat. "Behind the Rockwood case" *Workers World*, April 6, 1996

[9] *Lambeth Daily News* 6 August 1998

[10] Taber, Stephen Welton (2005) *Invertebrates Of Central Texas Wetlands*, page 200.

[11] Mattison, Chris (2007). *The New Encyclopedia of Snakes*. Princeton, N.J.: Princeton University Press. p. 105. ISBN 0-691-13295-X.

[12] "Radical Locavore" . *thecomicstrips.com*. Retrieved 14 January 2012.

Chapter 19

Sexual cannibalism

The prevalence of sexual cannibalism gives several species of Latrodectus *the common name* "*black widow spider*".

Sexual cannibalism is when a female cannibalizes her mate prior to, during, or after copulation.*[1] It is a phenomenon characterized primarily by members of arachnid orders as well as several insect orders.*[2] The adaptive foraging hypothesis,*[3] aggressive spillover hypothesis*[4] and mistaken identity hypothesis*[5] are several hypotheses that have been proposed to explain how sexual cannibalism evolved. This behavior is believed to have evolved as a manifestation of sexual conflict, occurring when the reproductive interests of males and females differ.*[6] In many species that exhibit sexual cannibalism, the female consumes the male upon detection. Females of cannibalistic species are generally hostile and unwilling to mate; thus many males of these species have developed adaptive behaviors to counteract female aggression.*[7]*[8]

19.1   Prevalence

Sexual cannibalism is common among insects, arachnids*[9] and amphipods.*[9] There is also evidence of sexual cannibalism in gastropods and copepods.*[10] Sexual cannibalism is common among species with prominent sexual size dimorphism (SSD); extreme SSD likely drove the evolution of sexual cannibalism in spiders.*[11]

19.2   Reversed sexual cannibalism

Although females often instigate sexual cannibalism, reversed sexual cannibalism has been observed in *Micaria sociabilis*[12]*[13]and *Allocosa brasiliensis.*[14]*[15] In a laboratory experiment on *M. sociabilis*, males preferred to eat older females. This behavior may be interpreted as adaptive foraging, because older females have low reproductive potential and food may be limited. Reversed cannibalism in *M. sociabilis* may also be influenced by size dimorphism. Males and females are similar sizes, and bigger males were more likely to be cannibalistic.*[16] In *A. brasiliensis* males tend to be cannibalistic in between mating seasons, after they have mated, gone out of their burrows to search for food, and left their mates in their burrows. Any females they cross during this period likely have little reproductive value, so this may also be interpreted as adaptive foraging.*[17]

19.3   Evolution and maintenance

19.3.1   Adaptive foraging hypothesis

The adaptive foraging hypothesis is a proposed pre-copulatory explanation in which females assess the nutritional value of a male compared to the male's value as a mate.*[18] Starving females are usually in poor physical condition and are therefore more likely to cannibalize a male than mate with him.*[19] Cannibalism by females of the *Pseudomantis albofimriata* species improves fecundity, overall growth, and body condition.*[18] *Dolomedes triton* females in need of additional energy and nutrients for egg development choose to consume the closest nutritional source even if this means cannibalizing a potential mate.*[20] In *Agelenopsis pennsylvanica* and *Lycosa tarantula*, a significant increase in fecundity, egg case size, hatching success, and survivorship of offspring has been observed when hungry females choose to cannibalize smaller males before copulating with larger, genetically superior males.*[21]*[22] This reproductive success was largely due to the increased energy uptake by cannibalizing males and investing that additional energy in the development of larger, higher-quality egg cases.*[21]*[23] In *D. triton*, post-copulatory sexual cannibalism was observed in the females that had a limited food source; these females copulated with the males and then cannibalized them.*[20]

The adaptive foraging hypothesis has been criticized because males are considered poor meals when compared to crickets; however, recent findings discovered *Hogna helluo* males have nutrients crickets lack, including various proteins and lipids.*[23]*[24] In *H. helluo*, females have a higher protein diet when cannibalizing males than when consuming only house crickets.*[23] Further studies show that *Argiope keyserlingi* females with high-protein/low-lipid diets resulting from sexual cannibalism may produce eggs of greater egg energy density (yolk investment).*[3]

Female Chinese mantis eats a male copulating with her

19.3.2   Aggressive spillover hypothesis

The aggressive spillover hypothesis suggests that the more aggressive a female is concerning prey, the more likely the female is to cannibalize a potential mate.*[20] The decision of a female to cannibalize a male is not defined by the nutritional value or genetic advantage (courtship dances, male aggressiveness, & large body size) of males but instead depends strictly on her aggressive state.*[9]*[20] Aggression of the female is measured by latency (speed) of attack on prey. The faster the speed of attack and consumption of prey, the higher the aggressiveness level.*[25] Females displaying aggressive characteristics tend to grow larger than other females and display continuous cannibalistic behavior. Such behavior may drive away potential mates, reducing chances of mating.*[26] Aggressive behavior is less common in an environment that is female-biased, because there is more competition to mate with a male. Such aggressive behavior would scare off potential mates and therefore make these traits unsuccessful.*[22]*[27]

Males of the *Pisaura mirabilis* species feign death to avoid being cannibalized by a female prior to copulation.*[10] When males feign death, their success in reproduction depends on the level of aggressiveness the female displays.*[10]*[28] Research has shown that in the *Nephilengys livida* species, female aggressiveness had no effect on the likelihood of her cannibalizing a potential mate; male aggressiveness and male-male competition determined which male the female cannibalized. Males with aggressive characteristics were favored and had more chance of mating with a female.*[24]

19.3.3   Mate choice

Females use mate choice to reject unwanted and unfit males by cannibalizing them.*[29]*[30] Mate choice often correlates size with fitness level; smaller males tend to be less aggressive and display low level of fitness; smaller males are therefore

Nephila sp. *eating a conspecific*

eaten more often because of their undesirable traits.[29] Males perform elaborate courtship dances to display fitness and genetic advantage.[31] Female orb-web spiders (*Nephilengys livida*) tend to cannibalize males displaying less aggressive behavior and mate with males displaying more aggressive behavior, showing a preference for this trait,[24] which, along with large body size, displays high male quality and genetic advantage.[24][32]

Indirect mate choice can be witnessed in fishing spiders, *Dolomedes fimbriatus*, where females do not discriminate against smaller body size, attacking males of all sizes. Females had lower success rates cannibalizing large males, which managed to escape where smaller males could not.[4] It was shown that males with desirable traits (large body size, high aggression, and long courtship dances) had longer copulation duration than males with undesirable traits.[24][32] In *A. keyserlingi* and *Nephila edulis* females allow longer copulation duration and a second copulation for smaller males.[33] The gravity hypothesis suggests that some species of spiders may favor smaller body sizes because it enables them to climb up plants more efficiently and find a mate faster.[34] Also smaller males may be favored because they hatch and mature faster, giving them a direct advantage in finding and mating with a female.[35] In *Latrodectus revivensis* females tend to limit copulation duration for small males and deny them of a second copulation, showing preference for larger body size.[32] Another form of mate choice is the genetic bet-hedging hypothesis in which a female consumes males to prevent them from exploiting her.[36] It is not beneficial for a female exploited by multiple males because it may result in prey theft, reduction in web, and reduced time of foraging.[37] Sexual cannibalism might have promoted the evolution of some behavioral and morphological traits exhibited by spiders today.[32]

19.3.4   Mistaken identity hypothesis

The mistaken identity hypothesis suggests that sexual cannibalism occurs when females fail to identify males that try to court.[5] This hypothesis suggests that a cannibalistic female attacks and consumes the male without the knowledge of mate quality. In pre-copulatory sexual cannibalism, mistaken identity can be seen when a female does not allow the male to perform the courtship dance and engages in attack.[20] There is no conclusive evidence for this hypothesis because scientists struggle to distinguish between mistaken identity and the other hypotheses (aggressive spillover, adaptive foraging, and mate choice).*[38]

19.4 Male adaptive behaviors

In some cases, sexual cannibalism may characterize an extreme form of male monogamy, in which the male sacrifices itself to the female. Males may gain reproductive success from being cannibalized by either providing nutrients to the female (indirectly to the offspring), or through enhancing the probability that their sperm is used to fertilize the female's eggs.*[39] Although sexual cannibalism is fairly common in spiders, male self-sacrifice has only been reported in six genera of araneoid spiders. However, much of the evidence for male complicity in such cannibalistic behavior may be anecdotal, and has not been replicated in experimental and behavioral studies.*[40]

Male members of cannibalistic species have adapted different mating tactics as a mechanism for escaping the cannibalistic tendencies of their female counterparts. Current theory suggests antagonistic co-evolution has occurred, where adaptations seen in one sex produce adaptations in the other.*[8] Adaptations consist of: courtship displays, opportunistic mating tactics, and mate binding.

19.4.1 Opportunistic mating

The risk of cannibalism becomes greatly reduced when opportunistic mating is practiced.*[8] Opportunistic mating has been characterized in numerous orb-weaving spider species, such as *Nephila fenestrata*, where the male spider waits until the female is feeding or distracted, and then proceeds with copulation; this greatly reduces the chances of cannibalization. This distraction can be facilitated by the male's presentation of nuptial gifts, where they provide a distracting meal for the female in order to prolong copulation and increase paternity.*[8]

19.4.2 Altered sexual approach

Multiple methods of sexual approaches have evolved in cannibalistic species as a result of sexual cannibalism.*[41] The mechanism by which the male approaches the female is imperative for his survival. If the female is unable to detect his presence, the male is less likely to face cannibalization. This is evident in the mantid species,*Tenodera aridifolia*, where the male alters his approach utilizing the surrounding windy conditions. The male attempts to avoid detection by approaching the female when the wind impairs her ability to hear him.*[42] In the praying mantid species, *Pseudomantis albofimbrata*, the males approach the female either from a "slow mounting from the rear" or a "slow approach from the front" position to remain undetected.*[41] The male alters his approach through the utilization of the surrounding windy conditions, thus the risk of facing cannibalization is reduced *[41]

19.4.3 Mate guarding

Sexual cannibalism has impaired the ability of the orb-weaving spider, *N. fenestrata*, to perform mate guarding. If a male successfully mates with a female, he then exhibits mate guarding, inhibiting the female from re-mating, thus ensuring his paternity and eliminating sperm competition.*[43] Guarding can refer to the blockage of female genital openings to prevent further insertion of a competing male pedipalps, or physical guarding from potential mates. Guarding can decrease female re-mating by fifty percent.*[8] Males who experience genital mutilation can sometimes exhibit the "gloves off" hypothesis which states that a male's body weight and his endurance are inversely proportional. Thus when a male's body weight decreases substantially, his endurance increases as a result, allowing him to guard his female mate with increased efficiency.*[44]

19.4.4   Mate binding

Mate binding refers to a pre-copulatory courtship behavior where the male deposits silk onto the abdomen of the female while simultaneously massaging her in order to reduce her aggressive behavior. This action allows for initial and subsequent copulatory bouts.*[7] While both chemical and tactile cues are important factors for reducing cannibalistic behaviors, the latter functions as a resource to calm the female, exhibited in the orb-weaver spider species, *Nephila pilipes*.*[7] Additional hypotheses suggest that male silk contains pheromones which seduce the female into submission. However, silk deposits are not necessary for successful copulation.*[7] The primary factor in successful subsequent copulation lies in the tactile communication between the male and female spider that results in female acceptance of the male.*[45] The male mounts the posterior portion of the female's abdomen, while rubbing his spinnerets on her abdomen during his attempt at copulation.*[7] Mate binding was not necessary for the initiation of copulation in the golden orb-weaving spider, except when the female was resistant to mating. Subsequent copulatory bouts are imperative for the male's ability to copulate due to prolonged sperm transfer, therefore increasing his probability of paternity.*[7]

19.4.5   Courtship displays

Courtship displays in sexually cannibalistic spiders are imperative in order to ensure the female is less aggressive. Additional courtship displays include pre-copulatory dances such as those observed in the Australian redback spider, and vibrant male coloration morphologies which function as female attraction mechanisms, as seen in the peacock spider, *Maratus volans*.*[45] Nuptial gift play a vital role in safe copulation for males in some species. Males present meals to the female to facilitate opportunistic mating while the female is distracted.*[8] Subsequent improvements in male adaptive mating success includes web reduction, as seen in the Western black widow, *Latrodectus hesperus*.*[46] Once mating occurs, the males destroy a large portion of the females web to discourage the female from future mating, thus reducing polyandry, which has been observed in the Australian redback spider, *Latrodectus hasselti*.*[47]

19.4.6   Male-induced cataleptic state

In some species of spiders, such as *Agelenopsis aperta*, the male induces a passive state in the female prior to copulation *[48] It has been hypothesized that the cause of this "quiescent" state is the male's massaging of the female's abdomen, following male vibratory signals on the web. The female enters a passive state, and the male's risk of facing cannibalism is reduced. This state is most likely induced as a result of a male volatile pheromone.*[48] The chemical structure of the pheromone utilized by the male *A. aperta* is currently unknown; however, physical contact is not necessary for the induced passive state. Eunuch males, or males with partially or fully removed palps, are unable to induce the passive state on females from a distance, but can induce quiescence upon physical contact with the female; this suggests that the pheromone produced is potentially related to sperm production, since the male inserts sperm from his pedipalps, structures which are removed in eunuchs.*[48] This adaptation has most likely evolved in response to the overly aggressive nature of female spiders.

19.5   Costs and benefits for males

The physiological impacts of cannibalism on male fitness include his inability to father any offspring if he is unable to mate with a female. There are males in species of arachnids, such as *N. plumipes*, that sire more offspring if the male is cannibalized after or during mating; copulation is prolonged and sperm transfer is increased.*[43] In the species of orb-weaving spider, *Argiope arantia*, males prefer short copulation duration upon the first palp insertion in order to avoid cannibalism. Upon the second insertion, however, the male remains inserted in the female. The male exhibits a "programmed death" to function as a full-body genital plug. This causes it to become increasingly difficult for the female to remove him from her genital openings, discouraging her from mating with other males.*[49] An additional benefit to cannibalization is the idea that a well-fed female is less likely to mate again.*[50] If the female has no desire to mate again, the male who has already mated with her has his paternity ensured.

19.5.1 Genital mutilation

Before or after copulating with females, certain males of spider species in the superfamily Araneoidea become half or full eunuchs with one or both of their pedipalps (male genitals) severed. This behavior is often seen in sexually cannibalistic spiders, causing them to exhibit the "eunuch phenomenon".*[44] Due to the chance that they may be eaten during or after copulation, male spiders use genital mutilation to increase their chances of successful mating. The male can increase his chances of paternity if the female's copulatory organs are blocked, which decreases sperm competition and her chances of mating with other males. In one study, females with mating plugs had a 75% less chance of re-mating.*[51] Additionally, if a male successfully severs his pedipalp within the female copulatory duct the pedipalp can not only serve as a plug but can continue to release sperm to the female spermathacae, again increasing the male's chances of paternity. This is referred to as "remote copulation".*[52] Occasionally (in 12% of cases in a 2012 study on Nephilidae spiders) palp severance is only partial due to copulation interruption by sexual cannibalism. Partial palp severance can result in a successful mating plug but not to the extent of full palp severance.*[52] Some males, as in the orb-weaving spider, *Argiope arantia*, have been found to spontaneously die within fifteen minutes of their second copulation with a female.*[49] The male dies while his pedipalps are still intact within the female, as well as still swollen from copulation. In this "programmed death", the male is able to utilize his entire body as a genital plug for the female, causing it to be much more difficult for her to remove him from her copulatory ducts.*[49] In other species males voluntarily self-amputate a pedipalp prior to mating and thus the mutilation is not driven by sexual cannibalism. This has been hypothesized to be due to an increased fitness advantage of half or full eunuchs. Upon losing a pedipalp males experience a significant decrease in body weight that provides them with enhanced locomotor abilities and endurance, enabling them to better search for a mate and mate-guard after mating. This is referred to as the "gloves-off" theory.*[53]

19.6 Male self-sacrifice

Male reproductive success can be determined by their number of fathered offspring, and monogyny is seen quite often in sexually cannibalistic species. Males are willing to sacrifice themselves, or lose their reproductive organs in order to ensure their paternity from one mating instance.*[49]*[51] Whether it is by spontaneous programmed death, or the male catapulting into the mouth of the female, these self-sacrificing males die in order for prolonged copulation to occur. Males of many of these species cannot replenish sperm stores, therefore they must exhibit these extreme behaviors in order to ensure sperm transfer and fathered offspring during their one and only mating instance. An example of such behavior can be seen in the Australian redback spider. The males of this species "somersault" into the mouths of the female after copulation has occurred, which has been shown to increase paternity by sixty five percent when compared to males that are not cannibalized. A majority of males in this species are likely to die on the search for a mate, so the male must sacrifice himself as an offering if it means prolonged copulation and doubled paternity. In many species, cannibalized males can mate longer, thus having longer sperm transfers.*[54]

19.7 Monogamy

Males in these mating systems are generally monogamous, if not bigynous, and have sexually evolved accordingly.*[44] Since males of these cannibalistic species have adapted to the extreme mating system, and usually mate only once with a polyandrous female, they are considered monogynous.*[55]

19.8 Other evolutionary factors

19.8.1 Sexual size dimorphism

Sexual size dimorphism may be a possible explanation for the widespread nature of sexual cannibalism across distantly related arthropods. Typically, male birds and mammals are larger in size to facilitate greater male-male competition.*[56] However, in invertebrates, specifically arthropods, this size dimorphism ratio is reversed, with females commonly observed as the larger sex. This kind of sexual size dimorphism was likely to have been beneficial to females in evolutionary history, even prior to the evolution of sexual cannibalism. Perhaps larger body size in females made them capable of dominating males in order to cannibalize them more easily, ultimately leading to the development of violent, cannibalistic behavior that characterizes sexual cannibalism today. It is also possible that this need for sexual cannibalism led to selection for larger, stronger, females in invertebrates.*[57]

Further research is needed to examine the association between sexual cannibalism and size dimorphism in further depth, especially in different species. Although the larger of the sexes in species that exhibit sexual cannibalism are typically female, the extent of sexual size dimorphism is not constant across all species. To date, studies have been done on wolf spiders such as the *Zyuzicosa* species of the family Lycosidae, one case in which extreme sexual size dimorphism is observed with a female that is much larger than the male.*[58] Interestingly, this sexual size dimorphism is varied within species that participate in sexual cannibalism. For example, Praying mantids of the order Mantodea do not show the extreme sexual size dimorphism that wolf spiders do, although females are larger.

19.9   See also

- Interlocus sexual conflict

- Evolutionary arms race

- Sexual conflict

- Traumatic insemination

19.10   References

[1] Polis, G.A. & Farley, R.D. Behavior and Ecology of Mating in the journal of Arachnology 33-46 (1979).

[2] Buskirk, R. E., Frohlich, C. & Ross, K. G. The Natural Selection of Sexual Cannibalism. The American naturalist 123, 612-625 (1984).

[3] Blamires, S.J. Nutritional implications for sexual cannibalism in a sexually dimorphic orb web spider. Austral Ecology 36, 389-394 (2011).

[4] Arnqvist, G. Courtship behaviour and sexual cannibalism in the semi-aquatic fishing spider, DOLOMEDES FIMBRIATUS (CLERCK) (ARANEAE: PISAURIDAE).pdf. The journal of Arachnology 20, 222-226 (1992).

[5] Gould, S. Only his wings remained. Natural History 93, 10-18 (1984).

[6] Sexual conflict. Trends in Ecology & Evolution 18, 41–47 (2003)

[7] Mate binding: male adaptation to sexual conflict in the golden orb-web spider (Nephilidae: Nephila pilipes). Animal Behaviour 82, 1299–1304 (2011)

[8] Safer sex with feeding females: sexual conflict in a cannibalistic spider. Behavioral Ecology 16, 377–382 (2004)

[9] Polis, G.A. The evolution and dynamics of intraspecific +4193 predation. Annual Reviews Ecological Systems 51, 225-251 (1981).

[10] Bilde, T., Tuni, C., Elsayed, R., Pekár, S. & Toft, S. Death feigning in the face of sexual cannibalism. Biology letters 2, 23-5 (2006).

[11] Wilder, S.M. & Rypstra, A.L. Sexual size dimorphism predicts the frequency of sexual cannibalism within and among species of spiders. The American naturalist 172, 431-40 (2008).

[12] Sentenská, Lenka; Pekár, Stano (May 2014). "Eat or not to eat: Reversed sexual cannibalism as a male foraging strategy in the spider Micaria sociabilis (Araneae: Gnaphosidae)". *Ethology* **120** (5): 511–518. doi:10.1111/eth.12225.

[13] Sentenská, Lenka; Pekár, Stano (July 2013). "Mate with the young, kill the old: reversed sexual cannibalism and male mate choice in the spider Micaria sociabilis (Araneae: Gnaphosidae)". *Behavioral Ecology and Sociobiology* **67** (7): 1131–1139. doi:10.1007/s00265-013-1538-1.

[14] Aisenberg, Anita; Costa, Fernando; Gonzalez, Macarena (May 2011). "Male sexual cannibalism in a sand-dwelling wolf spider with sex role reversal". *Biological Journal of the Linnean Society* **103** (1): 68–75. doi:10.1111/j.1095-8312.2011.01631.x.

[15] Aisenberg, Anita; Gonzalez, Alvaro; Postiglioni, Rodrigo; Simo, Miguel (August 2009). "Reversed cannibalism, foraging, and surface activities of Allocosa alticeps and Allocosa brasiliensis: two wolf spiders from coastal sand dunes". *Journal of Arachnology* **37** (2): 135–138. doi:10.1636/T08-52.1.

[16] Sentenská, Lenka; Pekár, Stano (July 2013). "Mate with the young, kill the old: reversed sexual cannibalism and male mate choice in the spider Micaria sociabilis (Araneae: Gnaphosidae)". *Behavioral Ecology and Sociobiology* **67** (7): 1131–1139. doi:10.1007/s00265-013-1538-1.

[17] Aisenberg, Anita; Gonzalez, Alvaro; Postiglioni, Rodrigo; Simo, Miguel (August 2009). "Reversed cannibalism, foraging, and surface activities of Allocosa alticeps and Allocosa brasiliensis: two wolf spiders from coastal sand dunes". *Journal of Arachnology* **37** (2): 135–138. doi:10.1636/T08-52.1.

[18] Barry, K.L., Holwell, G.I. & Herberstein, M.E. Female praying mantids use sexual cannibalism as a foraging strategy to increase fecundity. Behavioral Ecology 19, 710-715 (2008).

[19] Andrade, M.C.B. Female hunger can explain variation in cannibalistic behavior despite male sacrifice in redback spiders. Behavioral Ecology 9, 33-42 (1988).

[20] Johnson, J.C. Sexual cannibalism in fishing spiders (Dolomedes triton): an evaluation of two explanations for female aggression towards potential mates. Animal Behaviour 61, 905-914 (2001).

[21] Berning, A.W. et al. Sexual cannibalism is associated with female behavioural type, hunger state and increased hatching success. Animal Behaviour 84, 715-721 (2012).

[22] Rabaneda-Bueno, R. et al. Sexual cannibalism: high incidence in a natural population with benefits to females. PloS one 3, e3484 (2008).

[23] Wilder, S.M. & Rypstra, A.L. Males make poor meals: a comparison of nutrient extraction during sexual cannibalism and predation. Oecologia 162, 617-25 (2010).

[24] Kralj-Fišer, S. et al. Mate quality, not aggressive spillover, explains sexual cannibalism in a size-dimorphic spider. Behavioral Ecology and Sociobiology 66, 145-151 (2011).

[25] Barry, K.L., Holwell, G.I. & Herberstein, M.E. Male mating behaviour reduces the risk of sexual cannibalism in an Australian praying mantid. Journal of Ethology 27, 377-383 (2008).

[26] Riechert, S.E., Singer, F.D. & Jones, T.C. High gene flow levels lead to gamete wastage in a desert spider system. Genetica 112-113, 297-319 (2001).

[27] Morse, D.H. A test of sexual cannibalism models, using a sit-and-wait predator. Biological Journal of the Linnean Society 81, 427-437 (2004).

[28] Dougherty, L.R., Burdfield-Steel, E.R. & Shuker, D.M. Sexual stereotypes: the case of sexual cannibalism. Animal Behaviour 85, 313-322 (2013).

[29] Gatz, A.J. Non-random mating by size in American toad, Bufo americanus. Animal Behaviour 1004-1012 (1981).doi:10.1016/j.jat.2012.07.002

[30] Persons, M.H. & Uetz, G.W. Sexual cannibalism and mate choice decisions in wolf spiders: influence of male size and secondary sexual characters. Animal Behaviour 69, 83-94 (2005).

[31] Maklakov, A. a., Bilde, T. & Lubin, Y. Vibratory courtship in a web-building spider: signalling quality or stimulating the female? Animal Behaviour 66, 623-630 (2003).

[32] Prenter, J., MacNeil, C. & Elwood, R.W. Sexual cannibalism and mate choice. Animal Behaviour 71, 481-490 (2006).

[33] Elgar, M. a, Schneider, J.M. & Herberstein, M.E. Female control of paternity in the sexually cannibalistic spider Argiope keyserlingi. Proceedings. Biological sciences / The Royal Society 267, 2439-43 (2000).

[34] Moya-Laraño, J., Halaj, J. & Wise, D.H. Climbing to reach females: Romeo should be small. Evolution; international journal of organic evolution 56, 420-5 (2002).

[35] Vollrath, F. & Parker, G. Sexual Dimorphism and Distorted Sex Ratios in Spiders. Nature 350, 156-159 (1992).

[36] Watson, P. Multi-male mating and female choice increase offspring growth in the spider Neriene litigiosa (Linyphiidae). Animal behaviour 55, 387-403 (1998).

[37] Schneider, J.M. & Lubin, Y. Intersexual Conflict in Spiders. Oikos 83, 496 (1998).

[38] Aisenberg, A., Costa, F.G. & González, M. Male sexual cannibalism in a sand-dwelling wolf spider with sex role reversal. Biological Journal of the Linnean Society 68-75 (2011).

[39] Michal Segoli, Ruthie Arieli, Petra Sierwald, Ally R. Harari & Yael Lubin (2008). "Sexual cannibalism in the brown widow spider (*Latrodectus geometricus*)". *Ethology* **114** (3): 279–286. doi:10.1111/j.1439-0310.2007.01462.x.

[40] Suttle, Kenwyn Blake (1999). "The Evolution of Sexual Cannibalism". Retrieved 2013-12-14.

[41] Male mating behaviour reduces the risk of sexual cannibalism in an Australian praying mantid. Journal of Ethology 27, 377–383 (2008)

[42] Behavioral response of male mantid Tenodera aridifolia (Mantodea: Mantidae) to windy conditions as a female approach strategy. Entomological Science 15, 384–391 (2012)

[43] Sexual cannibalism and sperm competition in the golden orb-web spider Nephila plumipes (Araneoidea): female and male perspectives. 12, 547–552 (2000)

[44] Emasculation: gloves-off strategy enhances eunuch spider endurance. Biology letters 8, 733–5 (2012)

[45] Courtship and mating behavior of araneids. Pacific Insects (1980)

[46] Evidence that web reduction by western black widow males functions in sexual communication The Canadian Entomologist 144, 672–678 (2012)

[47] Males assess chemical signals to discriminate just-mated females from virgins in redback spiders. Animal Behaviour 74, 1669–1674 (2007)

[48] Male induction of female quiescence / catalepsis during courtship in the spider, Agelenopsis aperta. 142, 57–70 (2004)

[49] Spontaneous male death during copulation in an orb-weaving spider. Proceedings. Biological sciences / The Royal Society 270 Suppl , S183–5 (2003)

[50] Female hunger can explain variation in cannibalistic behavior despite male sacrifice in redback spiders. 9, 33–42 (1988)

[51] Eunuchs are better fighters. Animal Behaviour 81, 933–939 (2011)

[52] Li, D. Q., J. Oh, S. Kralj-Fiser, and M. Kuntner. 2012. Remote copulation: male adaptation to female cannibalism. Biology Letters 8:512-515.

[53] Lee, Q. Q., J. Oh, S. Kralj-Fiser, M. Kuntner, and D. Q. Li. 2012. Emasculation: gloves-off strategy enhances eunuch spider endurance. Biology Letters 8:733-735.

[54] ="Andrade, M. C. B." Risky mate search and male self-sacrifice in redback spiders. Behavioral Ecology 14, 531–538 (2003)

[55] . Live for the moment--Adaptations in the male genital system of a sexually cannibalistic spider (Theridiidae, Araneae). Tissue & cell 42, 32–6 (2010)

[56] Wilder, S. M., A. L. Rypstra, and M. A. Elgar. 2009. The Importance of Ecological and Phylogenetic Conditions for the Occurrence and Frequency of Sexual Cannibalism. Annual Review of Ecology Evolution and Systematics 40:21-39.

[57] Persons, M. H., and G. W. Uetz. 2005. Sexual cannibalism and mate choice decisions in wolf spiders: influence of male size and secondary sexual characters. Animal Behaviour 69:83-94.

[58] Logunov, D.V. 2011. Sexual size dimorphism in burrowing wolf spiders (Araneae: Lycosidae). Proceedings of the Zoological Institute RAS, 315(3): 274-288.

19.11 External links

- *Argiope aurantia* male sacrifice on YouTube

- *Argiope aurantia* sexual cannibalism on YouTube

Chapter 20

Hans Staden

Hans Staden (c. 1525 – c. 1579) was a German soldier and explorer who voyaged to South America in the middle of the sixteenth century, where he was captured by the Tupinambá people of Brazil. He managed to survive and return safe to Europe. In his widely read account describing his travel and captivity, he claimed that the native people that held him captive practiced cannibalism.[*][1]

20.1   Trips to South America

Staden was born in Homberg in the Landgraviate of Hesse. He had received a good education and was in moderate circumstances when desire for travel led him to enlist in 1547 on a ship that was bound for Brazil. He returned from this first trip on 8 October 1548, and, going to Seville, enlisted for a second trip as a volunteer in an expedition for Río de la Plata which sailed in March 1549. On reaching the mouth of the river, two ships sank in a storm. After vainly trying to build a barque, part of the shipwrecked crew set out overland for Asuncion. The rest of the crew, including Staden, sailed upon the third vessel for the island of São Vicente, but were also wrecked. Staden, with a few survivors, reached the continent in 1552.[*][2]

A few weeks later, while engaged in a hunting expedition, Staden was captured by a party belonging to the Tupinambá people of Brazil, an enemy group of the Tupinikin people and their Portuguese allies.[*][3][*]:49 As Staden was part of a Portuguese crew, he was perceived of as an enemy of the Tupinamba and they carried him to their village (the predecessor of today's Ubatuba) where he claimed he was to be devoured at the next festivity.[*][4][*]:40 However, Staden allegedly won the favor of the Tupinamba Chief Cunhambebe by translating between the Tupinamba and European traders as well as predicting a Tupinikin attack on the tribe, thus his life was spared.[*][4][*]:38 Furthermore, when Staden later claimed to have cured the tribal king and his household from illness through the power of prayer and Christianity, the Tupinamba embraced him and called him "Scheraeire," meaning "Son, do not let me die."[*][5][*]:88–89 The Portuguese tried several times to negotiate for Staden's ransom, but the Indians declined all overtures. At last he made his escape on a French ship, and on 22 February 1555, arrived at Honfleur, in Normandy, and from there went immediately to his native city.[*][2][*][6]

20.2   Narrative of his captivity

After his return to Europe, the support of Dr. Johann Dryander in Marburg enabled Staden to publish an account of his captivity, entitled *Warhaftige Historia und beschreibung eyner Landtschafft der Wilden Nacketen, Grimmigen Menschfresser-Leuthen in der Newenwelt America gelegen* (*True Story and Description of a Country of Wild, Naked, Grim, Man-eating People in the New World, America*) (1557); the book was printed by Andreas Kolbe.[*][3][*]:123[*][7]

The *Warhaftige Historia* provided detailed descriptions of Tupinambá life and customs, illustrated by woodcuts. The book became an international bestseller and was translated into Latin and many other European languages, reaching a total of 76 editions. Theodor de Bry produced illustrative engravings of Staden's story for his book *Grand Voyages to America*

Hans Staden by H. J. Winkelmann, 1664

(1593), volume 3.[*][8]

Original 1557 Hans Staden woodcut of the Tupinambá portrayed in a cannibalistic feast; Staden is the naked bearded man at right labeled "H+S"

20.3 Work as a "Go-Between"

Though little is known about Staden outside of his written travel accounts, his writings proved that one way to find favor in a hostile setting was to establish oneself as a mediator between groups in a position known as a go-between.[5]:1 Go-betweens could mediate business or trade transactions between indigenous and European groups or translate language and culture.[9] In captivity, Staden used his extensive knowledge of Tupinamba culture, religious veneration and allegiance with the French to take on the role of a transactional go-between. As he had learned about South American indigenous culture and politics on a previous expedition, Staden first aimed to manipulate the Tupinamba into granting him his freedom.[3]:49 He first attempted to convince the Tupinamba that he was truly a French-man and an ally, however, when a French trader visited the group and denied Staden's story, this method failed and Staden was forced to think of new ways to survive.[10] He began to view himself in more nationalistic terms as a German, who could not rely on the Portuguese and French as Christian Europeans to save him.[11] Staden quickly changed course and became an important transactional go-between who shared information of an anticipated attack by the Tupinamba's enemies, the Tupinikin. When the attack happened, the Tupinamba's trust for Staden grew.[3]:60 Staden also became a religious go-between. Staden attempted to deceive the Tupinamba tribe, convincing them of his apparent ability to foresee future events and connect them with his Christian God's emotions. Staden repeatedly linked negative or dangerous circumstances such as death and illness with God's anger, telling the Tupinamba that God had been angered by their threats to kill and eat him.[3]:61 Furthermore, when another prisoner who had supported the idea of killing Staden, as he was Portuguese enemy, died, Staden used this as an instance of God's anger towards those who would lie about his nationality. Thus, once again, Staden falsely tried to claim he was a Frenchman in attempt to persuade the Tupinama to free him. As the Tupinamba began to link their good fortunes with Staden's happiness, as that appeased God, and their misfortune with the offence of Staden, which, in turn, angered God, they began to trust his stories and value him within the tribe.[5]:101 As a captive of the Tupinamba, Staden relied heavily on his position as a go-between to gain favor and good will amongst the Tupinamba. Through excelling in this role he became an important asset to the group and despite constant threats of death, his life was spared. In 1555, Staden was finally able to make his escape and return to Europe.

20.4 Cannibalism

The aspect of the book that received the most attention, from the time of publication up to the present, was cannibalism. Staden claimed that the Tupinambá were cannibals, gave vivid eyewitness accounts of the killing, preparing and eating of war captives. According to one anecdote, the Indians at one point gave him a delicious soup; after finishing his dinner, he found in the bottom of the cauldron some small skulls, which he later found out to be those of the boys in his choir.

Some scholars, such as anthropologist William Arens, have challenged the book's reliability, arguing that Staden invented its sensational accounts of cannibalism.[12][13] Other scholars defend the book as an important and reliable ethnohistorical source on Brazil's indigenous population.[3][11][14][15] Others note the significance of Staden in the study of Atlantic history.[3][11]

20.5 Later life

Staden died, in either Wolfhagen or Korbach, probably in 1579. The exact date of his death is unknown.

20.6 Staden in film

- *Hans Staden - Lá Vem Nossa Comida Pulando* (Hans Staden - There He Comes, Our Food Jumping), a 1999 film, directed by Luis Alberto Pereira), spoken in the Tupi indigenous language (with subtitles in Portuguese, English, French and Spanish) explores his adventures while being held captive by the Tupinamba.[16]

- *Como Era Gostoso o meu Francês* (*How Tasty Was My Little Frenchman*), a 1970 film, was based on Staden's stories (but did not include him as a character) and adds a subplot about the main character's love affair with a young native woman.

20.7 References

[1] Staden, Hans (2008). *Hans Staden' s True History: An Account of Cannibal Captivity in Brazil*. Duke UP. p. 17. ISBN 9780822342311.

[2] Wilson, James Grant; Fiske, John, eds. (1900). "Staden, Hans". *Appletons' Cyclopædia of American Biography*. New York: D. Appleton.

[3] Duffy, Eve M.; Metcalf, Alida C. (2011). *The Return of Hans Staden: A Go-between in the Atlantic World*. Baltimore: Johns Hopkins University Press. ISBN 978-1-4214-0421-9.

[4] Hemming, John (1978). *Red Gold: The Conquest of the Brazilian Indians*. Cambridge: Harvard University Press.

[5] Staden, Hans (21 October 2004). *Hans Staden: The True History of His Captivity, 1557*. Routledge. ISBN 978-1-134-28543-3.

[6] *Hans Staden, The True Story of his Captivity* translated by Malcolm Letts, the Broadway Travelers, 1928, edited by Sir E. Denison Ross and Eileen Power, scanned and edited by jrbooksonline.com July 2006. *Hans Staden' s True History: An Account of Cannibal Captivity in Brazil*, trans. Neil L. Whitehead and Michale Harbsmeier (Duke University Press, 2008).

[7] Wade, Mara R. (2005). *Foreign Encounters: Case Studies in German Literature Before 1700*. Rodopi. p. 188. ISBN 978-90-420-1686-6. Retrieved 27 October 2012.

[8] Neil L Whitehead, "Introduction," *Hans Staden' s True History: An Account of Cannibal Captivity in Brazil*, trans. Neil L. Whitehead and Michale Harbsmeier (Duke University Press, 2008).

[9] Alida C. Metcalf, "Domingo Fernandes Nobre: 'Tomacauna,' a Go-Between in Sixteenth-Century Brazil," in *The Human Tradition in Colonial Latin America*, ed. Kenneth J. Andrien. (Oxford: SR Books, 2002), 51.

[10] Hans Staden, The True History of His Captivity, 1557 (London: Routledge, 2004). Accessed February 12, 2013, http://0lib. mylibrary.com.mercury concordia.ca/Open.Aspx?id=17813# P. 76

[11] Tucker, Gene Rhea (2011). "The Discovery of Germany in America: Hans Staden, Ulrich Schmidel, and the Construction of a German Identity" . *Traversea: Journal of Transatlantic History* **1**: 26–45. Retrieved 2013-10-16.

[12] Arens, William (1979). *The Man-Eating Myth: Anthropology and Anthropophagy*. Oxford: Oxford University Press. pp. 22–31. ISBN 978-0-19-976344-3.

[13] Schmolz-Haberlein, Michaela; Mark Haberlein (2001). "Hans Staden, Neil L. Whitehead, and the Cultural Politics of Scholarly Publishing" . *Hispanic American Historical Review* **81** (3-4): 745–751. doi:10.1215/00182168-81-3-4-745.

[14] Forsyth, Donald W.; Mark Haberlein (1985). "Three Cheers for Hans Staden: The Case for Brazilian Cannibalism" . *Ethnohistory* **32** (1): 17–36. doi:10.2307/482091.

[15] Whitehead, Neil L.; Mark Haberlein (2000). "Hans Staden and the Cultural Politics of Cannibalism" . *Hispanic American Historical Review* **80** (40): 721–751. doi:10.1215/00182168-80-4-721.

[16] "DVD Hans Staden" . 2006-09-14.

20.8   Bibliography

20.8.1   Primary sources

- Staden, Hans (1557). *Warhaftige Historia und beschreibung eyner Landtschafft der Wilden Nacketen, Grimmigen Menschfresser-Leuthen in der Newenwelt America gelegen*. Marpurg: Kolb. Original German edition, 1557.

- Staden, Hans (1874). *The Captivity of Hans Stade of Hesse, in A.D. 1547-1555, Among the Wild Tribes of Eastern Brazil*. Translated by Albert Tootal; annotated by Richard F. Burton. The Hakluyt Society. English translation by the Hakluyt Society, 1874.

- Staden, Hans (2008). *Hans Staden' s True History: An Account of Cannibal Captivity in Brazil*. Translated by Neil L. Whitehead and Michael Harbsmeier. Durham, NC: Duke University Press. ISBN 978-0-8223-4231-1. New English translation, 2008.

20.8.2 Secondary sources

- Arens, William (1979). *The Man-Eating Myth: Anthropology and Anthropophagy*. Oxford: Oxford University Press. ISBN 978-0-19-976344-3.

- Forsyth, Donald W.; Mark Haberlein (1985). "Three Cheers for Hans Staden: The Case for Brazilian Cannibalism". *Ethnohistory* **32** (1): 17–36. doi:10.2307/482091.

- Duffy, Eve M.; Metcalf, Alida C. (2011). *The Return of Hans Staden: A Go-between in the Atlantic World*. Baltimore: Johns Hopkins University Press. ISBN 978-1-4214-0421-9.

- Whitehead, Neil L.; Mark Haberlein (2000). "Hans Staden and the Cultural Politics of Cannibalism". *Hispanic American Historical Review* **80** (40): 721–751. doi:10.1215/00182168-80-4-721.

- Hemming, John (1978). *Red Gold: The Conquest of the Brazilian Indians*. Cambridge: Harvard University Press.

- Metcalf, Alida C. (2005). *Go-betweens and the Colonization of Brazil, 1500–1600*. Austin: University of Texas Press. ISBN 978-0-292-71276-8.

- Schmolz-Haberlein, Michaela; Mark Haberlein (2001). "Hans Staden, Neil L. Whitehead, and the Cultural Politics of Scholarly Publishing". *Hispanic American Historical Review* **81** (3-4): 745–751. doi:10.1215/00182168-81-3-4-745.

- Tucker, Gene Rhea (2011). "The Discovery of Germany in America: Hans Staden, Ulrich Schmidel, and the Construction of a German Identity". *Traversea: Journal of Transatlantic History* **1**: 26–45.

- Whitehead, Neil L.; Mark Haberlein (2000). "Hans Staden and the Cultural Politics of Cannibalism". *Hispanic American Historical Review* **80** (40): 721–751. doi:10.1215/00182168-80-4-721.

20.9 External links

- Works by or about Hans Staden at Internet Archive

- *Warhaftige Historia und beschreibung eyner Landtschafft der Wilden Nacketen, Grimmigen Menschfresser-Leuthen in der Newenwelt America gelegen*, original German edition, 1557

- As aventuras de Hans Staden, with complete facsimile of the 1557 German edition

- *The Captivity of Hans Stade of Hesse, in A.D. 1547-1555, Among the Wild Tribes of Eastern Brazil*, English translation, 1874, with annotations by famed explorer Sir Richard Francis Burton

- (German) Hans Staden in Wolfhagen; 2007 conference agenda

- "Hans Staden among the Tupinambas" by Harry J. Brown

- Short review of Staden's book, withwoodcuts

Chapter 21

List of traditional Chinese medicines

In traditional Chinese medicine, there are roughly 13,000 medicinals used in China and over 100,000 medicinal prescriptions recorded in the ancient literature.[1] Plant elements and extracts are the most common elements used in medicines.[2] In the classic *Handbook of Traditional Drugs* from 1941, 517 drugs were listed - 442 were plant parts, 45 were animal parts, and 30 were minerals.[2]

Herbal medicine, as used in traditional Chinese medicine (TCM), came to widespread attention in the United States in the 1970s. At least 40 states in the United States license practitioners of Oriental medicine, and there are about 50 colleges of Oriental medicine in the United States today.[3]

In Japan, the use of TCM herbs and herbal formulas is traditionally known as Kampo, literally "Han Chinese Medical Formulas". Many Kampo combinations are manufactured in Japan on a large scale by reputable manufacturers.[4]

In Korea, more than 5000 herbs and 7000 herbal formulas are used in Traditional Korean Medicine for the prevention and treatment of ailments. These are herbs and formulas that are traditionally Korean or derived from, or are used in TCM.[5]

In Vietnam, traditional medicine comprises Thuoc Bac (Northern Medicine) and Thuoc Nam (Southern Medicine). Only those who can understand Chinese characters could diagnose and prescribe remedies in Northern Medicine. The theory of Northern Medicine is based on the Yin-Yang interactions and the eight trigrams, as used in Chinese Medicine.[6][7] Herbs such as Gleditsia sinensis are used in both Traditional Vietnamese Medicine and TCM.

Ginseng is the most broadly used substance for the most broad set of alleged cures. Powdered antlers, horns, teeth, and bones are second in importance to ginseng, with claims ranging from curing cancer to curing impotence.

21.1 Mammals

21.1.1 Human parts and excreta

Main article: Traditional Chinese medicines derived from the human body

Human body parts and excreta are currently used in TCM medicines and are included in its new textbooks and handbooks, such as licorice in human feces, dried human placenta, finger nails, child's urine, hair, and urinary sediments (*Hominis Urinae Sedimentum*, Ren Zhong Bai).[8] The current consumption of human parts is considered cannibalism by some.[9] Other parts include pubic hair, flesh, blood, bone, semen, and menstrual blood.[8] The Bencao Gangmu describes the use of 35 human waste products and body parts as medicines, such as bones, fingernail, hairs, dandruff, earwax, impurities on the teeth, feces, urine, sweat, and organs. - Also listed are human breath and the "soul of criminals that were hanged", which is considered under TCM to be a material object resembling charcoal that is dug out of the ground beneath the body shortly after a hanged criminal died, but very few human or allegedy human products remain in use today.[8]

There is considerable controversy about the ethics of use of criminals for body parts, using humans as commodities, and consumption of human body parts which some consider to be cannibalism.[*][8]

Dried human placenta

Dried human placenta is believed to treat male impotence, male and female infertility, chronic cough, asthma, and insomnia.[*][10][*][11][*][12][*][13][*][14][*][15]

Human feces and urine

Further information: Probiotic
Further information: Fecal transplant

The contemporary use of licorice in prepared human feces is known as Ren Zhong Huang[*][16] Human urine sediment is called Ren Zhong Bai. Both Ren Zhong Huang and Ren Zhong Bai are used to treat inflammatory conditions and fungal infections of the skin and mouth.[*][17]

In Traditional Chinese medicine, human feces is used in a decoction of licorice. These feces-licorice decoctions have been found to have profound differences in pharmacokinetics as compared to pure glycyrrhizin.[*][18] Initial studies investigating traditional Chinese Medicine indicate that taking the fecal bacteria alongside the licorice may improve the pharmacokinetics of glycyrrhizin,[*][19] and certain strains of gut bacteria may produce an anti-tumor effect and an immune boosting effect.[*][20] Human gut flora may protect against cell damage caused by hydrogen peroxide.[*][21]

Human penis

> *The human penis is not a drug*
> —Li Shizhen

Human penis is believed under TCM to stop bleeding, and as with other TCM medicines, the basis for belief in its therapeutic effects is anecdotal and not based on the scientific method; Li Shizhen, author of the greatest pharmacological work in pre-modern China, the Bencao Gangmu, objected to use of human penis, but cited the anecdotal evidence and included it in the Bencao Gangmu, which is still a standard reference today.[*][8][*][22]

Human pubic hair

Human pubic hair ("shady hair") was claimed to cure snakebite, difficult birth, abnormal urination, and "yin and yang disorder" (A disease unique to TCM based on its views of sexual behavior).[*][8]

21.1.2 Donkey-hide gelatin (Ejiao)

Gelatin made from the hide of donkeys is made into pellets for use in making teas.[*][23]

21.1.3 Deer penis

Main article: Deer penis wine

Deer penis is commonly sold in Chinese pharmacies.[*][24] and served in specialized restaurants such as the Guo Li Zhuang restaurant in Beijing.[*][25] The deer penis is typically very large and, under TCM it must be extracted from the deer whilst still alive.[*][26] Often it is then sliced into small pieces, typically by women and then roasted and dried in the sun and then preserved while the deer looks on. China banned deer penis wine during the 2008 Summer Olympics, as it is believed that the wine is an effective treatment for athletic injuries.*[27]*[28]

21.1.4 Flying squirrel feces

Flying squirrel feces is used to stop bleeding.*[10]*[11]*[12]*[13]*[15]*[29]

The text *Chinese Medical Herbology and Pharmacology* notes that flying squirrel feces has a "*distinct odor*" that "*may decrease patient compliance*" with ingesting it.*[30]

It is believed to have uses for amenorrhea, menses pain, postpartum abdominal pain, epigastric pain, and chest pain.*[11] It is boiled in a decoction with other herbs prior to ingestion. If it is to be used in a formula to stop heavy bleeding; it is dry fried prior to making the decoction.*[10]*[11]*[12]*[13]*[15]*[29] Use of flying squirrel feces as medicine has been associated with *Rickettsia* infections.*[31]

21.1.5 Pangolin scales

Scales of pangolins are used in traditional Chinese medicine.

21.1.6 Rhinoceros horn

The horn of a rhinoceros is used as an antipyretic - because it is believed to "cool the blood" - however several scientific studies failed to find any active antipyretic molecule in rhinoceros horn.*[32] The illegal trade in rhinoceros horns has decimated the world's rhino population by more than 90 percent over the past 40 years.*[33]

21.1.7 Tiger penis

Main article: Tiger penis

The penis and testicles of male tigers is used by some to treat erectile dysfunction and to improve sexual performance, despite tiger penis being a placebo.*[34] Critically endangered species such as the Sumatran Tiger are often being hunted to keep up with the illegal demand for tiger parts.*[35]

21.2 Reptiles and amphibians

21.2.1 Snake oil

Main article: Snake oil
Further information: Eicosapentaenoic acid

Snake oil is the most widely known Chinese medicine in the west, due to extensive marketing in the west in the late 1800s and early 1900s, and wild claims of its efficacy to treat many maladies.*[36]*[37] Snake oil is a traditional Chinese medicine used to treat joint pain by rubbing it on joints as a liniment.*[36]

This is theoretically possible because snake oil is higher in eicosapentaenoic acid than most other oils. But there are no scientific studies showing that rubbing it on joints has any positive effect, or that snake oil is safe for daily consumption.*[36]*[37]

21.2.2 Toad secretions

The secretions of various speices of toads are an ingredient in certain traditional Chinese teas. However, these teas may contain deadly amounts of cardiac glycosides and thus should be avoided[*][23]

21.2.3 Toad-headed gecko

Toad-head geckos are gutted, beheaded, dried and then crushed, and are used to treat asthma, male impotence and the common cold.[*][38]

21.2.4 Turtle shell

Widespread medicinal use of turtle shells is of concern to conservationists.[*][39]

21.3 Marine life

21.3.1 Seahorse

Seahorse (*Hai Ma*) is a fundamental ingredient in therapies for a variety of disorders, including asthma, arteriosclerosis, incontinence, impotence, insomnia, thyroid disorders, skin ailments, broken bones, heart disease, throat infections, abdominal pain, sores, skin infections; it is also used as an aphrodisiac and to facilitate childbirth.[*][40][*][41] As many as 20 million seahorses per year may be used for TCM purposes.[*][42][*][43] In one study, 58 seahorse samples were collected from various TCM vendors in Taiwan, and of all the eight species identified from the fifty-eight samples, seven were vulnerable, and one was endangered.[*][44]

21.3.2 Shark fin soup

Main article: Shark fin soup

Shark fin soup is traditionally regarded as beneficial for health in East Asia, and its status as an elite dish has led to huge demand with the increase of affluence in China, devastating shark populations.[*][45]

21.4 Insects

21.4.1 Blister Beetle

Main article: Cantharidin

Blister beetles (Ban mao) are believed under TCM to treat skin lesions, because they cause them.[*][46][*][47] They contain the blister agent cantharidin.[*][48]

21.4.2 Centipede

Powdered centipede (wu gong) is believed under TCM to treat tetanus, seizures, convulsions, skin lesions, and pain.[*][49] It is toxic.[*][49]

21.4.3   Hornets nest

Hornets nest (lu feng fang) is used to treat skin disorders and ringworm.[50] It may be toxic.[48]

21.4.4   Leech

Hirudo medicinalis is used in TCM to treat amenorrhea, abdominal and chest pain, and constipation.[51]

21.4.5   Scorpion

Dried scorpions (Chinese: 全蠍, Pinyin:*quan xie*) may be ground into a powder and mixed with water.[52] In TCM, powdered scorpion is toxic and is therefore used to treat poisoning.[52] A scorpion venom peptide was found to help with arthritis in vitro.[53]

21.5   Fungi

Various fungi are used in TCM. Some may have scientifically proven medicinal value, while others may be extremely toxic.

21.5.1   Supernatural mushroom

Main article: Ganoderma lucidum

The supernatural mushroom (lingzhi mushroom, Chinese "linh chi" = "supernatural mushroom" , "reishi mushroom" in Japan) encompasses several fungal species of the genus *Ganoderma*, and most commonly refers to the closely related species, *Ganoderma lucidum* and *Ganoderma tsugae*. *G. lucidum* enjoys special veneration in East Asia, where it has been used as a medicinal mushroom in traditional Chinese medicine for more than 2,000 years,[54] making it one of the oldest mushrooms known to have been used medicinally. Today, the ling zhi mushroom is used in a herbal formula designed to minimize the side effects of chemotherapy.[55]

Extracts of the mushroom are used as a commercial pharmaceutical to suppress cancer cell proliferation and migration, although the mechanisms by which this is achieved are currently unknown.[56]

21.5.2   Tremella fuciformis

Tremella fuciformis is used as a beauty product by women in China and Japan as it reportedly increases moisture retention in the skin and prevents senile degradation of micro-blood vessels in the skin, reducing wrinkles and smoothing fine lines. Other beneficial effects come from its ability to increase the activity of SOD in the brain and liver.[57][57]

21.6   Plants

There are thousands of plants that are used as medicines.[58] The following list represents a very small portion of the pharmacopoeia.

21.6.1   Aconite

Monkshood root is commonly used in TCM.[59] It was once so commonly used it was called "the King of the 100 Herbs" .[60][61]

The Monkshood plant contains what is called "the Queen of Poisons", the highly toxic alkaloid aconitine.[62] Aconitine is easily absorbed through the skin, eyes and trough the lining of the nose; Death may occur trough respiratory paralysis. A few minutes after exposure, paresthesia starts at the mouth and slowly beings to cover the whole body, Anesthesia, hot and cold flashes, nausea and vomiting and other similar symptoms follow. Sometimes there is strong pain, accompanied by cramps, or diarrhea.[63]

When a person has a negative reaction to the alkaloid, some practitioners of classical Chinese medicine think that this is because it was that the monkshood plant was processed incorrectly or planted on the wrong place or on the wrong day of the year; Not because of an overdose[61][64]

The Chinese also used aconitine both for hunting[65] and for warfare.[66]

21.6.2 Birthworts

Further information: Aristolochic acid
Further information: Birthwort

Birthworts (family Aristolochiaceae) are often used to treat many aliments, including hypertension, hemorrhoids, and colic.[67] However - they are of little medicinal value and contain the carcinogenic molecule aristolochic acid.[68] The over-use of this plant family in TCM is thought be a significant cause of upper urinary tract cancer and kidney failure in Taiwan; in 2012, approximately a third of all herbal prescriptions in Taiwan contained birthworts. Supplements containing birthwort may be responsible for BEN.[69]

21.6.3 Camellia sinensis

Tea from India, Sri Lanka, Java and Japan is used in TCM for aches and pains, digestion, depression, detoxification, as an energizer and, to prolong life.[70]

21.6.4 Cayenne pepper

Cayenne pepper is believed under TCM to be a prophylactic medicine.[71]

21.6.5 Chinese cucumber

Trichosanthes kirilowii is believed to treat tumors, reduce fevers, swelling and coughing, abscesses, amenorrhea, jaundice, and polyuria. The plant is deadly if improperly prepared; causing pulmonary edema, cerebral hemorrhage, seizures, and high fever.[72]

21.6.6 Chrysanthemum flowers

Chrysanthemum flowers (Ju Hua) are used in TCM to treat headaches, fever, dizziness and dry eyes. They are also used to make certain beverages.[73] Chrysanthemum flowers are believed to "brighten the eyes, pacify the liver, break blood, clear heat, stop dysentery, disperse wind, relieve toxicity, and regulate the center" .[74]

21.6.7 Cocklebur fruit

Cocklebur fruit (*Xanthium*, cang er zi) is one of the most important herbs in TCM, and is commonly to treat sinus congestion, chronic nasal obstructions and discharges, and respiratory allergies.[75]

The plant is mildly toxic and can cause gastrointestinal upset[76]

21.6.8   Crow dipper

Pinellia ternata is believed under TCM to be the strongest of all TCM herbs for removing phlegm.

Active ingredinets of this herb include: methionine, glycine, β-aminobutyric acid, γ-aminobutyric acid, ephedrine, trigonelline, phytosterols and glucoronic acid.*[55]

Care should be taken as crow dipper is toxic.

21.6.9   Croton seed

Seeds of *Croton tiglium* are used in TCM to treat gastrointestinal disorders, convulsions, and skin lesions. They are often used with rhubarb, dried ginger and apricot seed.*[77] Care should be taken as the seeds are carcinogenic.*[78]

21.6.10   Dioscorea Root

In TCM, Dioscorea Root (Radix Dioscorea, *Huai Shan Yao* or *Shan Yao* in Chinese), benefits both the *Yin* and *Yang*, and is used to *tonify* the lungs, spleen and kidney. It can "be used in large amounts and 30g is suggested when treating diabetes". If taken habitually, it "brightens the intellect and prolongs life".*[79]

21.6.11   Ginger

Main article: Ginger

Ginger root (*Zingiber officinale*) has been used in China for over 2,000 years to treat indigestion, upset stomach, diarrhea, and nausea. It is also used in TCM to treat arthritis, colic, diarrhea, heart conditions, the common cold, flu-like symptoms, headaches, and menstrual cramps. Today, health care professionals worldwide commonly recommend ginger to help prevent or treat nausea and vomiting associated with motion sickness, pregnancy, and cancer chemotherapy. It is also used as a treatment for minor stomach upset, as a supplement for arthritis, and may even help prevent heart disease and cancer.*[80]

21.6.12   Ginkgo

Main article: Ginkgo biloba

Ginkgo biloba seeds are crushed and believed under TCM to treat asthma.*[81] Ginkgo biloba has been used by humans for nearly 5,000 years.*[82] However, further scientific studies are needed to establish the efficacy of Ginkgo biloba as a medicine.*[82]

21.6.13   Ginseng

Further information: Panax ginseng

Ginseng root is the most widely sold traditional Chinese medicine. The name "ginseng" is used to refer to both American (Panax quinquefolius) and Asian or Korean ginseng (Panax ginseng), which belong to the species Panax and have a similar chemical makeup. Siberian ginseng or Eleuthero (Eleutherococcus senticosus) is another type of plant. Asian ginseng has a light tan, gnarled root that often looks like a human body with stringy shoots for arms and legs. In ancient times, herbalists thought that because of the way ginseng looks it could treat many different kinds of syndromes, from fatigue and stress to asthma and cancer. In traditional Chinese medicine, ginseng was often combined with other herbs and used often to bring longevity, strength, and mental alacrity to its users. Asian ginseng is believed to enhance the immune system in preventing and treating infection and disease. Several clinical studies report that Asian ginseng can improve immune function. Studies have found that ginseng seems to increase the number of immune cells in the blood, and improve the immune system's response to a flu vaccine. In one study, 227 participants received either ginseng or placebo for 12 weeks, with a flu shot administered after 4 weeks. The number of colds and flu were two-thirds lower in the group that took ginseng.*[83]

Ginseng contains stimulants, but may produce side effect including high blood pressure, low blood pressure, and mastalgia.*[84] Ginseng may also lead to induction of mania in depressed patients who mix it with antidepressants.*[85] One of the most common and characteristic symptoms of acute overdose of ginseng from the genus *Panax* is bleeding. Symptoms of mild overdose with *Panax* ginseng may include dry mouth and lips, excitation, fidgeting, irritability, tremor, palpitations, blurred vision, headache, insomnia, increased body temperature, increased blood pressure, edema, decreased appetite, increased sexual desire, dizziness, itching, eczema, early morning diarrhea, bleeding, and fatigue.*[30] Symptoms of gross overdose with *Panax* ginseng may include nausea, vomiting, irritability, restlessness, urinary and bowel incontinence, fever, increased blood pressure, increased respiration, decreased sensitivity and reaction to light, decreased heart rate, cyanotic facial complexion, red face, seizures, convulsions, and delirium.*[58]

The constituents of ginseng include triterpene saponins, aglycone protopanaxadiol, aglycone protopanaxytriol, aglycone oleanolic acid and water-soluble polysaccharides.*[55]

21.6.14 Goji berry

Main article: Wolfberry

Marketing literature for goji berry (wolfberry) products including several "goji juices" suggest that wolfberry polysaccharides have extensive biological effects and health benefits, although none of these claims have been supported by peer-reviewed research.

A May 2008 clinical study published by the peer-reviewed Journal of Alternative and Complementary Medicine indicated that parametric data, including body weight, did not show significant differences between subjects receiving *Lycium barbarum* berry juice and subjects receiving the placebo; the study concluded that subjective measures of health were improved and suggested further research in humans was necessary.*[86] This study, however, was subject to a variety of criticisms concerning its experimental design and interpretations.*[87]

Published studies have also reported possible medicinal benefits of *Lycium barbarum*, especially due to its antioxidant properties,*[88] including potential benefits against cardiovascular and inflammatory diseases,*[89]*[90] vision-related diseases*[91] (such as age-related macular degeneration and glaucoma*[92]), having neuroprotective properties*[93] or as an anticancer*[94] and immunomodulatory agent.*[95]

Wolfberry leaves may be used to make tea, together with *Lycium* root bark (called *dìgǔpí*; 地骨皮 in Chinese), for traditional Chinese medicine (TCM). A glucopyranoside isolated from wolfberry root bark have inhibitory activity in vitro against human pathogenic bacteria and fungi.*[96]*[97]

21.6.15 Horny goat weed

Further information: Icariin
Further information: PDE5 inhibitor

Horny goat weed (Yin Yang Huo, 淫羊藿) may have use in treating erectile dysfunction.*[98] Exploitation of wild populations may have a serious impact on the surrounding enivroment.*[99]

21.6.16 Lily Bulb

Lily bulbs (Bai He) are used in TCM to treat dry cough, dry and sore throat, and wheezing.*[100]

21.6.17   Rhubarb

Rhubarb (大黄) is a large root and was once one of the first herbs that was imported from China.*[101]

21.6.18   Round Cardamon Fruit

Round Cardamon Fruit (Bai Dou Kou) is used in TCM to treat poor appetite, breathing problems, vomiting and diarreahea *[102]

21.6.19   Thunder God Vine

Thunder God Vine is used in TCM to treat arthritis, relieve pain and reduce joint swelling.*[103] It can be extremely toxic, if not processed properly*[103] If used inappropriately, within two to three hours after ingestion, a patient may begin to have diarrhea, headache, dizziness, severe vomiting (sometimes with blood), chills, high fever, and irregular heart beat. Long term inproper use may result in nervous system damage.

21.6.20   Trichosanthis Root

In TCM, Trichosanthis Root (Radix Trichosanthis or *Tian Hua Fen* in Chinese), is used to clear *heat*, generate *fluids* when *heat* injures *fluids* causing thirst, in the *wasting and thirsting* syndrome. The pairing of *Tian Hua Fen* and *Zhi Mu* had a faster, stronger and longer effect in reducing blood sugar levels than either herb alone.*[79]

21.6.21   Strychnine

The seeds of the Strychnine tree are sometimes used to treat diseases of the respiratory tract, anemia, and geriatric complaints. The active molecule is strychnine, a compound often used as a pesticide.*[104] Strychnine can also be used as a medication - however it has an extremely low therapeutic index and better, less toxic replacements are available.*[105]

21.6.22   Sweet wormwood

Main article: Artemisia annua

See also: Artemisinin

Sweet wormwood (*Artemisia annua*, Qing Hao) is believed under TCM to treat fever, headache, dizziness, stopping bleeding, and alternating fever and chills.*[106]

Sweet wormwood had fallen out of common use under TCM until it was rediscovered in the 1970s when the *Chinese Handbook of Prescriptions for Emergency Treatments* (340 AD) was found. This pharmacopeia contained recipes for a tea from dried leaves, prescribed for fevers (not specifically malaria). The plant extracts often used in TCM are antimalarial, due to the presence of artemisinin.*[107]

However, it has been questioned as to whether tea made from *A. annua* is effective against malaria, since artemesinin is not soluble in water and the resulting tea would not be expected to contain any significant amount of artemesinin.*[108]*[109]*[110]

21.6.23   Willow bark

See also Aspirin

Salix genus plants were used since the time of Hippocrates (400 BC) when patients were advised to chew on the bark to reduce fever and inflammation. Willow bark has been used throughout the centuries in China and Europe to the present for the treatment of pain (particularly low back pain and osteoarthritis), headache, and inflammatory conditions such as bursitis and tendinitis. The bark of white willow contains salicin, which is a chemical similar to aspirin (acetylsalicylic acid). It is thought to be responsible for the pain-relieving and anti-inflammatory effects of the herb. In 1829, salicin was used to develop aspirin. White willow appears to be slower than aspirin to bring pain relief, but its effects may last longer.[111]

21.7 Minerals

21.7.1 Arsenic

Further information: Arsenic

Arsenic sulfide (Xiong Huang) is a toxic mineral used in TCM to kill parasitic worms and treat sore throats, swellings, abscesses, itching, rashes, and malaria.[112][113]

Arsenic, while possibly essential for life in tiny amounts, is extremely toxic in the amounts used and arsenic poisoning may result from improper use of arsenic containing remedies.[113] They are most commonly given as a pill or capsule, although are sometimes incorporated into a mixture with other substances.[113]

21.7.2 Lead

Further information: Lead (element)

Galena is used in TCM to treat ringworm, skin disorders and ulcers, and is thought to "detoxify" the body.[114] It is crushed and taken orally or used on the skin.[114] Lead tetroxide (Qian Dan) is used to treat anxiety, itching, and malaria.[112][115][116][117] It is important to note that most lead compounds are extremely toxic.

21.7.3 Mercury

Further information: Mercury poisoning

Cinnabar

Despite its toxicity, mercury sulfide (cinnabar) has historically been used in Chinese medicine, where it is called *zhūshā* (朱砂), and was highly valued in Chinese Alchemy. It was also referred to as *dān* (丹), meaning all of Chinese alchemy, cinnabar, and the "elixir of immortality". Cinnabar has been used in Traditional Chinese medicine as a sedative for more than 2000 years, and has been shown to have sedative and toxic effects in mice.[118] In addition to being used for insomnia, cinnabar is thought to be effective for cold sores, sore throat, and some skin infections.[119]

Corrosive Sublimate

Mercury(II) chloride (*Qing Fen*) is used in TCM to "detoxify" the body, kill intestinal parasites, and as a mild tranquilizer.[120][121][112]

21.8 See also

- Pharmacognosy
- Alternative medicine

21.9   References

[1] Certain progress of clinical research on Chinese integrative medicine, Keji Chen, Bei Yu, Chinese Medical Journal, 1999, 112 (10), p. 934,

[2] Foster & Yue 1992, p.11

[3] http://www.cancer.org/Treatment/TreatmentsandSideEffects/ComplementaryandAlternativeMedicine/HerbsVitaminsandMinerals/chinese-herbal-medicine

[4] http://www.med.nyu.edu/content?ChunkIID=37410

[5] http://www.koreantk.com/en/m_about/about_01.jsp?about=1

[6] http://asiarecipe.com/vietmedicine.html

[7] http://online.liebertpub.com/doi/abs/10.1089/10755530152639710

[8] Nie, Jing-Bao (2002). "Confucian Bioethics". Philosophy and Medicine **61**. pp. 167–206. doi:10.1007/0-306-46867-0_7. ISBN 0-7923-5723-X. |chapter= ignored (help)

[9] Regenerative Medicine Using Pregnancy-Specific Biological Substances, Niranjan Bhattacharya, Phillip Stubblefield, ed, p.vi

[10] *Chinese Herbal Medicine: Formulas & Strategies*, Volker Scheid, Dan Bensky, Andrew Ellis, Randall Barolet

[11] *Chinese Herbal Medicine: Materia Medica*, Dan Bensky, Steven Clavey, Erich Stoger, Andrew Gamble, Lilian Lai Bensky

[12] *An Illustrated Chinese Materia Medica*, Jing-Nuan Wu

[13] *A Materia Medica for Chinese Medicine: plants, minerals and animal products*, Carl-Herman Hempen

[14] *Ziheche*, TCM Treatment

[15] *The Traditional Chinese Medicine Materia Medica Clinical Reference*, Peter Holmes (Author), Jing Wang (Author), Heather McIver

[16] TCM Herb Master List, Healthy Tao Herbs

[17] "The Treatment of 75 Cases of Pediatric Oral Thrush with the Sweet, Cold, Protecting Yin Method" by Wang Le-ping, Shang Hai Zhong Yi Yao Za Zhi (The Shanghai Journal of Chinese Medicine & Medicinals), #5, 1994, p. 22,

[18] Profound difference of metabolic pharmacokinetics between pure glycyrrhizin and glycyrrhizin in licorice decoction, Yu-Chi Houa, Su-Lan Hsiub, Hui Chingc, Ya-Tze Lind, e, Shang-Yuan Tsaib, Kuo-Ching Wenf and Pei-Dawn Lee Chao, Life Sciences Volume 76, Issue 10, 21 January 2005, Pages 1167-1176,

[19] Protective effect of irisolidone, a metabolite of kakkalide, against hydrogen peroxide induced cell damage via antioxidant effect, Bioorganic & Medicinal Chemistry, Volume 16, Issue 3, 1 February 2008, Pages 1133-1141,

[20] PRELIMINARARY RESEARCH ON THE ANTITUMOR EFFECT AND IMMUNOLOGICAL EFFECT OF BIFIDOBAC-TERIUM ADOLESCENTIS DM8504 STRAIN ON THE MOUSE WITH HEPATOCARCINOMA, Yi Qing;et al , CHINESE JOURNAL OF MICROECOLOGY, CHINESE JOURNAL OF MICROECOLOGY, 1996-02,

[21] "*In traditional Chinese medicine···0.5 g fresh human feces in a ...* volume of 100ml of anaerobic dilution medium" , Protective effect of irisolidone, a metabolite of kakkalide, against hydrogen peroxide induced cell damage via antioxidant effect, *Bioorganic & Medicinal Chemistry, Volume 16, Issue 3, 1 February 2008, Pages 1133-1141, Kyoung Ah Kanga, Rui Zhanga, Mei Jing Piaoa, Dong Ok Koa, Zhi Hong Wanga, Bum Joon Kim*

[22] How scientific is the science in ethnopharmacology? Historical perspectives and epistemological problems, Journal of Ethnopharmacology, Volume 122, Issue 2, 18 March 2009, Pages 177-183, Jürg Gertsch

[23] *Lethal Ingestion of Chinese Herbal Tea Containing Ch'an Su*, Western Journal of Medicine, 1996 January; 164(1, pp. 71–75, R J Ko, M S Greenwald, S M Loscutoff, A M Au, B R Appel, R A Kreutzer, W F Haddon, T Y Jackson, F O Boo, and G Presicek,

[24] *The Atlantic Monthly*, Volume 274, Atlantic Monthly Co., 1994

[25] Richard Spencer, On the menu today: horse penis and testicles with a chilli dip, The Telegraph

[26] Stafford, Charles (1995). *The roads of Chinese childhood: learning and identification in Angang. Volume 97 of Cambridge studies in social and cultural anthropology* (Cambridge University Press). p. 98. ISBN 0-521-46574-5.

[27] Harding, Andrew (September 23, 2006). "Beijing's penis emporium". BBC. Retrieved June 23, 2010.

[28] "Deer Penis Loses Favor as China's Olympians Fear Drug Testers". Bloomberg. March 23, 2008. Retrieved June 23, 2010.

[29] *Herbal Database*, Wu Ling Zhi

[30] Chinese Medical Herbology and Pharmacology, John Chen and Tina Chen, Art of Medicine Press, ISBN 0-9740635-0-9,

[31] *Flying Squirrel – Associated Typhus*, Infectious Diseases, 2003, Mary G. Reynolds, John W. Krebs, James A. Comer, John W. Sumner, Thomas C. Rushton, Carlos E. Lopez, William L. Nicholson, Jane A. Rooney, Susan E. Lance-Parker, Jennifer H. McQuiston, Christopher D. Paddock, James E. Childs

[32] *Facts about traditional Chinese medicine (TCM): rhinoceros horn*, Encucolpedia Britanica,

[33] "*Rhino horn: All myth, no medicine*", *National Geographic*, Rhishja Larson

[34] "Aphrodisiacs and the Myth of Tiger Penis Magical Cures", *Tigerhomes.org*

[35] 2008 report from TRAFFIC

[36] *Snake Oil*, Western Journal of Medicine, Aug 1989;151(2):208, R. A. Kunin

[37] *Fats that Heal: Fats that Kill*, Udo Erasmus, 1993, ISBN 0-920470-38-6

[38] Gecko, Ntritional Wellness

[39] Chen1, Tien-Hsi; Chang2, Hsien-Cheh; Lue, Kuang-Yang (2009). "Unregulated Trade in Turtle Shells for Chinese Traditional Medicine in East and Southeast Asia: The Case of Taiwan". *Chelonian Conservation and Biology* **8** (1): 11–18. doi:10.2744/CCB-0747.1.

[40] "NOVA Online | Kingdom of the Seahorse | Amanda Vincent". Pbs.org. Retrieved 2009-12-07.

[41] *Sea Horse*, Acupuncture Today.

[42] *Traditional Chinese Medicine and Endangered Animals*, Encyclopaedia Britannica Advocacy for Animals.

[43] "Seahorse Crusader Amanda Vincent" on *Nova* television show

[44] Chang *et al*, *Authenticating the use of dried seahorses in the traditional Chinese medicine market in Taiwan using molecular forensics*, Journal of Food and Drug Analysis Volume 21, Issue 3 , Pages 310-316, September 2013.

[45] "Shark Fin Soup: An Eco-Catastrophe?". Sfgate.com. 2003-01-20. Retrieved 2009-12-07.

[46] An Effective Supplemental Therapy for Cancer, Acupuncture Today, February, 2010, Vol. 11, Issue 02, Haitao Cao

[47] Ban Mao, Yin Yang House

[48] *Insect derived crude drugs in the Chinese song dynasty*, Namba Tsuneo, MA Yong-Hua, Inagaki Kenji, Journal of Ethnopharmacology, Volume 24, Issues 2-3, December 1988, Pages 247-285,

[49] Centipede, Acupuncture Today

[50] Lu Feng Fang, Materia Metrica

[51] Leech, Acupuncture Today

[52] Scorpion, Acupuncture Todady

[53] http://www.news.harvard.edu/gazette/2004/01.08/01-scorpion.html

[54] Jones, Kenneth (1990), *Reishi: Ancient Herb for Modern Times*, Sylvan Press, p. 6.

[55] http://maciociaonline.blogspot.sg/2012_05_01_archive.html

[56] http://lsb380.plbio.lsu.edu/Highway%20markers%20folder/Ganoderma.html

[57] Reshetnikov SV, Wasser SP, Duckman I, Tsukor K. (2000). "Medicinal value of the genus *Tremella* Pers. (Heterobasid-iomycetes) (review)". *International Journal of Medicinal Mushrooms* **2** (3): 345–67. doi:10.1615/IntJMedMushr.v2.i3.10.

[58] Chinese Medical Herbology and Pharmacology, by John K. Chen, Tina T. Chen

[59] "*Aconitum in Traditional Chinese, Medicine—A valuable drug or an unpredictable risk?*", *Journal of Ethnopharmacology*, Volume 126, Issue 1, 29 October 2009, Judith Singhuber, Ming Zhu, Sonja Prinz, Brigitte Kopp, Pages 18-30

[60] Yang Tianhui: Notes from My Visit to the Fuzi Growing Area of Zhangming County (Song Dynasty, 1099 CE), , Heiner Fruehauf,

[61] "*The Importance of Aconite (fuzi)*"

[62] Chan TY (April 2009). "Aconite poisoning". *Clinical Toxicology (Philadelphia, Pa.)* **47** (4): 279–85. doi:10.1080/15563650902904407. PMID 19514874.

[63] Roth, L., Daunderer, M. & Kormann, K. (1994): *Giftpflanzen - Pflanzengifte*. ISBN 3-933203-31-7.

[64] Pao Zhi: An Introduction to the Use of Processed Chinese Medicinals, Philippe Sionneau

[65] Sung, Ying-hsing. *T' ien kung k' ai wu*. Sung Ying-hsing. 1637. Published as *Chinese Technology in the seventeenth century*. Translated and annotated by E-tu Zen Sun and Shiou-chuan Sun. 1996. Mineola. New York. Dover Publications, p. 267.

[66] Chavannes, Édouard. "Trois Généraux Chinois de la dynastie des Han Orientaux. Pan Tch' ao (32-102 p.C.); – son fils Pan Yong; – Leang K' in (112 p.C.). Chapitre LXXVII du Heou Han chou." . 1906. *T' oung pao* 7, pp. 226-227.

[67]

[68] http://www.fda.gov/Food/RecallsOutbreaksEmergencies/SafetyAlertsAdvisories/ucm096374.htm

[69] C.-H. Chen, K. G. Dickman, M. Moriya, J. Zavadil, V. S. Sidorenko, K. L. Edwards, D. V. Gnatenko, L. Wu, R. J. Turesky, X.-R. Wu, Y.-S. Pu, A. P. Grollman. *Aristolochic acid-associated urothelial cancer in Taiwan*. Proceedings of the National Academy of Sciences, 2012; DOI: 10.1073/pnas.1119920109

[70] "*The distribution of minerals and flavonoids in the tea plant (Camellia sinensis)*", *Il Farmaco*, Volume 56, Issues 5-7, 1 July 2001, Lydia Ferrara, Domenico Montesanoa, and Alfonso Senatore, Pages 397-401

[71]

[72] Chinese Cucumber, Drugs.com

[73] Ju Hua, Yin Yang House

[74] http://www.koreantk.com/servlet/MedicDetailServlet?cmd=1&med_cd=M0000050&searchGbn=medic&ctrllist=undefined&pagesize=undefined&sorder=undefined&view_type=eng&langType=E

[75] Xanthium, Acupuncture Today

[76] Toxicological Risks of Chinese Herbs, Planta Med 2010; 76(17): 2012-2018, Debbie Shaw,

[77] Croton Seed, Acupuncture Today

[78] Predictive and preventive toxicology of innovative industrial crops of the spurge (Euphorbiaceae) family, Gminski, Richard; Hecker, Erich, Interdisciplinary Science Reviews, Volume 23, Number 2, June 1998 , pp. 99-112(14), []

[79] http://www.chineseherbacademy.org/articles/dm2.shtml

[80] *Ginger*, University of Maryland Medical Center

[81] Ginkgo, TCM Basics

[82] Dubey AK, Shankar PR, Upadhyaya D, Deshpande VY. Ginkgo biloba--an appraisal. Kathmandu University Medical Journal. 2004 Jul-Sep; 2(3): 225-9

[83]

[84] http://www.aafp.org/afp/20031015/1539.html

[85] Fugh-Berman, Adriane (2000). "Herb-drug interactions". *The Lancet* **355** (9198): 134–138. doi:10.1016/S0140-6736(99)06457-0. PMID 10675182.

[86] Amagase H, Nance DM (May 2008). "A randomized, double-blind, placebo-controlled, clinical study of the general effects of a standardized Lycium barbarum (Goji) Juice, GoChi". *J Altern Complement Med* **14** (4): 403–12. doi:10.1089/acm.2008.0004. PMID 18447631.

[87] Daniells S. (October 2008). "Questions raised over Goji science." . NutraIngredients.com-USA.

[88] Wu SJ, Ng LT, Lin CC (December 2004). "Antioxidant activities of some common ingredients of traditional Chinese medicine, Angelica sinensis, Lycium barbarum and Poria cocos". *Phytother Res* **18** (12): 1008–12. doi:10.1002/ptr.1617. PMID 15742346.

[89] Jia YX, Dong JW, Wu XX, Ma TM, Shi AY (June 1998). "[The effect of lycium barbarum polysaccharide on vascular tension in two-kidney, one clip model of hypertension]". *Sheng Li Xue Bao* (in Chinese) **50** (3): 309–14. PMID 11324572.

[90] Luo Q, Li Z, Huang X, Yan J, Zhang S, Cai YZ (July 2006). "Lycium barbarum polysaccharides: Protective effects against heat-induced damage of rat testes and H2O2-induced DNA damage in mouse testicular cells and beneficial effect on sexual behavior and reproductive function of hemicastrated rats". *Life Sci.* **79** (7): 613–21. doi:10.1016/j.lfs.2006.02.012. PMID 16563441.

[91] Cheng CY, Chung WY, Szeto YT, Benzie IF (January 2005). "Fasting plasma zeaxanthin response to Fructus barbarum L. (wolfberry; Kei Tze) in a food-based human supplementation trial". *Br. J. Nutr.* **93** (1): 123–30. doi:10.1079/BJN20041284. PMID 15705234.

[92] Chan HC, Chang RC, Koon-Ching Ip A, et al. (January 2007). "Neuroprotective effects of Lycium barbarum Lynn on protecting retinal ganglion cells in an ocular hypertension model of glaucoma". *Exp. Neurol.* **203** (1): 269–73. doi:10.1016/j.expneurol.2006.05.031. PMID 17045262.

[93] Yu MS, Leung SK, Lai SW, et al. (2005). "Neuroprotective effects of anti-aging oriental medicine Lycium barbarum against beta-amyloid peptide neurotoxicity". *Exp. Gerontol.* **40** (8-9): 716–27. doi:10.1016/j.exger.2005.06.010. PMID 16139464.

[94] Gan L, Hua Zhang S, Liang Yang X, Bi Xu H (April 2004). "Immunomodulation and antitumor activity by a polysaccharide-protein complex from Lycium barbarum". *Int. Immunopharmacol.* **4** (4): 563–9. doi:10.1016/j.intimp.2004.01.023. PMID 15099534.

[95] He YL, Ying Y, Xu YL, Su JF, Luo H, Wang HF (September 2005). "[Effects of Lycium barbarum polysaccharide on tumor microenvironment T-lymphocyte subsets and dendritic cells in H22-bearing mice]". *Zhong Xi Yi Jie He Xue Bao* (in Chinese) **3** (5): 374–7. doi:10.3736/jcim20050511. PMID 16159572.

[96] Lee DG, Park Y, Kim MR, et al. (July 2004). "Anti-fungal effects of phenolic amides isolated from the root bark of Lycium chinense". *Biotechnol. Lett.* **26** (14): 1125–30. doi:10.1023/B:BILE.0000035483.85790.f7. PMID 15266117.

[97] Lee DG, Jung HJ, Woo ER (September 2005). "Antimicrobial property of (+)-lyoniresinol-3alpha-O-beta-D-glucopyranoside isolated from the root bark of Lycium chinense Miller against human pathogenic microorganisms". *Arch. Pharm. Res.* **28** (9): 1031–6. doi:10.1007/BF02977397. PMID 16212233.

[98] Horny Goat Weed, Altmedicine.com

[99] Epimedium, ChemEurope.com

[100] http://www.yinyanghouse.com/theory/herbalmedicine/bai_he_tcm_herbal_database

[101] Optimized separation of pharmacologically active anthraquinones in Rhubarb by capillary electrochromatography, Yan Li, Huwei Liu, Xiuhong Ji, Junlin Li, ELECTROPHORESIS, Volume 21, Issue 15, pages 3109–3115, 1 September 2000,

[102]

[103] Lei Gong Teng (Radix Tripterygii Wilfordii): A Blessing or a Time Bomb?, John Chen, PhD, PharmD, OMD, Lac,

[104] Ma Qian Zi, Chinese Medical Tools, Acupuncture.com

[105] *Materia Medica, Dan Besky, p.1050*

[106] Qing Hao, TCM Herbal Database

[107] Duke SO, Paul RN (1993). "Development and Fine Structure of the Glandular Trichomes of *Artemisia annua L.*". *Int. J Plant Sci.* **154** (1): 107–18. doi:10.1086/297096. JSTOR 2995610.
Ferreira JFS, Janick J (1995). "Floral Morphology of *Artemisia annua* with Special Reference to Trichomes". *Int. J Plant Sci.* **156** (6): 807. doi:10.1086/297304.

[108] Mueller MS, Runyambo, Wagner I; et al. (2004). "Randomized controlled trial of a traditional preparation of *Artemisia annua* L. (Annual Wormwood) in the treatment of malaria". *Trans R Soc Trop Med Hyg* **98** (5): 318–21. doi:10.1016/j.trstmh.2003.09.001. PMID 15109558.

[109] Räth K, Taxis K, Walz GH, et al. (1 February 2004). "Pharmacokinetic study of artemisinin after oral intake of a traditional preparation of *Artemisia annua* L. (annual wormwood)". *Am J Trop Med Hyg* **70** (2): 128–32. PMID 14993622.

[110] Jansen FH (2006). "The herbal tea approach for artemesinin as a therapy for malaria?". *Trans R Soc Trop Med Hyg* **100** (3): 285–6. doi:10.1016/j.trstmh.2005.08.004. PMID 16274712.

[111]

[112] Genuis SJ, Schwalfenberg G, Siy A-KJ, Rodushkin I (2012) *Toxic Element Contamination of Natural Health Products and Pharmaceutical Preparations.* PLOS ONE 7(11): e49676. doi:10.1371/journal.pone.0049676

[113] Realgar, Acupuncture Today

[114] Galena, Acupuncture Today

[115] Qian Dan (Minium), TCM Assistant.

[116] Qian Dan, American Dragon.

[117] Qian Dan : lead elixir : minium, lead oxide, rootdown.us.

[118] "*Neurotoxicological effects of cinnabar (a Chinese mineral medicine, HgS) in mice*", *Toxicology and Applied Pharmacology*, Volume 224, Issue 2, 15 October 2007, Chun-Fa Huanga, Shing-Hwa Liua and Shoei-Yn Lin-Shiau, Pages 192-201,

[119] *Cinnabar*, Acupuncture Today.

[120] Qing Fen (Calomel), Yin Yang House.

[121] *Mercury and Chinese herbal medicine*, H.C. George Wong, MD, BCMJ, Vol. 46, No. 9, November 2004, page(s) 442 Letters.

Chapter 22

Transmissible spongiform encephalopathy

Transmissible spongiform encephalopathies (TSEs), also known as **prion diseases**, are a group of progressive conditions (encephalopathies) that affect the brain and nervous system of many animals, including humans. According to the most widespread hypothesis, they are transmitted by prions, though some other data suggest an involvement of a *Spiroplasma* infection.[*][1] Mental and physical abilities deteriorate and myriad tiny holes appear in the cortex causing it to appear like a sponge (hence **spongiform**) when brain tissue obtained at autopsy is examined under a microscope. The disorders cause impairment of brain function, including memory changes, personality changes and problems with movement that worsen over time. Prion diseases of humans include classic Creutzfeldt–Jakob disease, new variant Creutzfeldt–Jakob disease (nvCJD, a human disorder related to Bovine spongiform encephalopathy), Gerstmann–Sträussler–Scheinker syndrome, fatal familial insomnia, kuru, and the recently discovered Variably protease-sensitive prionopathy. These conditions form a spectrum of diseases with overlapping signs and symptoms.

Unlike other kinds of infectious disease, which are spread by microbes, the infectious agent in TSEs is believed to be a type of protein, called the prion protein. Misshapen prion proteins carry the disease between individuals and cause deterioration of the brain. TSEs are unique diseases in that their aetiology may be genetic, sporadic, or infectious via ingestion of infected foodstuffs and via iatrogenic means (e.g., blood transfusion).[*][2] Most TSEs are sporadic and occur in an animal with no prion protein mutation. Inherited TSE occurs in animals carrying a rare mutant prion allele, which expresses prion proteins that contort by themselves into the disease-causing conformation. Transmission occurs when healthy animals consume tainted tissues from others with the disease. In recent times, a type of TSE called bovine spongiform encephalopathy (BSE) spread in cattle in an epidemic fashion. This occurred because cattle were fed the processed remains of other cattle, a practice now banned in many countries.

Prions cannot be transmitted through the air or through touching or most other forms of casual contact. However, they may be transmitted through contact with infected tissue, body fluids, or contaminated medical instruments. Normal sterilization procedures such as boiling or irradiating materials fail to render prions non-infective.

22.1 Classification

22.2 History

In the 5th century BCE, Hippocrates described a disease like TSE in cattle and sheep, which he believed also occurred in man.[*][4] Publius Flavius Vegetius Renatus records cases of a disease with similar characteristics in the 4th and 5th centuries AD.[*][5] In 1755, an outbreak of scrapie was discussed in the British House of Commons and may have been present in Britain for some time before that.[*][6] Although there were unsupported claims in 1759 that the disease was contagious, in general it was thought to be due to inbreeding and countermeasures appeared to be successful. Early-20th-century experiments failed to show transmission of scrapie between animals, until extraordinary measures were taken such as the intra-ocular injection of infected nervous tissue. No direct link between scrapie and disease in man was suspected then or has been found since. TSE was first described in man by Alfons Maria Jakob in the 1921.[*][7] Daniel Carleton

Gajdusek's discovery that Kuru was transmitted by cannibalism accompanied by the finding of scrapie-like lesions in the brains of Kuru victims strongly suggested an infectious basis to TSE.[8] The priority given the search for a viral infectious agent almost cost Stanley Prusiner tenure when his research showed that a protein transferred the disease.[9] A paradigm shift to a non-nucleic infectious entity was required when the results were validated with an explanation of how a prion protein might transmit spongiform encephalopathy.[10] It wasn't until 1988 that the neuropathology of spongiform encephalopathy was properly described in cows.[11] The alarming amplification of BSE in the British cattle herd heightened fear of transmission to humans and reinforced the belief in the infectious nature of TSE. This was confirmed with the identification of a Kuru-like disease, called new variant Creutzfeldt–Jakob disease, in humans exposed to BSE.[12] Although the infectious disease model of TSE has been questioned in favour of a prion transplantation model that explains why cannibalism favours transmission,[13] the search for a viral agent is being continued in some laboratories.[14]

22.3   Features of TSE

The degenerative tissue damage caused by human prion diseases (CJD, GSS, and kuru) is characterised by four features: spongiform change, neuronal loss, astrocytosis, and amyloid plaque formation. These features are shared with prion diseases in animals, and the recognition of these similarities prompted the first attempts to transmit a human prion disease (kuru) to a primate in 1966, followed by CJD in 1968 and GSS in 1981. These neuropathological features have formed the basis of the histological diagnosis of human prion diseases for many years, although it was recognized that these changes are enormously variable both from case to case and within the central nervous system in individual cases.[15]

The clinical signs in humans vary, but commonly include personality changes, psychiatric problems such as depression, lack of coordination, and/or an unsteady gait (ataxia). Patients also may experience involuntary jerking movements called myoclonus, unusual sensations, insomnia, confusion, or memory problems. In the later stages of the disease, patients have severe mental impairment (dementia) and lose the ability to move or speak.[16]

Early neuropathological reports on human prion diseases suffered from a confusion of nomenclature, in which the significance of the diagnostic feature of spongiform change was occasionally overlooked. The subsequent demonstration that human prion diseases were transmissible reinforced the importance of spongiform change as a diagnostic feature, reflected in the use of the term "spongiform encephalopathy" for this group of disorders.

Prions appear to be most infectious when in direct contact with affected tissues. For example, Creutzfeldt-Jakob disease has been transmitted to patients taking injections of growth hormone harvested from human pituitary glands, from cadaver dura allografts and from instruments used for brain surgery (Brown, 2000) (prions can survive the "autoclave" sterilization process used for most surgical instruments). It is also believed that dietary consumption of affected animals can cause prions to accumulate slowly, especially when cannibalism or similar practices allow the proteins to accumulate over more than one generation. An example is kuru, which reached epidemic proportions in the mid 20th century in the Fore people of Papua New Guinea, who used to consume their dead as a funerary ritual.[17] Laws in developed countries now ban the use of rendered ruminant proteins in ruminant feed as a precaution against the spread of prion infection in cattle and other ruminants.

Note that not all encephalopathies are caused by prions, as in the cases of PML (caused by the JC virus), CADASIL (caused by abnormal NOTCH3 protein activity), and Krabbe disease (caused by a deficiency of the enzyme galactosylceramidase). Progressive Spongiform Leukoencephalopathy (PSL)—which is a spongiform encephalopathy—is also probably not caused by a prion, although the adulterant that causes it among heroin smokers has not yet been identified.[18][19][20][21] This, combined with the highly variable nature of prion disease pathology, is why a prion disease cannot be diagnosed based solely on a patient's symptoms.

22.4   Genetics

Mutations in the PRNP gene cause prion disease. Familial forms of prion disease are caused by inherited mutations in the PRNP gene. Only a small percentage of all cases of prion disease run in families, however. Most cases of prion disease are sporadic, which means they occur in people without any known risk factors or gene mutations. In rare circumstances, prion diseases also can be transmitted by exposure to prion-contaminated tissues or other biological materials obtained from individuals with prion disease.

The PRNP gene provides the instructions to make a protein called the prion protein (PrP). Under normal circumstances, this protein may be involved in transporting copper into cells. It may also be involved in protecting brain cells and helping them communicate. 24 Point-Mutations in this gene cause cells to produce an abnormal form of the prion protein, known as PrP*Sc. This abnormal protein builds up in the brain and destroys nerve cells, resulting in the signs and symptoms of prion disease.

Familial forms of prion disease are inherited in an autosomal dominant pattern, which means one copy of the altered gene in each cell is sufficient to cause the disorder. In most cases, an affected person inherits the altered gene from one affected parent.

In some people, familial forms of prion disease are caused by a new mutation in the PRNP gene. Although such people most likely do not have an affected parent, they can pass the genetic change to their children.

22.5 Competing hypotheses

22.5.1 Protein-only hypothesis

Protein could be the infectious agent, inducing its own replication by causing conformational change of normal cellular PrP*C into PrP*Sc. Evidence for this theory:

- infectivity titre correlates with PrP*Sc levels. However, this is disputed.*[22]
  - PrP*Sc is an isomer of PrP*C
  - Denaturing PrP removes infectivity*[23]

22.5.2 Multi-component hypothesis

While not containing a nucleic acid genome, prions may be composed of more than just a protein. Purified PrP*C appears unable to convert to the infectious PrP*Sc form, unless other components are added, such as RNA and lipids.*[26] These other components, termed cofactors, may form part of the infectious prion, or they may serve as catalysts for the replication of a protein-only prion.

22.5.3 Viral hypothesis

This hypothesis postulates that an infectious viral agent is the cause of the disease. Evidence for this hypothesis is as follows:

- **PrP-null mice cannot be infected*[24]**
- **PrP*C knockout in mice following inoculation with PrP*Sc reverses early spongeosis and behavioural deficits, halts further disease progression and increases life-span *[25]**
  Incubation time is comparable to a lentivirus
  - Strain variation of different isolates of PrP*Sc*[27]
  - An increasing titre of PrP*Sc as the disease progresses suggests a replicating agent.

22.6 Epidemiology

These spontaneous disorders in humans are very rare, affecting only about one person per million worldwide each year. However, transmissible spongiform encephalopathies can reach epidemic proportions, as was seen in the UK BSE outbreak of the 1980s and 1990s. It is very hard to map the spread of the disease due to the difficulty of identifying individual strains of the prions. This means that, if animals at one farm begin to show the disease after an outbreak on a nearby farm, it is very difficult to determine whether it is the same strain affecting both herds—suggesting transmission—or if the second outbreak came from a completely different source.

22.7   Possible cure or vaccine and diagnosis

There continues to be a very practical problem with diagnosis of prion diseases, including BSE and CJD. They have an incubation period of months to decades during which there are no symptoms, even though the pathway of converting the normal brain PrP protein into the toxic, disease-related PrP Sc form has started. At present, there is virtually no way to detect PrP*Sc reliably except by examining the brain using neuropathological and immunohistochemical methods after death. Accumulation of the abnormally folded PrP*Sc form of the PrP protein is a characteristic of the disease, but it is present at very low levels in easily accessible body fluids like blood or urine. Researchers have tried to develop methods to measure PrP*Sc, but there are still no fully accepted methods for use in materials such as blood.

In 2010, a team from New York described detection of PrP*Sc even when initially present at only one part in a hundred billion (10^*-11) in brain tissue. The method combines amplification with a novel technology called Surround Optical Fiber Immunoassay (SOFIA) and some specific antibodies against PrP*Sc. After amplifying and then concentrating any PrP*Sc, the samples are labelled with a fluorescent dye using an antibody for specificity and then finally loaded into a micro-capillary tube. This tube is placed in a specially constructed apparatus so that it is totally surrounded by optical fibres to capture all light emitted once the dye is excited using a laser. The technique allowed detection of PrP*Sc after many fewer cycles of conversion than others have achieved, substantially reducing the possibility of artefacts, as well as speeding up the assay. The researchers also tested their method on blood samples from apparently healthy sheep that went on to develop scrapie. The animals' brains were analysed once any symptoms became apparent. The researchers could therefore compare results from brain tissue and blood taken once the animals exhibited symptoms of the diseases, with blood obtained earlier in the animals' lives, and from uninfected animals. The results showed very clearly that PrP*Sc could be detected in the blood of animals long before the symptoms appeared.*[28]*[29]

Recent research from the University of Toronto and Caprion Pharmaceuticals has discovered one possible avenue that might lead to quicker diagnosis, a vaccine or possibly even treatment for prion diseases. The abnormally folded proteins that cause the disease have been found to expose a side chain of amino acids that the properly folded protein does not expose. Antibodies specifically coded to this side-chain amino acid sequence have been found to stimulate an immune response to the abnormal prions and leave the normal proteins intact.*[30]

Another idea involves using custom peptide sequences. Since some research suggests prions aggregate by forming beta barrel structures, work done *in vitro* has shown that peptides made up of beta barrel-incompatible amino acids can help break up accumulations of prion. Yet, a third idea concerns genetic therapy, whereby the gene for encoding protease-resistant protein is considered to be an error in several species, and therefore something to be inhibited.

22.8   See also

- Proteopathy

- Prion

22.9   Further reading

- *Deadly Feasts: The "Prion" Controversy and the Public's Health,*[31] by Richard Rhodes

- *The Pathological Protein: Mad Cow, Chronic Wasting, and Other Deadly Prion Diseases*, Phillip Yam, 2003, Springer, ISBN 0-387-95508-9

- *The Family That Couldn't Sleep* by D. T. Max provides a history of prion diseases.

- *Fatal Flaws: How a Misfolded Protein Baffled Scientists and Changed the Way We Look at the Brain*, by Jay Ingram, 2012, HarperCollins Publishers.

22.10 References

- *This entry incorporates public domain text originally from the National Institute of Neurological Disorders and Stroke, National Institutes of Health and the U.S. National Library of Medicine*

[1] Bastian FO, Sanders DE, Forbes WA, Hagius SD, Walker JV, Henk WG, Enright FM, Elzer PH; Sanders; Forbes; Hagius; Walker; Henk; Enright; Elzer (2007). "*Spiroplasma* spp. from transmissible spongiform encephalopathy brains or ticks induce spongiform encephalopathy in ruminants". *Journal of Medical Microbiology* **56** (9): 1235–1242. doi:10.1099/jmm.0.47159-0. PMID 17761489.

[2] Brown P, Preece M, Brandel JP, Sato T, McShane L, Zerr I, Fletcher A, Will RG, Pocchiari M, Cashman NR, d'Aignaux JH, Cervenakova L, Fradkin J, Schonberger LB, Collins SJ; Preece; Brandel; Sato; McShane; Zerr; Fletcher; Will; Pocchiari; Cashman; d'Aignaux; Cervenáková; Fradkin; Schonberger; Collins (2000). "Iatrogenic Creutzfeldt-Jakob disease at the millennium". *Neurology* **55** (8): 1075–81. doi:10.1212/WNL.55.8.1075. PMID 11071481.

[3] Believed to be identical to the BSE prion.

[4] McAlister, V (June 2005). "Sacred disease of our times: failure of the infectious disease model of spongiform encephalopathy". *Clin Invest Med* **28** (3): 101–4. PMID 16021982. Retrieved 2011-06-20.

[5] Digesta Artis Mulomedicinae, Publius Flavius Vegetius Renatus

[6] Brown P, Bradley R; Bradley (December 1998). "1755 and all that: a historical primer of transmissible spongiform encephalopathy". *BMJ* **317** (7174): 1688–92. doi:10.1136/bmj.317.7174.1688. PMC 1114482. PMID 9857129.

[7] Katscher F. (May 1998). "It's Jakob's disease, not Creutzfeldt's". *Nature* **393** (6680): 11. Bibcode:1998Natur.393Q..11K. doi:10.1038/29862. PMID 9590681.

[8] Gajdusek DC (Sep 1977). "Unconventional viruses and the origin and disappearance of kuru". *Science* **197** (4307): 943–60. Bibcode:1977Sci...197..943C. doi:10.1126/science.197.4307.943 (inactive 2015-02-01). PMID 142303.

[9] Prusiner S. "Autobiography". *Nobel Prize in Physiology or Medicine 1997*. Retrieved 2011-11-20.

[10] Collins SJ, Lawson VA, Masters CL.; Lawson; Masters (Jan 2004). "Transmissible spongiform encephalopathies". *Lancet* **363** (9204): 51–61. doi:10.1016/S0140-6736(03)15171-9. PMID 14723996.

[11] Hope J, Reekie LJ, Hunter N, Multhaup G, Beyreuther K, White H, Scott AC, Stack MJ, Dawson M, Wells GA.; Reekie; Hunter; Multhaup; Beyreuther; White; Scott; Stack; Dawson; et al. (Nov 1988). "Fibrils from brains of cows with new cattle disease contain scrapie-associated protein". *Nature* **336** (6197): 390–2. Bibcode:1988Natur.336..390H. doi:10.1038/336390a0. PMID 2904126.

[12] Will RG, Ironside JW, Zeidler M, Cousens SN, Estibeiro K, Alperovitch A, Poser S, Pocchiari M, Hofman A, Smith PG.; Ironside; Zeidler; Cousens; Estibeiro; Alperovitch; Poser; Pocchiari; Hofman; Smith (April 1996). "A new variant of Creutzfeldt-Jakob disease in the UK". *Lancet* **347** (9006): 921–5. doi:10.1016/S0140-6736(96)91412-9. PMID 8598754.

[13] McAlister, V (June 2005). "Sacred disease of our times: failure of the infectious disease model of spongiform encephalopathy". *Clin Invest Med* **28** (3): 101–4. PMID 16021982. Retrieved 2011-06-20.

[14] Manuelidis L, Yu ZX, Barquero N, Banquero N, Mullins B; Yu; Banquero; Mullins (February 2007). "Cells infected with scrapie and Creutzfeldt-Jakob disease agents produce intracellular 25-nm virus-like particles". *Proceedings of the National Academy of Sciences of the United States of America* **104** (6): 1965–70. Bibcode:2007PNAS..104.1965M. doi:10.1073/pnas.0610999104. PMC 1794316. PMID 17267596.

[15] Jeffrey M, Goodbrand IA, Goodsir CM; Goodbrand; Goodsir (1995). "Pathology of the transmissible spongiform encephalopathies with special emphasis on ultrastructure". *Micron* **26** (3): 277–98. doi:10.1016/0968-4328(95)00004-N. PMID 7788281.

[16] Collinge J (2001). "Prion diseases of humans and animals: their causes and molecular basis". *Annu Rev Neurosci* **24**: 519–50. doi:10.1146/annurev.neuro.24.1.519. PMID 11283320.

[17] Collins S, McLean CA, Masters CL; McLean; Masters (2001). "Gerstmann-Straussler-Scheinker syndrome, fatal familial insomnia, and kuru: a review of these less common human transmissible spongiform encephalopathies". *J Clin Neurosci* **8** (5): 387–97. doi:10.1054/jocn.2001.0919. PMID 11535002.

[18] "hafci.org". Archived from the original on November 1, 2004. Retrieved 2007-12-02.

[19] Kriegstein AR; Shungu DC; Millar WS; et al. (1999). "Leukoencephalopathy and raised brain lactate from heroin vapor inhalation ("chasing the dragon")". *Neurology* **53** (8): 1765–73. doi:10.1212/WNL.53.8.1765. PMID 10563626.

[20] Chang YJ, Tsai CH, Chen CJ; Tsai; Chen (1997). "Leukoencephalopathy after inhalation of heroin vapor". *J. Formos. Med. Assoc.* **96** (9): 758–60. PMID 9308333.

[21] Koussa S, Zabad R, Rizk T, Tamraz J, Nasnas R, Chemaly R; Zabad; Rizk; Tamraz; Nasnas; Chemaly (2002). "[Vacuolar leucoencephalopathy induced by heroin: 4 cases]". *Rev. Neurol. (Paris)* (in French) **158** (2): 177–82. PMID 11965173.

[22] Barron RM; Campbell SL; King D; et al. (December 2007). "High titers of transmissible spongiform encephalopathy infectivity associated with extremely low levels of PrPSc in vivo". *The Journal of Biological Chemistry* **282** (49): 35878–86. doi:10.1074/jbc.M704329200. PMID 17923484.

[23] Supattapone S; Wille H; Uyechi L; et al. (April 2001). "Branched Polyamines Cure Prion-Infected Neuroblastoma Cells". *Journal of Virology* **75** (7): 3453–61. doi:10.1128/JVI.75.7.3453-3461.2001. PMC 114138. PMID 11238871.

[24] Sakudo A; Lee DC; Saeki K; et al. (August 2003). "Impairment of superoxide dismutase activation by N-terminally truncated prion protein (PrP) in PrP-deficient neuronal cell line". *Biochemical and Biophysical Research Communications* **308** (3): 660–7. doi:10.1016/S0006-291X(03)01459-1. PMID 12914801.

[25] Mallucci G; Dickinson A; Lineham J; et al. (October 2003). "Depleting Neuronal PrP in Prion Infection Prevents Disease and Reverses Spongiosis". *Science* **302** (5646): 871–874. Bibcode:2003Sci...302..871M. doi:10.1126/science.1090187. PMID 14593181.

[26] Deleault NR, Harris BT, Rees JR, Supattapone S; Harris; Rees; Supattapone (June 2007). "Formation of native prions from minimal components in vitro". *Proc. Natl. Acad. Sci. U.S.A.* **104** (23): 9741–6. Bibcode:2007PNAS..104.9741D. doi:10.1073/pnas.0702662104. PMC 1887554. PMID 17535913.

[27] Bruce ME (2003). "TSE strain variation". *British Medical Bulletin* **66**: 99–108. doi:10.1093/bmb/66.1.99. PMID 14522852.

[28] "Detecting Prions in Blood" (PDF). *Microbiology Today*.: 195. August 2010. Retrieved 2011-08-21.

[29] "SOFIA: An Assay Platform for Ultrasensitive Detection of PrP*Sc in Brain and Blood" (PDF). SUNY Downstate Medical Center. Retrieved 2011-08-19.

[30] Paramithiotis E; Pinard M; Lawton T; et al. (July 2003). "A prion protein epitope selective for the pathologically misfolded conformation". *Nature Medicine* **9** (7): 893–9. doi:10.1038/nm883. PMID 12778138. Lay summary – *ScienceDaily* (2003-06-02).

[31] *Deadly Feasts: The "Prion" Controversy and the Public's Health*, Richard Rhodes, 1998, Touchstone, ISBN 0-684-84425-7

22.11 External links

- Transmissible spongiform encephalopathy at DMOZ

Chapter 23

Gilberto Valle

Gilberto Valle III (born April 14, 1984) is a former New York City police officer who was convicted in March 2013 of conspiracy to kidnap. Valle was arrested after his wife discovered he was spending time in chat rooms describing detailed plans to abduct, torture, rape and cannibalize women; Valle claimed all scenarios he described were mere fantasy. The case drew widespread attention for its unusual nature—Valle was dubbed the "**Cannibal Cop**"—and because of the legal issue of whether describing criminal activities crosses the line into criminal intent.*[1]

23.1 Background

Valle was born in Queens, New York, in 1984, and attended Archbishop Molloy High School.*[2] He attended the University of Maryland, graduating in 2006 with a degree in psychology.*[3]

Valle joined the New York City Police Department in 2006, and was assigned to the 26th Precinct in Morningside Heights, Manhattan. He married Kathleen Cooke Mangan, who he met on the dating website OKCupid, in 2010 in Spokane, Washington. They had a daughter born in early 2012.*[4]*[5]

He was fired from the NYPD following his arrest.*[6]

23.2 Chats and arrest

On October 25, 2012, Valle was arrested and charged with conspiracy to commit kidnapping.*[7] The arrest occurred after his wife reported to police that she had found in his Internet search engine history a series of chat room communications on Dark Fetish Net, a forum dedicated to sexual fetishes and fantasies involving torture, rape, murder and cannibalism. Valle had been chatting with another user about torturing and murdering her, as well as murdering and cannibalizing more than 100 other women.*[8]

23.3 Trial

Valle faced a maximum of life in prison for the conspiracy charge, and a maximum of five years for accessing the federal National Crime Information Center database without authorization. Valle's wife testified against him during the trial.*[4] Throughout the trial, Valle claimed that the chat room communications were mere fantasy, and that he had no intention of acting on them.*[4] He was found guilty of all charges in March 2013. *[6]

Judge Paul G. Gardephe of Federal District Court overturned Valle's conviction on the conspiracy charge in June 2014, saying the evidence supported his contention that he was engaged in only "fantasy role-play". Valle had at this point served 21 months in prison.*[9] The lesser conviction regarding the database remained standing, but Valle was sentenced to time served and released.*[6] The government appealed the dismissal of the conspiracy charge to the Second Circuit.*[10]

23.4 Documentary

A documentary film, *Thought Crimes: The Case of the Cannibal Cop*, chronicled Valle's arrest, trial, imprisonment and release. Directed by Erin Lee Carr, the film debuted on HBO on May 11, 2015.*[11]

An episode of *Law & Order: Special Victims Unit* titled "Thought Criminal" was inspired by Valle's case.*[12]

23.5 References

[1] Weiser, Benjamin (July 1, 2014). "Officer's Conviction in Cannibalism Case Overturned". *The New York Times*. Retrieved June 1, 2015.

[2] Weiser, Benjamin (February 26, 2013). "At Trial, Officer's Friend Recalls Abduction Threat". *The New York Times*. Retrieved June 1, 2015.

[3] Rosenwald, Michael S. (October 26, 2012). "Alleged cannibal cop is UMd grad". *Washington Post*. Retrieved June 1, 2015.

[4] "'Cannibal Cop's' wife takes the stand as horrific details of former NYPD officer's twisted bondage fetish emerge in first day of trial". *New York Daily News*. February 25, 2013. Retrieved June 2, 2015.

[5] Collins, Laura (November 21, 2012). "EXCLUSIVE: 'Cannibal cop' pictured with wife who tipped-off police . . . as it is claimed he craved 'girl meat' for Thanksgiving dinner". *The Daily Mail*. Retrieved 2 June 2015.

[6] "NY policeman Gilberto Valle acquitted in cannibal plot" bbc.com. 1 July 2014.

[7] Goldstein, Joseph (October 26, 2014). "Officer Plotted to Abduct, Cook and Eat Women, Authorities Say". *The New York Times*. Retrieved June 2, 2015.

[8] "NYC 'cannibal cop' case man Gilberto Valle sentenced on lesser charge." 13 November 2014. bbc.com.

[9] Weiser, Benjamin. "Gilberto Valle, Ex-New York Police Officer Talks About His Cannibalism Fantasies in Film." *The New York Times*. April 16, 2015

[10] "United States v. Gilberto Valle". *Electronic Frontier Foundation*. Retrieved 19 August 2015.

[11] Newman, Jason. "'Cannibal Cop' Doc Questions Line Between Fantasy and Murder." *Rolling Stone*. May 5, 2015.

[12] Leotta, Allison. "SVU's 'Thought Criminal'" *Huffington Post*. May 15, 2014.

23.6 External links

- United States v. Gilbert Valle initial criminal complaint

Chapter 24

Cannibalism (zoology)

For human cannibalism, see Cannibalism. For cannibalism in poultry, see Cannibalism in poultry.
In zoology, **cannibalism** is the act of one individual of a species consuming all or part of another individual of the same

Three Mormon crickets eating a fourth Mormon cricket

species as food. To consume the same species or show cannibalism is a common ecological interaction in the animal kingdom and has been recorded for more than 1,500 species.*[1] It does not, as once believed, occur only as a result of extreme food shortages or artificial conditions, but commonly occurs under natural conditions in a variety of species.*[1]*[2]*[3] Cannibalism seems to be especially prevalent in aquatic communities, in which up to approximately 90% of the organisms engage in cannibalism at some point of the life cycle. Cannibalism is also not restricted to carnivorous species, but is commonly found in herbivores and detritivores.*[2]

24.1   Sexual cannibalism

Main article: Sexual cannibalism

Sexual cannibalism is a special case of cannibalism in which a female organism kills and consumes a conspecific male before, during, or after copulation. Rarely, these roles are reversed.*[4]*[5] Sexual cannibalism has been recorded in the female redback spider, black widow spider, praying mantis, and scorpion, among others.

24.2   Size-structured cannibalism

Size-structured cannibalism is cannibalism in which older, larger, more mature individuals consume smaller, younger conspecifics. In size-structured populations, (where populations are made of individuals of various sizes, ages, and maturities), cannibalism can be responsible for 8% (Belding's ground squirrel) to 95% (dragonfly larvae) of the total mortality,*[6] making it a significant and important factor for population*[7] and community dynamics.*[8]

Size-structured cannibalism has commonly been observed in the wild for a variety of taxa. Vertebrate examples include chimpanzees, where groups of adult males have been observed to attack and consume infants.*[9]*[10]*[11]

24.2.1   Filial cannibalism

Main article: Filial cannibalism

Filial cannibalism, is a specific type of size-structured cannibalism in which adults eat their own offspring.*[12] Though most often thought of as parents eating live young, filial cannibalism includes parental consumption of stillborn infants and miscarried fetuses as well as infertile and still-incubating eggs. Vertebrate examples include pigs, where savaging accounts for a sizable percentage of total piglet deaths, and cats.*[13]

Filial cannibalism is particularly common in teleost fishes, appearing in at least seventeen different families of teleosts.*[14] Within this diverse group of fishes, there have been many, variable explanations of the possible adaptive value of filial cannibalism. One of these is the energy-based hypothesis, which suggests that fish eat their offspring when they are low on energy as an investment in future reproductive success.*[12] This has been supported by experimental evidence, showing that male three-spined sticklebacks,*[12]*[15]*[16] male tessellated darters,*[17] and male sphinx blenny fish*[18] all consume or absorb their own eggs to maintain their physical conditions. In other words, when males of a fish species are low on energy, it might sometimes be beneficial for them to feed on their own offspring to survive and invest in future reproductive success.

Another hypothesis as to the adaptive value of filial cannibalism in teleosts is that it increases density-dependent egg survivorship. In other words, filial cannibalism simply increases overall reproductive success by helping the other eggs make it to maturity by thinning out the numbers. Possible explanations as to why this is so include increasing oxygen availability to the remaining eggs,*[19] the negative effects of accumulating embryo waste,*[20] and predation.*[20]

In some species of eusocial wasps, such as *P. chinensis*, the reproducing female will kill and feed younger larvae to her older brood. This occurs under food stressed conditions in order to ensure that the first generation of workers emerges without delay. *[21] Further evidence also suggests that occasionally filial cannibalism might be the unfortunate by-product of cuckoldry in fish. Males consume broods, which may include their own offspring, when they believe a certain percentage of the brood contains genetic material that is not theirs.*[15]*[22]

The dinosaur *Coelophysis* was once suspected to have a degree in this form of cannibalism but this turned out to be wrong, although *Deinonychus* may have been. Skeletal remains from subadults with missing parts are suspected of having been eaten by other *Deinonychus*, mainly full-grown adults.

24.2.2 Infanticide

Main article: Infanticide (zoology)

Infanticide is the killing of a non-adult animal by an adult of the same species. Infanticide is often, but not always, accompanied by cannibalism. It is often displayed in lions; a male lion encroaching on the territory of a rival pride will often kill any existing cubs fathered by other males; this brings the lionesses into heat more quickly, enabling the invading lion to sire his own young. This is a good example of cannibalistic behavior in a genetic context.

24.3 Intrauterine cannibalism

Intrauterine cannibalism is a behaviour in some carnivorous species, in which multiple embryos are created at impregnation, but only one or two are born. The larger or stronger ones consume their less-developed siblings as a source of nutrients.

In **adelphophagy** or **embryophagy**, the fetus eats sibling embryos, while in oophagy it feeds on eggs.[23][24]

Adelphophagy occur in some marine gastropods (calyptraeids, muricids, vermetids, and buccinids) and in some marine annelids (*Boccardia proboscidia* in Spionidae).[25]

Intrauterine cannibalism is known to occur in lamnoid sharks[26] such as the sand tiger shark, and in the Fire Salamander,[27] as well as in some teleost fishes.[24] The Carboniferous period chimaera, *Delphyodontos dacriformes*, is suspected of having practiced intrauterine cannibalism, also, due to the sharp teeth of the recently born (or possibly aborted) juveniles, and the presence of fecal matter in the juveniles' intestines.[28]

Further information: Oophagy

24.4 See also

- Cannibalism (poultry)

24.5 References

[1] G. A. Polis, The evolution and dynamics of intraspecific predation. Annual Review of Ecology and Systematics 12, 225-251 (1981).

[2] Laurel R. Fox, Cannibalism in natural populations. Annual Review of Ecology and Systematics 6, 87-106 (1975).

[3] M. A. Elgar and B. J. (eds) Crespi, Cannibalism: Ecology and evolution among diverse taxa. (Oxford University Press, New York, 1992).

[4] Kenwyn Blake Suttle (1999). "The Evolution of Sexual Cannibalism" . University of California, Berkeley.

[5] Min-Li Tsai & Chang-Feng Dai (2003). "Cannibalism within mating pairs of the parasitic isopod *Ichthyoxenus fushanensis*" (abstract page). *Journal of Crustacean Biology* **23** (3): 662–668. doi:10.1651/C-2343.

[6] G. A. Polis, The evolution and dynamics of intraspecific predation. Annual Review of Ecology and Systematics 12, 225-251 (1981)

[7] David Claessen, A. M. De Roos, and L. Persson, Population dynamic theory of size-dependent cannibalism. Proceedings of the Royal Society of London Series B-Biological Sciences 271 (1537), 333-340 (2004)

[8] V. H. W. Rudolf, Consequences of stage-structured predators: Cannibalism, behavioral effects and trophic cascades. Ecology 88, 2991-3003 (2007)

[9] A. C. Arcadi and R. W. Wrangham, Infanticide in chimpanzees: Review of cases and a new within-group observation from the Kanyawara study group in Kibale National Park. Primates 40 (2), 337-351 (1999).

[10] M. L. Wilson, W. R. Wallauer, and A. E. Pusey, New cases of intergroup violence among chimpanzees in Gombe National Park, Tanzania. International Journal Of Primatology 25 (3), 523-549 (2004).

[11] D. P. Watts, J. C. Mitani, and H. M. Sherrow, New cases of inter-community infanticide by male chimpanzees at Ngogo, Kibale National Park, Uganda. Primates 43 (4), 263-270 (2002)

[12] Rohwer, S. 1978. Parent Cannibalism of Offspring and Egg Raiding as a Courtship Strategy. American Naturalist 112:429-440.

[13] Hartwell, S, Cats that kill kittens

[14] Manica, A. 2002. Filial cannibalism in teleost fish. Biological Reviews 77:261-277.

[15] Mehlis, M., T. C. M. Bakker, L. Engqvist, and J. G. Frommen. 2010. To eat or not to eat: egg-based assessment of paternity triggers fine-tuned decisions about filial cannibalism. Proceedings of the Royal Society B-Biological Sciences 277:2627-2635.

[16] Mehlis, M., T. C. M. Bakker, and J. G. Frommen. 2009. Nutritional benefits of filial cannibalism in three-spined sticklebacks (Gasterosteus aculeatus). Naturwissenschaften 96:399-403.

[17] DeWoody, J. A., D. E. Fletcher, S. D. Wilkins, and J. C. Avise. 2001. Genetic documentation of filial cannibalism in nature. Proceedings of the National Academy of Sciences of the United States of America 98:5090-5092.

[18] Kraak, S. B. M. 1996. Female preference and filial cannibalism in Aidablennius sphynx (Teleostei, Blenniidae); a combined field and laboratory study. Behavioural Processes 36:85-97.

[19] Payne, A. G., C. Smith, and A. C. Campbell. 2002. Filial cannibalism improves survival and development of beaugregory damselfish embryos. Proceedings of the Royal Society of London Series B-Biological Sciences 269:2095-2102.

[20] Klug, H., K. Lindstrom, and C. M. S. Mary. 2006. Parents benefit from eating offspring: density-dependent egg survivorship compensates for filial cannibalism. Evolution 60:2087-2095.

[21] Kudo, K.; Shirai, A. (5 January 2012). "Effect of food availability on larval cannibalism by foundresses of the paper wasp Polistes chinensis antennalis". Insect Soc. 59: 279–284.

[22] Gray, S. M., L. M. Dill, and J. S. McKinnon. 2007. Cuckoldry incites cannibalism: male fish turn to cannibalism when perceived certainty of paternity decreases. American Naturalist 169:258-263.

[23] Thierry Lodé 2001. Les stratégies de reproduction des animaux (reproduction strategies in animal kingdom). Eds Dunod Sciences, Paris

[24] Crespi, Bernard; Christina Semeniuk (2004). "Parent-Offspring Conflict in the Evolution of Vertebrate Reproductive Mode". The American Naturalist 163 (5): 635–654. doi:10.1086/382734. PMID 15122484.

[25] Thomsen O., Collin R. & Carrillo-Baltodano A. (2014). "The Effects of Experimentally Induced Adelphophagy in Gastropod Embryos". PLoS ONE 9(7): e103366. doi:10.1371/journal.pone.0103366.

[26] Hamlett, William C.; Allison M. Eulitt; Robert L. Jarrell; Matthew A. Kelly (1993). "Uterogestation and placentation in elasmobranchs". Journal of Experimental Zoology 266 (5): 347–367. doi:10.1002/jez.1402660504.

[27] Stebbins, Robert C.; Nathan W. Cohen (1995). A Natural History of Amphibians. Princeton, NJ: Princeton University Press. p. 9. ISBN 0-691-10251-1.

[28] Lund, R. 1980. Viviparity and intrauterine feeding in a new holocephalan fish from the Lower Carboniferous of Montana. Science, 209: 697-699.

24.6   Further reading

- M. A. Elgar and Bernard J. Crespi (eds.). 1992. *Cannibalism: Ecology and Evolution of Cannibalism among Diverse Taxa* Oxford University Press, New York. (361pp) ISBN 0-19-854650-5

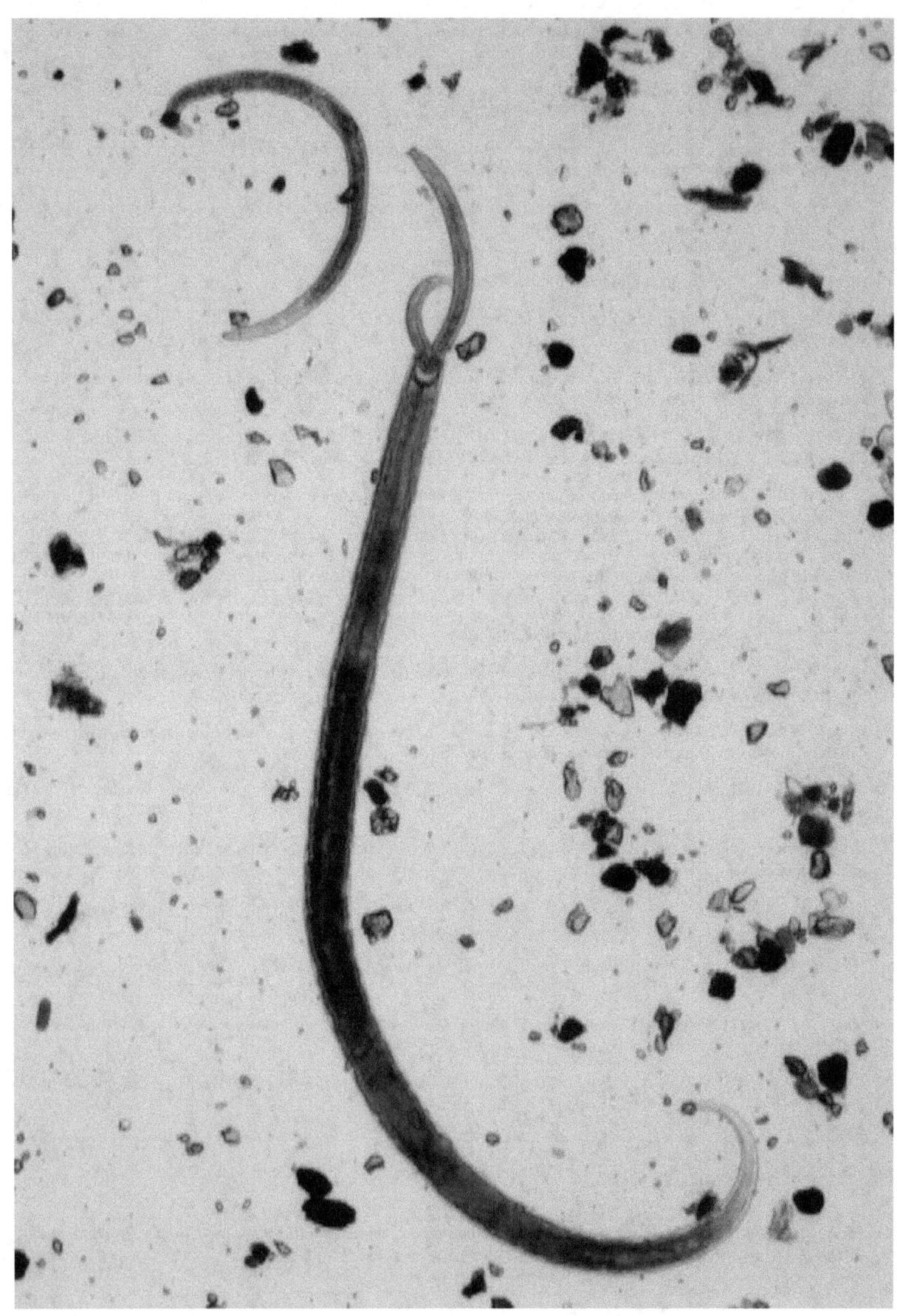

Nematode Mononchidae eating another Mononchidae.

24.7 Text and image sources, contributors, and licenses

24.7.1 Text

- **Cannibalism** *Source:* https://en.wikipedia.org/wiki/Cannibalism?oldid=687598346 *Contributors:* Damian Yerrick, Magnus Manske, Lee Daniel Crocker, Brion VIBBER, Eloquence, Bryan Derksen, MarXidad, The Anome, Aidan Elliott-McCrea, Eclecticology, Christopher Mahan, Darius Bacon, Rmhermen, Ortolan88, Roadrunner, DavidLevinson, KF, Hephaestos, Susano, Olivier, Rickyrab, Ericd, AntonioMartin, Frecklefoot, Patrick, Infrogmation, D, Llywrch, Lexor, Jrcrin001, Dante Alighieri, Dominus, Nixdorf, Liftarn, Dculberson, Wwwwolf, Ixfd64, Skysmith, Paul A, Shimmin, Tregoweth, Ahoerstemeier, Jpatokal, TUF-KAT, Bueller 007, Александър, Error, Rossami, Ruhrjung, Lee M, Eirik (usurped), Smack, Etaoin, Mydogategodshat, RodC, Adam Bishop, PaulinSaudi, Dcoetzee, Nohat, Viz, Ike9898, Fuzheado, Andrewman327, Jogloran, AHands, Haukurth, Foodman, Imc, Saltine, Itai, Nv8200pa, Sabbut, Ed g2s, Ann O'nyme, Floydian, Jeeves, Joy, Rls, Wetman, Hajor, Jeffq, Owen, Rossumcapek, Huangdi, Phil Boswell, Robbot, Hankwang, Fnunez~enwiki, Fredrik, Kizor, PBS, Tomchiukc, Chris 73, RedWolf, Donreed, Goethean, Altenmann, Naddy, Mirv, Babbage, P0lyglut, Academic Challenger, Texture, Auric, DHN, Jondel, Andrew Levine, Sunray, Hadal, Toiyabe, Michael Snow, Fuelbottle, Kent Wang, Takinc, Anthony, Pifactorial, Arnyek~enwiki, Oobopshark, Pengo, Nanahuatzin, Pablo-flores, Acm, Matt Gies, Exploding Boy, Paul Richter, Jyril, Lethe, Meursault2004, Mark Richards, Obli, Peruvianllama, Everyking, Subsolar, No Guru, TomViza, Pashute, Wolfe, Leonard G., Chinasaur, DO'Neil, FriedMilk, Mboverload, Ferdinand Pienaar, Evilweevil, Gzornenplatz, Mateuszica, Btphelps, Shakeer, MSTCrow, OldakQuill, Pinnecco, PeterC, Michael Paiewonsky, Pamri, Mike R, SURIV, Jpkoester1, Abu badali, Sonjaaa, Gzuckier, Antandrus, Beland, MisfitToys, Scottperry, MacGyverMagic, Girolamo Savonarola, DragonflySixtyseven, Tothebarricades.tk, Semenko, SimonLyall, ErikNY, Kevin143, Sam Hocevar, NoPetrol, Darksun, Asbestos, Eric B. and Rakim, Lindberg G Williams Jr, Joyous!, Positron, Mschlindwein, Leo Trollstoy, Laca, Jh51681, MementoVivere, JavaTenor, Trevor MacInnis, Rickvaughn, Smiller933, Mike Rosoft, Jayjg, PZFUN, Fpga, Lifefeed, Lan56, RTCearly, Discospinster, Rich Farmbrough, Guanabot, Caesar, Cnwb, N^O^el, GoD, Barista, MeltBanana, Too Old, R.123, Berkut, Zh, Dbachmann, Pavel Vozenilek, Bumhoolery, Stereotek, Horsten, Stbalbach, Bender235, Kjoonlee, Calair, Verbalcontract, Ground, Dataphile, Commonbrick, Brian0918, Jremington, Ben Webber, Carlon, Kwamikagami, Laurascudder, Spearhead, Peaceful, Sietse Snel, Dennis Brown, Markussep, CeeGee, Bobo192, Ypacaraí, Func, Enric Naval, Tronno, Viriditas, Kashasu, ZayZayEM, Larsie, L33tminion, Russ3Z, Yuje, Townmouse, Idleguy, Jonathunder, Nsaa, Licon, Espoo, Alansohn, Anthony Appleyard, Hektor, Snojoe, Nik42, Sherurcij, Elpincha, Eric Kvaalen, Philosophistry, Skradley, SpaceFalcon2001, Demi, MarkGallagher, Harburg, Tchalvak, InShaneee, Phocks, XLR8TION, Differentgravy, Cdc, BernardH, WikiParker, Hu, Bart133, DreamGuy, Marianocecowski, Wtmitchell, SidP, Suruena, Leoadec, Shadowolf, Tony Sidaway, Gpvos, Carioca, RainbowOfLight, Birdmessenger, TenOfAllTrades, Sciurinæ, Rhialto, Gpaliot, Sazerac, Computerjoe, Ianblair23, Versageek, SteinbDJ, Mattbrundage, Zereshk, GringoInChile, DonQuixote87, Mosesofmason, Jävligsvengelska, Zntrip, Klestrob44, Xanthar, Angr, Bacteria, Richard Arthur Norton (1958-), Simetrical, Laubzega, Roboshed, Woohookitty, Mindmatrix, TigerShark, LOL, StradivariusTV, Thivierr, TomTheHand, Broquaint, Pol098, Jeff3000, Kelisi, Lawrence O'Neil, Ilyusha, Akira625, Macaddct1984, Karmosin, Male1979, Watchmands, Brendanconway, Mtloweman, Rudeboy87, Sin-man, RichardWeiss, Graham87, Deltabeignet, Cuchullain, BD2412, Kbdank71, Xxpor, Nlsanand, Amorrow, NebY, Dpv, Dvyost, Edison, Canderson7, Coneslayer, Dubkiller, Rjwilmsi, Logmasd, Koavf, CyberGhostface, XP1, Mo-Al, Billbaitsg, XLerate, Miserlou, ScottJ, Aechris, Brighterorange, DoubleBlue, Fred Bradstadt, JamesEG, Yamamoto Ichiro, Pmc, Stepanovas, Saksham, Mvavrek, Wragge, Ian Pitchford, Xmoogle, Old Moonraker, Musical Linguist, Margosbot~enwiki, El Cid, Vsion, Nivix, Oedalis, Celestianpower, Fritz9000, RexNL, Gurch, Nimur, Str1977, Quuxplusone, Stigmaticllama, OrbitOne, Losecontrol, Wingsandsword, Kkragenbrink, Vidkun, Butros, King of Hearts, CJLL Wright, Shauni, Algebraist, B.~enwiki, Wack'd, Jak722, Satanael, YurikBot, Wavelength, TexasAndroid, RobotE, Hairy Dude, Rtkat3, Ryz05, Tznkai, Theredstarswl, Arjuna909, Red Slash, Garglebutt, Zafiroblue05, Hede2000, Pigman, ZacharyS, Chensiyuan, Stephenb, Okedem, Gaius Cornelius, Mike Young, CambridgeBayWeather, Eleassar, Alex Bakharev, Bovineone, Wimt, Dmlandfair, Bullzeye, Nawlin-Wiki, Wiki alf, BrainyBroad, Chick Bowen, Moop2000, WAS, Welsh, Kvn8907, ONEder Boy, Julien Deveraux, Apokryltaros, Ngorongoro, Anetode, Francis Ocoma, Kazuhite, Brian Crawford, Peter Delmonte, Jpbowen, Decapod73, Kermitmorningstar, Raven4x4x, Ezeu, Froth, Jeremy Franey, Iicatsii, Alex43223, Dbfirs, Mission9801, Peter.m.ng, DeadEyeArrow, Asarelah, FiggyBee, Barnabypage, BoonDock, Stefeyboy, IceCreamAntisocial, Maunus, Black Falcon, Wknight94, Smoove K, Salmanazar, WAS 4.250, Johndoyle, Encephalon, Nikkimaria, Ketsuekigata, SMcCandlish, DGaw, JoanneB, Vicarious, LeonardoRob0t, Danharms, Airodyssey, Garion96, Chris1219, Sugar Bear, Nightside eclipse, Robertcornell68, Allens, Aliza250, Hirudo, Nekura, DVD R W, Trolleymusic, Tom Morris, Qero, Hiddekel, MaeseLeon, SmackBot, Macgreco, Mr Curly, Nsayer, Reedy, Dangherous~enwiki, Hanchi, KnowledgeOfSelf, C.Fred, Vald, Pennywisdom2099, Paxse, Hskf4, Geoff B, Edgar181, HalfShadow, Evanreyes, Commander Keane bot, Pathless, Ellipsis, Sloman, Gilliam, Donama, Quidam65, Ohnoitsjamie, James xeno, Hmains, Squiddy, Schmiteye, Anwar saadat, Mirokado, Valley2city, Chris the speller, Bluebot, TimBentley, Agateller, Persian Poet Gal, Bjmullan, Gilthoniel, Thumperward, Fuzzform, Jgera5, Merlin Cox, Roscelese, Rediahs, JoeBlogsDord, Sadads, Dustimagic, Nbarth, Baa, Azeira, Aridd, Colonies Chris, Hongooi, Konstable, ChristopherM, Mladifilozof, XSG, Xeryus, Mimson, Rvcx, Tsca.bot, Can't sleep, clown will eat me, MisterHand, Kidvicious, Shalom Yechiel, Amber388, Onorem, Jennica, KaiserbBot, Sommers, OOODDD, Geoffrey Gibson, Bisected8, Yidisheryid, Rrburke, Tommyjb, VMS Mosaic, KerathFreeman, Chcknwnm, Anaugirain, Crboyer, Khoikhoi, Jmlk17, Krich, Gothmog.es, Fuhghettaboutit, Savidan, Detruncate, OutRIAAge, Dreadstar, Johnpf, DMighton, TechPurism, RandomP, G716, Paroxysm, Hgilbert, Smerus, Maelnuneb, Edd17, N Shar, Sturm, Mostlyharmless, Skinnyweed, Ohconfucius, Snowgrouse, Digana, Robotforaday, Rory096, Mykha, Minaker, Dsantesteban, Kuru, Ergative rlt, AmiDaniel, Writtenonsand, Hbriem, Mathiasrex, Grimhim, Heimstern, Gobonobo, Shlomke, Perfectblue97, MrJim, Shadowcaster187, Saigon punkid, Riley Gillis, Kransky, IronGargoyle, Camilo Sanchez, FrostyBytes, The Man in Question, A. Parrot, Dekkappai, Makyen, Bdruss, Mr Stephen, Kliqjaw, AdultSwim, Midnightblueowl, Ryulong, Halaqah, Digsdirt, MrDolomite, KJS77, DabMachine, Norm mit, Hropt1421, JoeBot, Discordia23, Twas Now, Ramshackle Man, Pinochii, Colin McLaughlin, Ewulp, Maleabroad, Courcelles, Esn, Tawkerbot2, Pudeo, Rdunn, Jack's Revenge, Miholvr125, J Milburn, JForget, Adam Keller, KyleGardiner, CmdrObot, Dycedarg, Eric, Tristan benedict, Skeletor2112, GHe, ShelfSkewed, MetaruKoneko, Ballista, Shandris, Kalemika, Chazsylvester, Neelix, Ken Gallager, Penbat, BigDaddy93, Fordmadoxfraud, TheAdventMaster, Gregbard, Fairsing, Jac16888, Pit-yacker, Ganryuu, Tiphareth, AniMate, Treybien, Gogo Dodo, Bellerophon5685, Jkelley, Frosty0814snowman, Drur93, MetalFreak2000, Myscrnnm, Blicious, Dusty relic, Svizzi, DumbBOT, Lsell@duke.edu, Ngopikrishna, Garik, Omicronpersei8, Vanished User jdksfajlasd, Zalgo, Pustelnik, Rayt5, Krylonblue83, Richhoncho, SianMycock, TSBoncompte, BetacommandBot, Thegoodson, Thijs!bot, Kaoruchan, Epbr123, Biruitorul, Qwyrxian, Olahus, Xaurtmj, Ucanlookitup, N5iln, PerfectStorm, Mojo Hand, Trouble tim, Oliver202, Headbomb, Trevyn, Marek69, John254, Kathovo, Pmrobert49, Mr pand, E. Ripley, QuitsMum, Big Bird, Orfen, Dawnseeker2000, Grandin, Mentifisto, Porqin, CerealBabyMilk, AntiVandalBot, Richard

Warner, Chubbles, Opelio, QuiteUnusual, EarthPerson, John Mathai, AaronY, Rockdave, TimVickers, RogueNinja, Clamster5, SSJPabs, Spencer, Spartaz, Pixelface, Ingolfson, JAnDbot, Dusty duster, Dan D. Ric, CosineKitty, Reduxx, Fetchcomms, Roleplayer, Airbreather, Flying tiger, PhilKnight, ResurgamII, Lord Crayak, Joshua, Geniac, SteveSims, Skele, Gert7, Majinvegeta, Hypershock, Bakilas, Bongwarrior, VoABot II, MiguelMunoz, Vordabois, Wikidudeman, Adam keller, JamesBWatson, Mclay1, Ling.Nut, Canniball, Tedickey, CTF83!, Nyttend, Prestonmcconkie, Froid, Wikied~enwiki, Catgut, ClovisPt, EagleFan, Almost Anonymous, RahadyanS, 28421u2232nfenfcenc, Cpl Syx, SlamDiego, Fang 23, Gerry D, DerHexer, Esanchez7587, Patpend, WLU, Cocytus, NatureA16, Ethron, Custardninja, MartinBot, Freezing the mainstream, Healkids, Arjun01, Hehehe111, Thiskidiscool, Ultraviolet scissor flame, Icenine378, R'n'B, CommonsDelinker, AlexiusHoratius, KTo288, Nono64, Boston, Cyrus Andiron, JBC3, J.delanoy, Pharaoh of the Wizards, Weissmann~enwiki, Trusilver, Specialclifford, Honx~enwiki, Bogey97, ChrisfromHouston, Tikiwont, Uncle Dick, Hierophantasmagoria, Bhavesh.Chauhan, Mike.lifeguard, Jerry, Ian.thomson, Captain Infinity, Paris1127, It Is Me Here, Skullketon, DarkFalls, Caitifty, Koven.rm, Philthe25th, Hillock65, Gurchzilla, Dexter prog, (jarbarf), HiLo48, Plasticup, Merceris, El monty, Belovedfreak, NewEnglandYankee, Cadwaladr, DadaNeem, Cmichael, Joshua Issac, Marcion, Juliancolton, Tiggerjay, Echoica, Coyote02, Remember the dot, Gwen Gale, Donmike10, Jgiam, Yellowfiver, Nomi887, Colinrobinson, Untitled and unidentified1, Motsa, Vkt183, Halmstad, ACSE, Craitman17, Vranak, VolkovBot, CWii, Anthonyh1010, ABF, Jeff G., Daleks and Davros, Dark paladin x, Blackoutdaddy, LeilaniLad, Philip Trueman, Roarshocker, TXiKiBoT, Deleet, Vipinhari, Technopat, Hqb, Gelatine5, Ann Stouter, ElinorD, Chaosflame210, Aholladay, Qxz, JezWegierski, Searching for Orion, Anna Lincoln, Steven J. Anderson, Lradrama, Sladek, Claidheamohmor, Martin451, Leafyplant, CanOfWorms, Gauge00, Mzmadmike, LeaveSleaves, Nicornal, PDFbot, Optigan13, Hepcat65, Snowbot, Frosty120985, Mr. Absurd, Liderbuksen, Dirkbb, Hari Anderson, Itzcoatl, Joseph A. Spadaro, Falcon8765, Enviroboy, Drutt, Zhouzhenning, Seresin, The Devil's Advocate, Insanity Incarnate, Nibios, Doc James, Quantpole, Angelastic, Ryan spencer, Karl23, Rontrigger, Farnsworth1968, Tingeling5, Adancingmonk, EJF, Gomr, Royaljared, Fooker69, Sonicology, Timrfrench61, Scarian, Sharkentile, Caltas, Spideyfan1227, Wideeyedraven, Zellss, Dr.Florence Magoo, Yintan, Jonas Poole, Wateva101, Mr.Z-bot, Keilana, ChronicFaith, Bentogoa, Hobbit fingers, Manofsecrets~enwiki, Albertrothschild, Candt Sparkle, Oliveguy, Antonio Lopez, Nuttycoconut, Ryan125, ViennaUK, Ageslimit, Lightmouse, Helikophis, Poindexter Propellerhead, Manway, Ks0stm, Xanman117, Thirteen squared, Mikeewen 19, IdreamofJeanie, StaticGull, Benny the wayfarer, Chrisrus, Mangledorf, Harel Newman, Sean.hoyland, Paulinho28, Asikhi, Florentino floro, Blackcat52, Verdadero, Bpeps, Denisarona, Q montanto esq, Ainlina, ImageRemovalBot, RobinHood70, SallyForth123, Kinkyturnip, Martarius, ClueBot, Grammar Vigilante, The Thing That Should Not Be, Radioangel, TableManners, Hongthay, Cygnis insignis, Jsarratt, Shark96z, Pakaal, Drmies, Mild Bill Hiccup, EscapeMIT, Nam1974, Niceguyedc, Alex Mazor, LebOneez, Blanchardb, RafaAzevedo, Confusious, Kabir pal, Arunsingh16, Vulture19, Tanketz, Shizznit789, DragonBot, Rvobrien, Excirial, Thegreatestwalrusintheworld, Coralmizu, Tiniti, Iceglass, Mattjm24, Gillfactor, Kathrynroscheborre, Gtstricky, Zaharous, Tyler, NuclearWarfare, Subdolous, EhJJ, TheRedPenOfDoom, DeltaQuad, Trogadoore, Steffy111588, Dekisugi, Frozen4322, Bearerofthecup, Ark25, Muro Bot, Thehelpfulone, Rui Gabriel Correia, Thingg, The Always Trusted Scholar, Hniyer, SoxBot III, Gikü, Editor2020, SteelMariner, Vanished User 1004, DumZiBoT, Hethurs, Mr Larrington, MichaelQSchmidt, XLinkBot, Enallagma, Spitfire, Rankiri, Stickee, Jovianeye, Kick-the-kannibal, Hadrianvs et antinovs, Mitch Ames, Anturiaethwr, Billwhittaker, Tezza UK, Badgernet, Spoonkymonkey, Bawjaws123, Sonyray, Notuncurious, Good Olfactory, Q Valda, Surtsicna, Princessinblack, Me as in me, Ekkyekkyekkyparkyptang, DOI bot, Tcncv, Friginator, AnnaJGrant, I vunder, Trasman, Uskill, Livedanddied, GeneralAtrocity, Ronhjones, Movingboxes, Fieldday-sunday, Electron, CanadianLinuxUser, Leszek Jańczuk, Fluffernutter, Medleystudios72, Teamsofmany, Twiceshook2, Sebastian scha., Mario CUSENZA, Uzgeek, Download, Tehcheese, CarsracBot, Redheylin, 1archie99, Glane23, Johnnyharry2571, Chzz, Favonian, Tallan, Kyle1278, Alliem16, 5 albert square, Tyw7, Tassedethe, Habitualsurfer4, Tide rolls, OlEnglish, Mjquinn id, Al3xil, Gail, Beeskneestrees, Erictheplaya, Halaster, Koustav2007, Genius101, Ben Ben, Legobot, Luckas-bot, Yobot, Wheelsthem, Cyanoa Crylate, KHP2, Smoke Trail, Melaena, Brendansykes, Jack5150, THEN WHO WAS PHONE?, Gongshow, Mrmcdonnell, Jimjilin, Againme, Eric-Wester, Jessi1989, AnomieBOT, Dukebutts123, This gives me the jitters!, Rjanag, Death666666, Cavarrone, Hadrian89, Th1nk ur b4d, Piano non troppo, AdjustShift, Knowledgekid87, Ulric1313, Flewis, Algorithme, UltimateDarkloid, Materialscientist, TheTechieGeek63, Citation bot, Zeroimpl, E2eamon, La comadreja, AlguzarA, Rvd4life, Monkeys1234, Hgriggs, ReallyUltraSuperSecretGuy, Ieuan Sant, I-10, Emma21mcr, Xqbot, Ywaz, Intelati, JimVC3, Capricorn42, AL3X TH3 GR8, Poetaris, Timmyshin, Clearly Toughpick, That1guy137, 661kts, Srich32977, Kithira, Wes52353, P00nc00s, J04n, Canadianbiker999, Ramboinwalmart6, Wikieditor1988, Bellerophon, Anthonymayne, Doulos Christos, Trafford09, Applied Research, GhalyBot, Bpselvam, DarkElrad, Cannibalchildren, Prezbo, Amdapoop, Theguy123456, Napstein, Foreverlove10, RetiredWikipedian789, A robustus, Fungusblimp, GT5162, George2001hi, FrescoBot, Itatchi83, Sandgem Addict, Vampiric jesus, Ryryrules100, Hookthemhorns, Tobby72, Jibtazzle, Chace22, Lothar von Richthofen, RicHard-59, Recognizance, Galorr, Moloch09, America09, MADaboutforests, Citation bot 1, Bobmack89x, Pinethicket, I dream of horses, Edderso, 3rd is mint, Getonthebus, Jonesey95, Supreme Deliciousness, Calmer Waters, Bejinhan, A8UDI, Vehement, RedBot, Yutsi, Lcw27, Nijgoykar, Coolknot, Tamsier, Full-date unlinking bot, Fartherred, Write2me today, White Shadows, Tim1357, Yunshui, MikeAllen, Spotsgoalie, Dinamikbot, Vrenator, Frenchruby, Nataev, Lynn Wilbur, Thespicytaco, Diannaa, Yoggsaron, Keegscee, G2sean, Race911, LoveSNSD, Whisky drinker, RjwilmsiBot, Joseph Spadaro, ButOnMethItIs, Jonnytruluv2009, VernoWhitney, Yaush, NerdyScienceDude, Lavhbti, Tigermyboo, CaitsMeow, EmausBot, Santamoly, Riptideyoutube, WikitanvirBot, Avenue X at Cicero, Gfoley4, Alphateam2003, Ajraddatz, Iznor19, Natalie29, Kbokassa, RenamedUser01302013, AlanSiegrist, Tommy2010, Spookyland, Devillian, Tuxedo junction, Werieth, CoffeeColossus, Susfele, Zdfghsfd, Traxs7, Jcpobrien, Rexodus, Refinnejann, Mobius Bot, H3llBot, GeeGollyJeepers, Cymru.lass, Siddell, 234bbbvvvccc, Brandmeister, Maalaaa1, L Kensington, Flannelbean, Puffin, Taulant Kastrati, Sgphillips, Taotao2010, Peter Karlsen, SmilingMonster, Pifferz, Pasoccerplaya95, J.Smithmans, Warewolph, Wolfrunner1996, 3oWh pF0wHz, ClueBot NG, Gothicartech, Rich Smith, Therealchella, Qbobdole, Adair2324, Dragongirl5678, Cntras, Karl 334, Amelia1532, Crystal Linux, DrChrissy, Pudge MclameO, AkbarHuAkbar, Helpful Pixie Bot, Syed8551, Nightenbelle, Curb Chain, Calabe1992, Rodigyen, Gorbachev96, Lowercase sigmabot, Plumu2010, BG19bot, Yo2485, Engranaje, Nattvv, Ketih King, Yakoj, Duelingaces18, Northamerica1000, Noobdestroyer123, Eladynnus, Babill123, Hallows AG, Smcg8374, Badon, Solomon7968, Canoe1967, BreakfastHorse, TEHASophannah, Ahmadtauseef, Cryptiddude, Troll 26, 12DECDEC, Nbahaji, Zdude28, Vitusberingbg, Ἑρμῆς, MattBaxter, Zombehstross, Jediknightelectro1997, Jonadin93, Zondrah89, TigerDover, Bumchum123, JinxYou'reIt!, Vanished user lt94ma34le12, Tlbastian, Wagon66, ChrisGualtieri, DoctorKubla, Davidvacca, JBGeorge77, Khazar2, FixingError, TinyTed-Danson, Pophorror, Harsh 2580, Mylemurlua, Pippy79, Katerina (Katherine) Petrova, Lady Chosa, Darekk2, ZombieMonkeyNZ, Emmakh86, Vannahpollock, Mogism, Inayity, FedtotheGhouls, Smithman123, JRYon, Freedomcali7, RotlinkBot, JamieSc, Automaton wiki, Bladesmulti, Monkbot, Daffodillday, Freshness For Lettuce, Tepehuan, Nøkkenbuer, Zezima5625, KasparBot, Mariojack3, Eldizzino, IllusIon, Philipfolta and Anonymous: 1675

- **List of incidents of cannibalism** *Source:* https://en.wikipedia.org/wiki/List_of_incidents_of_cannibalism?oldid=688230443 *Contributors:* Dante Alighieri, Woohookitty, Rjwilmsi, WriterHound, Wavelength, Deville, E Wing, Chris the speller, Colonies Chris, Jennica, B.S. Lawrence,

Dashiellx, IdreamofJeanie, Niceguyedc, Excirial, TheRedPenOfDoom, Yohananw, Ark25, 1archie99, SPat, Yobot, AnomieBOT, Jim1138, Sionk, FrescoBot, LittleWink, Lotje, RjwilmsiBot, K6ka, Sundostund, Natt39, K kisses, ClueBot NG, Catlemur, Rlees42, Antiqueight, BG19bot, Engranaje, BattyBot, Miszatomic, Darylgolden, ZappaOMati, DoctorKubla, Tandrum, Khazar2, Koopatrev, Mogism, IainChSh, Bowtiecamera, NFLisAwesome, Bluebasket, Lilneige~enwiki, Rajmaan, Epicgenius, Thegreatestever21, Changsunil, Tentinator, Automaton wiki, Bladesmulti, Altansh, Monkbot, TrapBeatz402, Cannibal719, WikiOriginal-9, ScrapIronIV, Modmouse1324, NekoKatsun, Supdiop, Srednuas Lenoroc, ThorLorn123 and Anonymous: 46

- **The Baby-Roast** *Source:* https://en.wikipedia.org/wiki/The_Baby-Roast?oldid=669482928 *Contributors:* Malcolma, Gilliam, Ser Amantio di Nicolao, Gatoclass, Amandajm, SL93, Lucas Thoms, PumpkinSky, MrBill3, Bonkers The Clown, DoctorKubla, Jyg, Bouowmx, Datadoggieein, Jerodlycett and Anonymous: 1

- **Child cannibalism** *Source:* https://en.wikipedia.org/wiki/Child_cannibalism?oldid=686014295 *Contributors:* Auric, Dbachmann, Beau99, ADM, Ricky81682, Sfacets, Sonic Mew, WAS, SigPig, Chunky Rice, Asarelah, Jeff Silvers, Attilios, SmackBot, Bluebot, Francisx, Terminal157, Kingurth, Serpent-A, Scottandrewhutchins, Pie Man 360, MarshBot, Majorly, VoABot II, WLU, Jmm6f488, Mewmuffin, BeIsKr, Hebele, Carlygnarly, Helenkilla, Otolemur crassicaudatus, Ngebendi, Mlaffs, DumZiBoT, XLinkBot, Yutsi, John of Reading, Smittee, ClueBot NG, Widr, BG19bot, Altaïr, EagerToddler39, Applemad, Paraloco, Datbubblegumdoe and Anonymous: 37

- **Custom of the sea** *Source:* https://en.wikipedia.org/wiki/Custom_of_the_sea?oldid=656123783 *Contributors:* GTBacchus, Adam Conover, Donreed, Mervyn, Cutler, SYSS Mouse, Silly Dan, Espoo, LinkTiger, Hairy Dude, Cliffb, Mike Young, Anetode, Warreed, Jeff Silvers, Squiddy, WSaindon, Bisected8, Cybercobra, Johncmullen1960, Chovain, Superbeatles, Shirt58, Skomorokh, Max Hyre, Robotman1974, Cpl Syx, Gurko, Hillock65, VolkovBot, AlleborgoBot, AdRock, Beligaronia, Jonas Poole, Jaredtwalker, Radioangel, CowboySpartan, Shem1805, DumZiBoT, Doc9871, Addbot, Evasuneva, PMLawrence, Citation bot, Slowingpulse, GrouchoBot, Napstein, FrescoBot, Helpful Pixie Bot, Hmainsbot1, Cornersss and Anonymous: 28

- **Endocannibalism** *Source:* https://en.wikipedia.org/wiki/Endocannibalism?oldid=684069654 *Contributors:* 20040302, Rich Farmbrough, Dbachmann, BD2412, Rjwilmsi, Nihiltres, Jpbowen, Aldux, SmackBot, Thumperward, RMHED, Gregbard, TSBoncompte, SteveSims, WLU, Potatoswatter, Moblinmaniac, HairyWombat, Twinsday, John Nevard, Editor2020, Jakedsnyder, Trasman, Zubrahim, Yobot, AnomieBOT, LilHelpa, Gilo1969, DeNoel, Trappist the monk, RjwilmsiBot, John of Reading, Parusaro, ClueBot NG, Slowking4, Helpful Pixie Bot, LNCP, SouthclawWiki, Monkbot, Jaycs.554, Trjeffers, Maddelamia, Kmp42, Kmgrow, Killgrove, Zygomatic12 and Anonymous: 17

- **Exocannibalism** *Source:* https://en.wikipedia.org/wiki/Exocannibalism?oldid=688544912 *Contributors:* Wtmitchell, Woohookitty, BD2412, Phantomsteve, SmackBot, TSBoncompte, Snideology, Niceguyedc, Yobot, ClueBot NG, BG19bot, Maddelamia and Anonymous: 16

- **Filial cannibalism** *Source:* https://en.wikipedia.org/wiki/Filial_cannibalism?oldid=681871233 *Contributors:* Stemonitis, Rjwilmsi, Invertzoo, Good Olfactory, Bakerb4379, Jarble, AnomieBOT, Alvin Seville, Cold Season, Mobydickens, Katheefwah, Rey ks and Anonymous: 6

- **Human placentophagy** *Source:* https://en.wikipedia.org/wiki/Human_placentophagy?oldid=688480311 *Contributors:* Bearcat, Rjwilmsi, MZMcBride, Whoisjohngalt, Hairy Dude, RussBot, Malcolma, Romarin, BullRangifer, Lesion, Cydebot, Jmg38, Reedy Bot, Bearian, De728631, Niceguyedc, CallidoraBlack, SoxBot, Yobot, Bluerasberry, Citation bot, RjwilmsiBot, KLBot2, Austinprince, Filing Flunky, Westcoastmd, Lambfc4, Khazar2, Antunesi, Steveballou, EvergreenFir, MeAliasX and Anonymous: 20

- **Keep the River on Your Right: A Modern Cannibal Tale** *Source:* https://en.wikipedia.org/wiki/Keep_the_River_on_Your_Right%3A_ A_Modern_Cannibal_Tale?oldid=684183115 *Contributors:* Bearcat, Shawn in Montreal, BG19bot, Everymorning and Culturezoom

- **Francisco Leóna** *Source:* https://en.wikipedia.org/wiki/Francisco_Le%C3%B3na?oldid=685153870 *Contributors:* JackofOz, ÀrdRuadh21, Niceguyedc, Gareth Griffith-Jones, Lakun.patra and Anonymous: 1

- **Manifesto Antropófago** *Source:* https://en.wikipedia.org/wiki/Manifesto_Antrop%C3%B3fago?oldid=685121531 *Contributors:* GVOLTT, Ricardo Carneiro Pires, AKeen, SmackBot, Elonka, Gilliam, Werdan7, JamesAM, Jlove88, Skullketon, BaseballDetective, Oneprincesslea, No such user, MovementLessRestricted, Jargonash, Good Olfactory, Addbot, Yobot, Prburley, Trafford09, MxxL, 550brock, IluvatarBot, Giso6150, Vanished user 31lk45mnzx90 and Anonymous: 12

- **Pishtaco** *Source:* https://en.wikipedia.org/wiki/Pishtaco?oldid=686600864 *Contributors:* Rvolz, Woohookitty, Rjwilmsi, Asarelah, Seishin17, Gonzalo84, CaTi0604, PhJ, Gonzalo M. Garcia, Uyvsdi, Grsz11, GlassCobra, Excirial, MatthewVanitas, Addbot, Power.corrupts, Willking1979, Alexjgunn, Luckas-bot, Yobot, McKaot, Dneyder, Tim1357, Victor Victoria, Trappist the monk, RjwilmsiBot, Amerias, Vukskaradzic, We hope, WIERDGREENMAN, Helpful Pixie Bot, BG19bot, Pilarrr, CitationCleanerBot, Monkbot, Vieque, GinAndChronically and Anonymous: 11

- **Placentophagy** *Source:* https://en.wikipedia.org/wiki/Placentophagy?oldid=687155365 *Contributors:* The Anome, Infrogmation, EvanProdromou, Lexor, Karada, Delirium, Radicalsubversiv, Error, Dpol, Jengod, JesseW, Decumanus, Dbenbenn, Mshonle~enwiki, Nunh-huh, Everyking, Varlaam, Rick Block, Bovlb, Shane Lin, Sonjaaa, Sam Hocevar, Poccil, Rhobite, John Vandenberg, Viriditas, Chuck F, Reithy, ReithySockPuppet, Okiedokie, JennyBicks, Calton, RoppongiHillsTempleU, EyeBall, GeorgeStepanek, Aranae, Wtmitchell, AlbertCahalan~enwiki, FreplySpang, Rjwilmsi, IlanaWarnack, Florihupf, Naraht, Avalyn, Hairy Dude, Lavenderbunny, Obarskyr, Lexicon, Ckamaeleon, 2over0, Coqsportif, Closedmouth, Dbarefoot, SmackBot, Melchoir, Bwithh, BiT, Cazort, Gilliam, OrphanBot, Elendil's Heir, Sspecter, Symbionese, Mbkristal, CmdrObot, Metanoid, Jfredericksen, Natalie Erin, Flauta~enwiki, RobotG, Kimwiki, Kmaguir1, SwiftBot, Wormcast, Enquire, WLU, Pomte, Plasticup, Bucinka, Bradman3001, Bearian, 2literhero, EugeneOleinik, Bsradams, ClueBot, Drmies, Loupdebois, Lx 121, XLinkBot, Addbot, Elainecs, Grubel, ThreeOfCups, Norman21, Anxietycello, مlان, Gail, Yobot, DerechoReguerraz, AnomieBOT, Citation bot, SpaceRocket, Homer2009, Citation bot 1, Pinethicket, Full-date unlinking bot, Mancy Houghton-Freund, RjwilmsiBot, Tomchen1989, John of Reading, Jodiselander, ZéroBot, H3llBot, RaptureBot, Donner60, DM4242, ClueBot NG, Gravyb, Boaschic1, InstantNull, Bapplebeet, NewbTopolis Rex and Anonymous: 116

- **Cannibalism in popular culture** *Source:* https://en.wikipedia.org/wiki/Cannibalism_in_popular_culture?oldid=682614851 *Contributors:* Andrewman327, Donreed, Altenmann, Khaosworks, D6, Discospinster, Andrew Maiman, Dbachmann, Pavel Vozenilek, CanisRufus, Spearhead, Bendono, Balok, Beau99, Philip Cross, Ricky81682, Echuck215, Piggen, Sfacets, Firsfron, Woohookitty, Whitehorse1, Tabletop, SteveCrook, WBardwin, BD2412, Rjwilmsi, MZMcBride, Vclaw, RussBot, RadioFan, Stephen Burnett, Kvn8907, Xdenizen, GracieLizzie, Misza13,

Rwalker, Nikkimaria, Ladysway1985, SmackBot, Nsayer, Hmains, Valley2city, Chris the speller, Robocoder, NickPenguin, Crouchbk, Kransky, Jaiwills, Bwalko, Krispos42, ISD, Barfbagger, The Haunted Angel, J Milburn, CmdrObot, Calibanu, Cyrus XIII, Palendrom, WLior, ShelfSkewed, Cydebot, Barticus88, Jpark3909, Xaurtmj, John254, Bobblehead, Mr pand, JustAGal, CharlotteWebb, Edokter, Warhawk159, Daggoth, KrijnMossel, Omeganian, Cpoirot, Lord Crayak, Geniac, Majinvegeta, Bakilas, VoABot II, Bluebeetle, Froid, Mr. Garrison, JaGa, Custardninja, CommonsDelinker, A Nobody, Reedy Bot, Hundred-Man, Lee Kay, Mega00byte, Dijeratti, Jevansen, Vranak, X!, Hammersoft, Ikf5, Jomasecu, The holy barnacle, Davehi1, JLThorpe, TravelingCat, Magiclite, Horus86, Witchkraut, JL-Bot, Hoplon, Sfan00 IMG, Ideal gas equation, EoGuy, Sleeming88, Arjayay, Ngebendi, Dementia13, Feddx, DumZiBoT, Dmacewen, OpusAtrum, Apo-kalypso, Dthomsen8, Tassedethe, Sammy theeditor, TheOriginalObbie, Yobot, Guy1890, Rogerb67, Jmaddux23, MinorProphet, AnomieBOT, Neurolysis, Ubcule, Technowarrior, J04n, LyleHoward, Eugene-elgato, Cannibalchildren, FrescoBot, Patchy1, Abetheeagle, DooDahDave, SkyMachine, Landon1014, Greenleaf547, Skip Zipper, M4pnt, ClueBot NG, Focusedontruth, BG19bot, Bmusician, Mark Arsten, Miraclewhipped224, Cleanelephant, BattyBot, Kbrokamp14, Soulparadox, Jihadcola, Editfromwithout, Applemad, Hmainsbot1, Abyssopelagic, Hayesthemanmythlegend, Liz, BethNaught, MohammadF12, Hienafant and Anonymous: 163

- **Cannibalism in poultry** *Source:* https://en.wikipedia.org/wiki/Cannibalism_in_poultry?oldid=664657032 *Contributors:* Bearcat, Kurt Shaped Box, Rjwilmsi, Steven Walling, Chiswick Chap, Good Olfactory, Download, Pinethicket, Onel5969, ClueBot NG, CopperSquare, DrChrissy, Melcous, LukasMatt, Joerockzzz, FourViolas and Anonymous: 5

- **Sacamantecas** *Source:* https://en.wikipedia.org/wiki/Sacamantecas?oldid=683621612 *Contributors:* Error, ÀrdRuadh21, Editor2020, Dthomsen8, Yobot, AnomieBOT, J04n, GrindtXX, Miszatomic and WikiOriginal-9

- **Self-cannibalism** *Source:* https://en.wikipedia.org/wiki/Self-cannibalism?oldid=688678409 *Contributors:* Error, Altenmann, Auric, Moink, Jleedev, Graeme Bartlett, DocWatson42, Gtrmp, Risk one, Dumbo1, Tonymaric, Jackcsk, Beland, Joyous!, Mike Rosoft, Ouro, Wfaulk, DanielCD, Adrian~enwiki, CyberSkull, Keenan Pepper, Calton, Mailer diablo, ClockworkSoul, Abanima, Pictureuploader, Graham87, Ligulem, Eubot, MacRusgail, Fragglet, Klosterdev, Introvert, Satanael, YurikBot, Hairy Dude, Icarus3, Anetode, Natliskeliguten, CNichols, Nikkimaria, Arundhati bakshi, Allens, SmackBot, InverseHypercube, Niayre, Evanreyes, Gilliam, Portillo, Lady Serena, Nzd, Rmosler2100, Tyciol, RDBrown, Evangelista, Шизомби, Exoir, Wizardman, Soap, Mary Read, Stwalkerster, Serephine, Nehrams2020, Kernow, Dunne409, Squanto1, Courcelles, Wikivigilante, CmdrObot, Rogerborg, Shandris, Slazenger, AniMate, Reywas92, Daniel J. Leivick, Optimist on the run, Rusl, Trappleton, Trevyn, Hmrox, CommanderCool1654, MoogleDan, Opelio, Spencer, Albany NY, Smith Jones, GoodDamon, Mclay1, Girdi, WhatamIdoing, Xsmasher, Lilac Soul, Ginsengbomb, Breadcult, Temporarily Insane, Holme053, Reptile654, Barneca, Meters, Angelastic, Mygerardromance, ClueBot, Niceguyedc, Krobey, Kakofonous, MatthewVanitas, Skyezx, Idbelange, Tassedethe, Peridon, Al3xil, Jarble, Ihavingamingebag, AnomieBOT, Citation bot, LilHelpa, DSisyphBot, Anon423, FrescoBot, Lord Oblivion, Dltcentennial, Full-date unlinking bot, Abcbe, Comet Tuttle, Reaper Eternal, Bloodrinker 666, EmausBot, Wikfr, AManWithNoPlan, Donner60, ClueBot NG, Widr, HominidMachinae, Davidiad, Gautehuus, DraceEmpressa, Backendgaming, Absinthe pretty 27, Monkbot, Cgs17, Roy101AC, KingZogKing-Zog, NewbTopolis Rex, 15zulu and Anonymous: 139

- **Sexual cannibalism** *Source:* https://en.wikipedia.org/wiki/Sexual_cannibalism?oldid=684070393 *Contributors:* Subsolar, Zeimusu, Rosemaryamey, Dr.frog, Xezbeth, Sole Soul, Larry V, 99of9, Stuartyeates, Stemonitis, Daniel Case, Rjwilmsi, Eyu100, VincentG, Bensin, Nogburt, SmackBot, Melchoir, Gilliam, J. Spencer, Epastore, Eliyahu S, Richard001, LtPowers, Mgiganteus1, IronGargoyle, Jack O'Neill, Afghana~enwiki, AshLin, Anil1956, Metanoid, Alfirin, Shirulashem, Thijs!bot, Headbomb, Luigifan, Danger, Catgut, Boston, Sman789, Sneeka2, Sphayros, Mizusajt, Wikiisawesome, Brianga, Xenobiologista, Flyer22 Reborn, Oxymoron83, Badger Drink, Blanchardb, Robert Skyhawk, Excirial, Tim010987, Addbot, Offenbach, DOI bot, Anxietycello, Yobot, AnomieBOT, Citation bot, Xqbot, Tyrol5, FrescoBot, Citation bot 1, Pinethicket, Inthecaliforniasun, HRoestBot, Jonesey95, Callanecc, Fastilysock, CCEvo-danrath, EmausBot, John of Reading, Aha231, The Mysterious El Willstro, Tuxedo junction, Natirips, Jcaraballo, DemonicPartyHat, Mjbmrbot, ClueBot NG, Matthewilfoe, Bibcode Bot, Plantdrew, FamousPplRCuul, Supernerd11, Schmooble, Skbobade, Mogism, Berudagon, Ccevo2012, 296.x, Cleverdickie, Agasso26, Elleinad1122, Ccevol2013, Sachio999, Swahyeh, KitKatKlobber, Zumoarirodoka, TranquilHope, Crystallizedcarbon, Ed Agyei, Ccevol2014, Dr. K. Smith, Srednuas Lenoroc, Jdvh1985 and Anonymous: 73

- **Hans Staden** *Source:* https://en.wikipedia.org/wiki/Hans_Staden?oldid=676578397 *Contributors:* AxelBoldt, Deb, Dimadick, JackofOz, Varlaam, Matthead, Mateuszica, Mschlindwein, Discospinster, PochWiki, Polylerus, SlaveToTheWage, Carbon Caryatid, Grenavitar, Zootm, FeanorStar7, Rjwilmsi, ABot, FlaBot, Gulielmus Cumrotae, Bgwhite, YurikBot, RussBot, Dysmorodrepanis~enwiki, Jaxl, Howcheng, Tuckerresearch, Donald Albury, Cotoco, SmackBot, Betacommand, Ser Amantio di Nicolao, OAlexander, Tawkerbot2, George100, Logical2u, Cydebot, Natezomby, Lsell@duke.edu, Knarf-bz~enwiki, Missvain, Dmitri Lytov, Felipe Menegaz, Adam keller, Waacstats, Valerius Tygart, CommonsDelinker, Numbo3, VolkovBot, Magafuzula, Andreas Kaganov, Hyleg, Jalo, Llajwa, SISLEY, Monegasque, XPTO, Drmies, Niceguyedc, RafaAzevedo, Dthomsen8, Addbot, Lightbot, Luckas-bot, Bob Burkhardt, Green Cardamom, FrescoBot, Igallards7, Rjwilmsi-Bot, Sander Moholi, Tuxedo junction, PBS-AWB, Engranaje, ChrisGualtieri, Khazar2, Lorelei, Hmainsbot1, Luismanu, JordanaStarkman, OccultZone, Monkbot, KasparBot and Anonymous: 35

- **List of traditional Chinese medicines** *Source:* https://en.wikipedia.org/wiki/List_of_traditional_Chinese_medicines?oldid=688230263 *Contributors:* Bearcat, Rolfmueller, Rjwilmsi, Wavelength, Welsh, Apokryltaros, Malcolma, Pegship, Chris the speller, Deli nk, Keahapana, Colonel Warden, LadyofShalott, CmdrObot, Reywas92, Rothorpe, Jeff G., Lamro, Xenobiologista, JohnnyMrNinja, Wikievil666, EoGuy, ImperfectlyInformed, Doseiai2, AnomieBOT, LilHelpa, Melmann, PPdd, John of Reading, Look2See1, Frglz, ClueBot NG, Herbxue, Helpful Pixie Bot, Curb Chain, Jblaska, Plantdrew, Arminden, CitationCleanerBot, Arcandam, Khazar2, Bluebasket, Willowtits, 4pillars, Sfdkljsd, CensoredScribe, Monkbot, Kaciemonster, Isabellajemas, Mfernflower, Naturalllybalance, Coen122 and Anonymous: 20

- **Transmissible spongiform encephalopathy** *Source:* https://en.wikipedia.org/wiki/Transmissible_spongiform_encephalopathy?oldid=686169994 *Contributors:* Mav, Alex.tan, Edward, Michael Hardy, CesarB, Jdforrester, Surfer97301, Charles Matthews, Ike9898, Adoarns, Steinsky, Gestumblindi, Phil Boswell, Robbot, Rhombus, Reytan, Jfdwolff, Oniamien, ShakataGaNai, Jossi, Karl Dickman, Stephenpratt, Alexrexpvt, Rich Farmbrough, RoyBoy, CDN99, Viriditas, Wisdom89, ZayZayEM, Arcadian, AlanH, Unused000701, Eric Kvaalen, Wouterstomp, CJ, Velella, Alfvaen, TenOfAllTrades, Benbest, Before My Ken, Fred Bradstadt, FlaBot, Str1977, Chobot, Bgwhite, FrankTobia, Wavelength, Purple, Mushin, Cyferx, RussBot, Zwobot, Slicing, Esprit15d, NetRolller 3D, SmackBot, The Angriest Man Alive, DocKrin, Jakken, Nbarth, Kingdon, Acdx, Clicketyclack, Joelmills, Mathias-S, Matt Kurz, Arstchnca, DabMachine, Nehrams2020, Ruslik0, LittleT889, Cydebot, Calvero JP, Oleksii0, Jasonisme, Headbomb, Lfstevens, Tstrobaugh, Magioladitis, VoABot II, Arno Matthias, Recurring dreams, Sabedon, Dredsina,

Tygrrr, Shiggity, VolkovBot, Sporti, Eyejuice, Mbangert, AlleborgoBot, Michael Frind, SieBot, Moonriddengirl, ToePeu.bot, Faradayplank, Movalley, ClueBot, The Thing That Should Not Be, Mild Bill Hiccup, Rockfang, PixelBot, XLinkBot, Addbot, DOI bot, Toyokuni3, Looie496, LaaknorBot, PRL42, דוד55, Legobot, Luckas-bot, Langthorne, AnomieBOT, Letuño, Metalhead94, Citation bot, ArthurBot, Xqbot, Jimwoulfe, FrescoBot, Citation bot 1, Citation bot 4, RjwilmsiBot, WikitanvirBot, H3llBot, AManWithNoPlan, Alexsr100, Whoop whoop pull up, ClueBot NG, Paula.pe, Bibcode Bot, Regulov, PhnomPencil, Miniscus777, Raquel.taylor, Cyberbot II, Sgspecker, Davidlwinkler, Michipedian, Mqassem, Raymond C. Noyes, Brainiacal, Anrnusna, Monkbot, Lizichell2 and Anonymous: 71

- **Gilberto Valle** *Source:* https://en.wikipedia.org/wiki/Gilberto_Valle?oldid=686944079 *Contributors:* Asc85, Treybien, Wikimandia, Scott Illini, JL-Bot, Yobot, Mczebroski and Versus001

- **Cannibalism (zoology)** *Source:* https://en.wikipedia.org/wiki/Cannibalism_(zoology)?oldid=681871884 *Contributors:* SebastianHelm, Nv8200pa, Ruakh, Tobias Bergemann, Subsolar, Beland, DragonflySixtyseven, Dbachmann, ZayZayEM, DodgerOfZion, Rjwilmsi, XP1, Gurch, Nimur, CambridgeBayWeather, Snek01, Grafen, Apokryltaros, Barnabypage, Sandstein, Sagsaw, SmackBot, Kintetsubuffalo, Gilliam, Bidgee, Thumperward, J. Spencer, Richard001, Sturm, Mgiganteus1, Halaqah, Sheep81, IronChris, Ræv, Boingo the Clown, Davidhorman, Sophie means wisdom, Celithemis, Mclay1, Brusegadi, Mattinbgn, Boston, Inter16, Harveyhanson, Michaeldsuarez, Rps5, Funkamatic, Matthew Yeager, Cannibal baboon, Chrisrus, Imac.vincent, DumZiBoT, Enallagma, Ost316, Good Olfactory, Addbot, DOI bot, Electron, Anxietycello, ماني, Yobot, TaBOT-zerem, Sharayanan, Karthickbala, Citation bot, Capricorn42, Gigemag76, Aaaaaaahh, Gatorgirl7563, Omnipaedista, ئاسوﯨ, Geopersona, Citation bot 1, DrilBot, Animalparty, Bhudh, Devin, Tuxedo junction, ZéroBot, Donner60, Ego White Tray, ClueBot NG, Trigrinum76, DrChrissy, MerlIwBot, Helpful Pixie Bot, BendelacBOT, The Mark of the Beast, JSWHU, Ccevo2011, Xanderman0923, JYBot, Babitaarora, Monkbot, Micah.Steinbrecher, H0tb0y212, Rednose1234 and Anonymous: 60

24.7.2   Images

- **File:Albarelli_Axung_Hominis.jpg** *Source:* https://upload.wikimedia.org/wikipedia/commons/b/b6/Albarelli_Axung_Hominis.jpg *License:* CC BY-SA 3.0 *Contributors:* Own work *Original artist:* Bullenwächter

- **File:Albert_Eckhout_Tapuia_woman_1641.jpg** *Source:* https://upload.wikimedia.org/wikipedia/commons/9/9d/Albert_Eckhout_Tapuia_woman_1641.jpg *License:* Public domain *Contributors:* scanned from the book Albert Eckhout: een Hollandse kunstenaar in Brazilië ISBN 9040089299 *Original artist:* Albert Eckhout (circa 1610–circa 1666)

- **File:Ambox_important.svg** *Source:* https://upload.wikimedia.org/wikipedia/commons/b/b4/Ambox_important.svg *License:* Public domain *Contributors:* Own work, based off of Image:Ambox scales.svg *Original artist:* Dsmurat (talk · contribs)

- **File:Anchor.svg** *Source:* https://upload.wikimedia.org/wikipedia/commons/8/80/Anchor.svg *License:* CC0 *Contributors:* ? *Original artist:* ?

- **File:Black_widow_ventral_1370.jpg** *Source:* https://upload.wikimedia.org/wikipedia/commons/8/8c/Black_widow_ventral_1370.jpg *License:* CC-BY-SA-3.0 *Contributors:* Image taken by Pollinator, released under GFDL *Original artist:* User Pollinator on en.wikipedia

- **File:Blake_Hell_33_Ugolino.jpg** *Source:* https://upload.wikimedia.org/wikipedia/commons/3/3c/Blake_Hell_33_Ugolino.jpg *License:* Public domain *Contributors:* Unknown *Original artist:* William Blake

- **File:Bokassa_portrait.jpg** *Source:* https://upload.wikimedia.org/wikipedia/commons/b/b9/Bokassa_portrait.jpg *License:* Attribution *Contributors:*

- Bokassa_with_Ceausescu.jpg *Original artist:* Bokassa_with_Ceausescu.jpg: unknown, image comes from the National Archives

- **File:Cannibalism.jpg** *Source:* https://upload.wikimedia.org/wikipedia/commons/9/9b/Cannibalism.jpg *License:* Public domain *Contributors:* Deutsche Rundschau für Geographie und Statistik *Original artist:* own scan

- **File:Cannibalism_during_Russian_famine_1921.jpg** *Source:* https://upload.wikimedia.org/wikipedia/commons/8/80/Cannibalism_during_Russian_famine_1921.jpg *License:* Public domain *Contributors:* selfmade copy of photimages published in the book "Russia 1904-1924. The Revolutionary Years" by Eric Baschet *Original artist:* Unknown

- **File:Cannibalism_on_Tanna.jpeg** *Source:* https://upload.wikimedia.org/wikipedia/commons/8/82/Cannibalism_on_Tanna.jpeg *License:* Public domain *Contributors:* Bonhams *Original artist:* Charles E. Gordon Frazer (1863-1899)

- **File:Cannibalization(silk_spider).jpg** *Source:* https://upload.wikimedia.org/wikipedia/commons/b/b1/Cannibalization%28silk_spider%29.jpg *License:* CC BY 2.0 *Contributors:* Flickr *Original artist:* Kumon

- **File:Cannibals.23232.jpg** *Source:* https://upload.wikimedia.org/wikipedia/commons/f/f7/Cannibals.23232.jpg *License:* Public domain *Contributors:* ? *Original artist:* ?

- **File:Caribou_from_Wagon_Trails.jpg** *Source:* https://upload.wikimedia.org/wikipedia/commons/e/e0/Caribou_from_Wagon_Trails.jpg *License:* CC BY-SA 2.5 *Contributors:* ? *Original artist:* ?

- **File:Cercophonius_squama.jpg** *Source:* https://upload.wikimedia.org/wikipedia/commons/6/60/Cercophonius_squama.jpg *License:* CC BY-SA 3.0 *Contributors:* Own work *Original artist:* Noodle snacks

- **File:Commons-logo.svg** *Source:* https://upload.wikimedia.org/wikipedia/en/4/4a/Commons-logo.svg *License:* ? *Contributors:* ? *Original artist:* ?

- **File:Cord_&_Placenta.jpg** *Source:* https://upload.wikimedia.org/wikipedia/commons/e/ef/Cord_%26_Placenta.jpg *License:* CC BY-SA 3.0 *Contributors:* Own work (Original text: *self-made*) *Original artist:* sarindam7 (talk)

- **File:Edit-clear.svg** *Source:* https://upload.wikimedia.org/wikipedia/en/f/f2/Edit-clear.svg *License:* Public domain *Contributors:* The *Tango! Desktop Project.* *Original artist:*

  The people from the Tango! project. And according to the meta-data in the file, specifically: "Andreas Nilsson, and Jakub Steiner (although minimally)."

- **File:Folder_Hexagonal_Icon.svg** *Source:* https://upload.wikimedia.org/wikipedia/en/4/48/Folder_Hexagonal_Icon.svg *License:* Cc-by-sa-3.0 *Contributors:* ? *Original artist:* ?

- **File:Francisco_de_Goya,_Saturno_devorando_a_su_hijo_(1819-1823).jpg** *Source:* https://upload.wikimedia.org/wikipedia/commons/8/82/Francisco_de_Goya%2C_Saturno_devorando_a_su_hijo_%281819-1823%29.jpg *License:* Public domain *Contributors:* [1] *Original artist:* Francisco Goya

- **File:Goat_eating_placenta.jpg** *Source:* https://upload.wikimedia.org/wikipedia/commons/2/20/Goat_eating_placenta.jpg *License:* CC-BY-SA-3.0 *Contributors:* Transferred from en.wikipedia; Transfer was stated to be made by User:Fernandopascullo. *Original artist:* Original uploader was Fir0002 at en.wikipedia

- **File:Hans_Staden,_Tupinamba_portrayed_in_cannibalistic_feast.jpg** *Source:* https://upload.wikimedia.org/wikipedia/commons/8/8a/Hans_Staden%2C_Tupinamba_portrayed_in_cannibalistic_feast.jpg *License:* Public domain *Contributors:* Retrieved from http://www.athenapub.com/staden1.htm on December 2, 2006. *Original artist:* Hans Staden

- **File:Hans_Staden.jpg** *Source:* https://upload.wikimedia.org/wikipedia/commons/a/a6/Hans_Staden.jpg *License:* Public domain *Contributors:* http://www.regionalmuseum-wolfhager-land.de/hans_staden.htm *Original artist:* H. J. Winkelmann

- **File:Hansel-and-gretel-rackham.jpg** *Source:* https://upload.wikimedia.org/wikipedia/commons/d/d1/Hansel-and-gretel-rackham.jpg *License:* Public domain *Contributors:* ? *Original artist:* ?

- **File:Homo_antecessor_female.jpg** *Source:* https://upload.wikimedia.org/wikipedia/commons/f/f2/Homo_antecessor_female.jpg *License:* CC BY-SA 2.0 *Contributors:* Homo antecessor hembra *Original artist:* Jose Luis Martinez Alvarez from Asturias, España

- **File:Issoria_lathonia.jpg** *Source:* https://upload.wikimedia.org/wikipedia/commons/2/2d/Issoria_lathonia.jpg *License:* CC-BY-SA-3.0 *Contributors:* ? *Original artist:* ?

- **File:Magliabchanopage_73r.jpg** *Source:* https://upload.wikimedia.org/wikipedia/commons/1/11/Magliabchanopage_73r.jpg *License:* Public domain *Contributors:* ? *Original artist:* ?

- **File:Manticore_-_British_Library_Royal_12_F_xiii_f24v_(detail).jpg** *Source:* https://upload.wikimedia.org/wikipedia/commons/f/f4/Manticore_-_British_Library_Royal_12_F_xiii_f24v_%28detail%29.jpg *License:* Public domain *Contributors:* This file has been provided by the British Library from its digital collections.It is also made available on a British Library website. *Original artist:* ?

- **File:Mantis_Tenodera_aridifolia01.jpg** *Source:* https://upload.wikimedia.org/wikipedia/commons/4/4e/Mantis_Tenodera_aridifolia01.jpg *License:* CC BY 3.0 *Contributors:* Own work (Photo by myself) *Original artist:* Apple2000

- **File:Mononchidae_eating_a_Mononchidae_1.jpg** *Source:* https://upload.wikimedia.org/wikipedia/commons/3/31/Mononchidae_eating_a_Mononchidae_1.jpg *License:* Public domain *Contributors:* Personal picture *Original artist:* Vincent

- **File:Mormon_cricket_cannibals.jpg** *Source:* https://upload.wikimedia.org/wikipedia/commons/e/ed/Mormon_cricket_cannibals.jpg *License:* CC-BY-SA-3.0 *Contributors:* ? *Original artist:* ?

- **File:Ouroboros_1.jpg** *Source:* https://upload.wikimedia.org/wikipedia/commons/8/87/Ouroboros_1.jpg *License:* Public domain *Contributors:* ? *Original artist:* ?

- **File:P_human_body.svg** *Source:* https://upload.wikimedia.org/wikipedia/commons/0/09/P_human_body.svg *License:* CC-BY-SA-3.0 *Contributors:* Own work *Original artist:* Yosi I

- **File:Question_book-new.svg** *Source:* https://upload.wikimedia.org/wikipedia/en/9/99/Question_book-new.svg *License:* Cc-by-sa-3.0 *Contributors:*
Created from scratch in Adobe Illustrator. Based on Image:Question book.png created by User:Equazcion *Original artist:*
Tkgd2007

- **File:Raft_of_the_Medusa_-_Theodore_Gericault.JPG** *Source:* https://upload.wikimedia.org/wikipedia/commons/f/ff/Raft_of_the_Medusa_-_Theodore_Gericault.JPG *License:* Public domain *Contributors:* en.wikipedia *Original artist:* ?

- **File:Retablo11-Pistaku.jpeg** *Source:* https://upload.wikimedia.org/wikipedia/commons/6/64/Retablo11-Pistaku.jpeg *License:* Public domain *Contributors:* ? *Original artist:* ?

- **File:Sacamantecas.jpg** *Source:* https://upload.wikimedia.org/wikipedia/commons/a/a8/Sacamantecas.jpg *License:* Public domain *Contributors:* Juan Díaz de Garayo. Fot. Archivo José Luis Sáenz de Ugarte, http://www.euskomedia.org/ImgsAuna/09024404.jpg *Original artist:* Unknown prior to 1881.

- **File:Starling_Feeding_Offspring.jpg** *Source:* https://upload.wikimedia.org/wikipedia/commons/5/5f/Starling_Feeding_Offspring.jpg *License:* CC BY-SA 3.0 *Contributors:* Own work *Original artist:* Ian Dunster

- **File:Video-x-generic.svg** *Source:* https://upload.wikimedia.org/wikipedia/en/e/e7/Video-x-generic.svg *License:* Public domain *Contributors:* ? *Original artist:* ?

- **File:Wiki_letter_w.svg** *Source:* https://upload.wikimedia.org/wikipedia/en/6/6c/Wiki_letter_w.svg *License:* Cc-by-sa-3.0 *Contributors:* ? *Original artist:* ?

- **File:Wiki_letter_w_cropped.svg** *Source:* https://upload.wikimedia.org/wikipedia/commons/1/1c/Wiki_letter_w_cropped.svg *License:* CC-BY-SA-3.0 *Contributors:*

- Wiki_letter_w.svg *Original artist:* Wiki_letter_w.svg: Jarkko Piiroinen

- **File:Wikibooks-logo-en-noslogan.svg** *Source:* https://upload.wikimedia.org/wikipedia/commons/d/df/Wikibooks-logo-en-noslogan.svg *License:* CC BY-SA 3.0 *Contributors:* Own work *Original artist:* User:Bastique, User:Ramac et al.

- **File:Ziheche.jpg** *Source:* https://upload.wikimedia.org/wikipedia/commons/6/68/Ziheche.jpg *License:* CC BY-SA 2.0 *Contributors:* http://www.flickr.com/photos/hellobobo/3858965235/ *Original artist:* 胶花妹妹 ~hellobobo~

24.7.3 Content license

www.ingramcontent.com/pod-product-compliance
Lightning Source LLC
Chambersburg PA
CBHW081215280526
45787CB00006B/2409